www.ingramcontent.com/pod-product-compliance
Lightning Source LLC
Chambersburg PA
CBHW081218230426
43666CB00015B/2783

TEACHER'S EDITION

The New Hebrew Through Prayer

2

Roberta Osser Baum

Consultants:
Rabbi Martin Cohen
Ellen Rank

Behrman House, Inc.

Book and Cover Design: Irving S. Berman
Electronic Composition and Page Production:
21st Century Publishing and Communications, Inc.
Special Needs Education Consultant:
Sara Rubinow Simon

Copyright © 2002 Behrman House, Inc.
Springfield, New Jersey
www.behrmanhouse.com
ISBN 0-87441-134-3

CONTENTS

I. **INTRODUCTION AND OVERVIEW** — 4
   - Preface — 4
   - Using This Teacher's Edition — 4
   - Overview of Lesson Planning — 5
   - Reinforcing Prayer Awareness — 5
   - Teaching Aids — 5
   - Developing Reading Skills — 6
   - Classroom Games — 9

II. **USING THE TEXTBOOK** — 12
   - Introducing the Textbook — 12
   - Lesson 1 ... אָבוֹת/אָבוֹת וְאִמָהוֹת — 13
   - Lesson 2 ... גְבוּרוֹת — 27
   - Lesson 3 ... קְדוּשָׁה — 41
   - Lesson 4 ... הוֹדָאָה — 51
   - Lesson 5 ... בִּרְכַּת שָׁלוֹם: שָׁלוֹם רָב/שִׂים שָׁלוֹם — 63
   - Lesson 6 ... עֹשֶׂה שָׁלוֹם — 77
   - Lesson 7 ... לְכָה דוֹדִי — 89
   - Lesson 8 ... וְשָׁמְרוּ — 99
   - Lesson 9 ... שָׁלוֹם עֲלֵיכֶם — 111

III. **ENRICHMENT AND SUPPLEMENTARY MATERIALS** — 123
   - Family Education — 123
   - Techniques for Use With Special Needs Students — 133
   - Answers to Worksheets — 134

I. INTRODUCTION AND OVERVIEW

PREFACE

You are about to embark on a sacred task, the task of teaching our children how to worship, to pray in the Hebrew language. In doing so, you will help them connect with our God, with our ancestors, and with our heritage.

As Jewish educators, we want to help our students develop positive attitudes toward our rich Jewish tradition. Toward this end, *Hineni—The New Hebrew Through Prayer* is designed to deepen our students' understanding of Jewish ritual and the concepts inherent in our mitzvot, while teaching them to read Hebrew and to pray. The prayer selections introducing each lesson encourage participation in the rituals of synagogue and home. And the enrichment activities aid students in developing reading fluency, allowing for active participation in the classroom setting. This approach encourages students to feel comfortable in their learning environment, where they sharpen their reading skills and develop a familiarity and understanding of ritual and mitzvot.

USING THIS TEACHER'S EDITION

This Teacher's Edition contains the entire text of *Hineni—The New Hebrew Through Prayer 2*, reproduced in reduced size. The pages are annotated with suggested activities, teaching methods, and other information to assist you. Black-line masters that supplement the material are also provided in this Teacher's Edition.

Keep in mind that students learn in different ways, and any student's primary learning mode may be aural, visual, or tactile. Similarly, teachers teach in different ways. Don't feel obligated to use a method that does not feel comfortable with your teaching style. By the same token, remember that since students learn in different ways, you should vary your teaching methods accordingly. Feel free to repeat an activity or method that worked especially well for you and your students.

> The information and suggestions in this Teacher's Edition are intended to assist you in developing your own teaching plan. You do not need to follow every suggestion on every page. Rather, the guide provides you with many different options from which to choose.

Pacing

Students differ in ability. Teachers differ in style. Schools differ in the number of class sessions scheduled each week. Ultimately, you must decide how to pace your class through the text.

The lessons in *Hineni* vary in length. Some lessons may take three or more sessions, while others will take one or two. A short but more difficult lesson may take more time to teach than a longer, simpler lesson.

Homework

Whether or not to give homework is a question that should be addressed to your school principal. Keep in mind that homework can provide students with the additional contact, repetition, and reinforcement of what has already been learned in class. Homework should not be used as a tool to teach new information.

If you do give homework, *Hineni* makes assigning homework easy. At the end of each lesson in the Teacher's Edition is a review worksheet. These review worksheets can be duplicated and completed for homework, or, of course, they can be used for in-class evaluation.

Be sure to review each homework assignment during the class session following the assignment. Doing this reinforces the importance of the homework and reassures the students that their efforts were noted and were a worthwhile expenditure of time.

Family Education

A partnership between home and school can help your students reach their greatest potential in their Hebrew studies. Parents can be important allies in the education of your students, and every effort should be made to facilitate this partnership. To aid you in this endeavor, black-line masters to duplicate and send home for the family are included in this Teacher's Edition.

OVERVIEW OF LESSON PLANNING

Timing is an important factor in planning your classes. Keep in mind the objectives of the program as you plan your lesson for the day. Foremost in your mind should be not how quickly you move through the text, but rather how effectively you teach the material and how thoroughly the students master it. Remember that review and reinforcement are essential ingredients for mastery.

There are nine lessons in *Hineni 2*. How you pace your class should depend on the number of classroom sessions each week, your students' reading ability, and the length of the particular passages. It is important to decide beforehand which activities you will cover in each session and how much time you will allot to each activity. Make sure that reading is a part of *every* lesson. The materials in the textbook and in this Teacher's Edition, as well as teacher reinforcement through games and Word Card work, should all come into play to ensure the success of the program.

REINFORCING PRAYER AWARENESS

Developing comfort and familiarity with the prayers on the part of your students is an important aspect of your goal. Several strategies can help you to achieve this objective.

Prayer Service

Begin each class with a short (two- to five-minute) prayer service, including the prayers learned to date. Ask individual students to take turns as leaders.

You may choose to end the service by having the class recite this blessing.

בָּרוּךְ אַתָּה, יְיָ אֱלֹהֵינוּ, מֶלֶךְ הָעוֹלָם,
אֲשֶׁר קִדְּשָׁנוּ בְּמִצְוֹתָיו וְצִוָּנוּ לַעֲסוֹק
בְּדִבְרֵי תוֹרָה.

Praised are You, Adonai our God, Ruler of the world, who makes us holy with commandments and commands us to be involved with the words of Torah.

Create Your Own Prayerbook

After learning each prayer, you may ask students to write the prayer and its English meaning in a personal prayerbook. Students may wish to write the prayers in calligraphy (see below) and illustrate or illuminate their work. These prayerbooks can then be used at every class prayer service.

Calligraphy

Most lessons offer an opportunity for students to practice Hebrew calligraphy. This can be done on a variety of levels: simple printing, copying a text, or learning formal calligraphy as practiced by a *sofer* (scribe).

Students can use any writing medium, but we recommend investing in felt-tip pens specifically designed for calligraphy. They are inexpensive, and the results justify the expenditure.

You may wish to exhibit students' efforts on bulletin boards and in other displays.

TEACHING AIDS

Chalkboard

Use the chalkboard to introduce new words and prayers, to answer questions, to play games, and to present assignments.

Remember to vary the way in which you use the chalkboard. This can be as simple as changing the chalk color or varying the size of the letters you write.

Draw a picture on the chalkboard to illustrate the lesson. (The less polished an artist you are, the more the class will love your drawings.)

Incorporate children's need for physical movement. Plan quick-paced exercises that involve coming to the board. For example, have students copy a word that you have written on the board. There is really nothing more special about writing on a chalkboard than on paper—unless you are a child. Coming to the front of the room and writing on the board is exciting to many students. If they enjoy using the board, let them do so.

Flannelboard

A flannelboard can be used with the entire class, with small groups, or by a single student. It saves writing time at the chalkboard and presents letters and words exactly as they appear in a printed book. It also offers students the opportunity to manipulate words to form whole phrases.

Flannelboards can be purchased at a school supplies store or may be easily constructed by covering a large piece of cardboard with flannel. You can make flannelboard words by gluing a small piece of velcro or sandpaper onto the back of existing Word Cards or by cutting flashcards out of rough-textured construction paper. Most flannelboard techniques will also work with a magnetic board.

The flannelboard can be used to introduce new words and display them clearly. It is also useful for drill or review.

DEVELOPING READING SKILLS

Alef-Bet Review

Begin the year with a thorough review of the letters and vowels in the Hebrew alphabet. Use an *alef-bet* poster, *alef-bet* flashcards, or the Word Cards for *Hineni 1*. You can also use a transitional reading text such as the *Back-to-School Hebrew Reading Refresher* to review and drill Hebrew decoding before students begin *Hineni 2*.

Stopwatch and Tape Recorder

A stopwatch is an easy way to assess improvement in reading fluency. It can be used to time the speed at which a student reads a passage. Many students enjoy the experience of competing against and trying to improve their own best time.

A tape recorder also provides students with tangible evidence of their improvement. Record members of the class as they read a passage. Remember the order in which they have read. Two or three weeks later, record the students, in the same order, while they read the passage on a second tape, then play back both and compare.

Word Cards

There is a set of Word Cards available for use with *Hineni 2*. These cards, printed on durable, heavy cardboard, include all key words covered by the book. (Each Word Card is numbered for easy reference to activities included in this Teacher's Edition.) The English meaning is on the back of each Word Card.

Word Cards may be used by individuals or small groups of students, or by the class as a whole. Activities should be both teacher and student initiated, to reinforce reading skills. Possible games and teaching strategies using Word Cards are endless, and each teacher will develop many ways of using them. The following suggestions may be implemented as presented here or adapted as necessary.

Remember to use the Word Cards regularly and with a variety of techniques.

General Word Card Techniques and Games

1. Display a number of Word Cards on the edge of the chalkboard or in a pocket chart. Provide a clue about one of the words and ask the students to read the correct word. For example, "This is the Jewish state"—*Yisrael*.

2. Distribute Word Cards to the class. Call out, one at a time, the Hebrew words and phrases found on the individual cards. Ask the student with the matching card to supply the correct answer by standing up, displaying the card, and reading the word or phrase.

3. Make a packet of ten Word Cards. Arrange the class in a circle (sitting or standing) and have the students pass the packet around the circle while playing music on a tape or CD player. (Try to use Jewish or Israeli music.) When the music stops, the student holding the packet should read and/or translate the top card. This card is then placed at the bottom of the pile and the game continues in the same fashion.

4. Create two rows of Word Cards with six cards in each row. Ask students individually (or in two teams) to choose a row. Taking turns, ask the individual students or teams to read the six Hebrew words, then switch and read the words in the other row. You can also play the game by translating the words instead of reading them.

5. Post at least six words in a column on the board. Ask individuals or teams to take turns "climbing up the ladder" by reading and translating the words in the column in ascending order. Score one point for each word read correctly and two points for each word translated correctly. Then play again by having students read the words in descending order to climb down the ladder.

6. Place Word Cards on the edge of the chalkboard in full view of the class. Read the words one at a time, calling on students to go to the board and remove the identified card. Variation: Have one of the students read the words.

7. You can play a memory game with double sets of Word Cards (two identical cards for each word). Lay out eight pairs of words (sixteen cards in all) upside down and shuffled, in rows. Call on a student to pick a card and read it aloud, then try to find its match. If successful, the student must then tell the meaning of the word in order to keep the pair. On successfully giving the meaning, the student keeps the cards and two new cards are put down. If the student is unsuccessful, then the initial cards are returned to their place face down. Then the next student goes.

Pronunciation and Translation

1. Show a card and ask for volunteers to read.

2. Show a card and read together with the class.

3. Lightning Review: Show a card to one student, who has 5–10 seconds to pronounce the word; immediately show the next card to another student until everyone has participated.

4. Ask students to drill each other.

Reinforcing Word Order

1. Place cards on a flannelboard in the correct order; have students read the prayer (as a group and individually).

2. Ask students to close their eyes; remove one or more cards. Ask which words are missing.

3. Scramble all the cards for the words in a prayer. Ask students to place the cards in the correct order.

4. Scramble all the cards for the words in a prayer and put one or more aside. Ask students to place cards in the correct order and determine what is missing.

5. Distribute all the cards in a prayer, one per student. Ask students to come to the front of the room and stand in the order of the words of the prayer.

6. Distribute all the cards in a prayer, one per student, plus extra words not from the prayer. Proceed as in step 5 above, but ask students holding the extra words to step aside.

Word Cards

The following is a list of words included in *Hineni 2*:

1.	אָבוֹת	fathers		47.	עַמְּךָ	your people
2.	אֲבוֹתֵינוּ	our fathers		48.	וְטוֹב	and may it be good
3.	אֱלֹהֵי	God of		49.	בְּעֵינֶיךָ	in your eyes
4.	אַבְרָהָם	Abraham		50.	לְבָרֵךְ	to bless
5.	יִצְחָק	Isaac		51.	בִּשְׁלוֹמֶךָ	with your peace
6.	יַעֲקֹב	Jacob		52.	שִׂים	grant, put
7.	אִמָּהוֹת	mothers		53.	טוֹבָה	goodness
8.	אִמּוֹתֵינוּ	our mothers		54.	חֵן	graciousness
9.	שָׂרָה	Sarah		55.	אָבִינוּ	our parent
10.	רִבְקָה	Rebecca		56.	כֻּלָּנוּ כְּאֶחָד	all of us as one
11.	לֵאָה	Leah		57.	נָתַתָּ	you gave
12.	רָחֵל	Rachel		58.	תּוֹרַת חַיִּים	Torah of life
13.	הַגָּדוֹל	the great		59.	וְאַהֲבַת חֶסֶד	and a love of kindness
14.	הַגִּבּוֹר	the mighty		60.	עֹשֶׂה	makes
15.	וְהַנּוֹרָא	and the awesome		61.	יַעֲשֶׂה	(will) make
16.	עֶלְיוֹן	supreme		62.	עָלֵינוּ	for us, on us
17.	חֲסָדִים טוֹבִים	acts of loving-kindness		63.	וְעַל	and for, and on
18.	מֶלֶךְ	ruler		64.	כָּל	all
19.	עוֹזֵר	helper		65.	וְאִמְרוּ	and say
20.	וּמוֹשִׁיעַ	and rescuer		66.	אָמֵן	Amen
21.	וּמָגֵן	and shield		67.	לְכָה	go
22.	אַתָּה	you (are)		68.	דוֹדִי	my beloved
23.	גִּבּוֹר	mighty, powerful		69.	כַּלָּה	bride
24.	לְעוֹלָם	eternally		70.	פְּנֵי	the face of
25.	מְחַיֶּה	give life		71.	נְקַבְּלָה	let us receive
26.	לְהוֹשִׁיעַ	to save		72.	שָׁמוֹר	keep
27.	חַיִּים	life, the living		73.	זָכוֹר	remember
28.	בְּרַחֲמִים	with compassion, mercy		74.	בֹּאִי	come
29.	מִי כָמוֹךָ	who is like you?		75.	וְשָׁמְרוּ	and shall keep
30.	נְקַדֵּשׁ	let us sanctify		76.	בְּנֵי	the children of
31.	שִׁמְךָ	your name		77.	לַעֲשׂוֹת	to make
32.	כְּבוֹדוֹ	God's glory		78.	לְדֹרֹתָם	for their generations
33.	יִמְלֹךְ	will rule		79.	בְּרִית	covenant
34.	לְדוֹר וָדוֹר	from generation to generation		80.	עוֹלָם	eternal
35.	נַגִּיד	we will tell		81.	הַשָּׁמַיִם	the heavens
36.	גָּדְלֶךָ	your greatness		82.	הָאָרֶץ	the earth
37.	מוֹדִים	thank, give thanks		83.	יוֹם הַשְּׁבִיעִי	the seventh day
38.	אֲנַחְנוּ	we		84.	שָׁבַת	rested
39.	נוֹדֶה	we will thank, give thanks		85.	עֲלֵיכֶם	upon you
40.	תְּהִלָּתֶךָ	your praises		86.	מַלְאֲכֵי	angels of
41.	וִיהַלְלוּ	(they) will praise		87.	מֶלֶךְ מַלְכֵי הַמְּלָכִים	Ruler of Rulers
42.	בֶּאֱמֶת	in truth		88.	הַקָּדוֹשׁ בָּרוּךְ הוּא	the Holy Blessed One
43.	לְהוֹדוֹת	to thank		89.	בּוֹאֲכֶם	come
44.	שָׁלוֹם	peace		90.	בָּרְכוּנִי	bless me
45.	רַב	great		91.	צֵאתְכֶם	depart
46.	יִשְׂרָאֵל	Israel				

CLASSROOM GAMES

Games can add variety and interest to a lesson. They reinforce learning through a medium that quickly catches the students' attention. As you plan to use the games found below, or others you develop on your own, keep the following considerations in mind:

1. Use games that move quickly.
2. Stop when students' interest begins to lag.
3. Choose games appropriate to the age group.
4. When playing a game with the entire class, see that all students become actively involved.
5. Choose games that contribute to improving specific skills and reading fluency.
6. Use games that are easy to follow and organize. Explain rules clearly. Avoid complicated directions. You want students' attention focused on the skills being reinforced, not on rules.
7. Maintain control of the class.

What's Missing?

Decide on a set of lines in a prayer passage from which to draw words. Divide the class into two teams, then choose a word and write it without vowels in two different places on the chalkboard. Each team (with members playing individually, one at a time, or as a group) must locate the word in the set of lines, go to the board and, using the book for reference, add the vowels. The first team to do so then gets the chance to read the word correctly (from either the board or the book), and if correct, they score a point. If incorrect, then the other team (having located the word and written in the vowels) gets a chance to read and score a point.

Word Search

This game will help students recognize phrases within a prayer passage. Each student has a pencil, paper, and text open to a prayer passage. (The teacher might choose to focus the students' attention on a given set of lines within the passage.) The class is divided into two teams. The teacher reads a word aloud. Students search for the word and write it down, along with the word immediately following it, to complete a phrase. (A word is often found more than once in a prayer passage; therefore, more than one answer is possible.) Students are given a specified amount of time to search for the word and write the phrase. The teacher calls "Stop" and pencils are put down. A point is given for each team member who found and wrote the phrase in the allotted time.

Variation: Instead of writing the phrase, the teacher calls out the first word in a phrase, then the two team players search for the word and race to the chalkboard (or any other "target"). The first to hit the "target" reads the phrase and earns a point for the team.

Speed Reading

Individual Competition

Using a watch with a second hand, or a stopwatch, time individual students reading an assigned set of lines three separate times. The goal is for the students to improve their previous record. If the student reads a word incorrectly, ask the student to repeat the word correctly in order to proceed. Allow each student a maximum time of 60 seconds before proceeding to the next student. You may also allow students their own choice of lines to read.

Teams

Divide the class into two teams—Team A and Team B. Select a prayer passage (or set of lines) for students to read. Ask each student on Team A to read a word or line in turn until the passage is completed, while timing the team. Then ask Team B to try to achieve a better time while reading the same selection in the same manner. Then reverse, using a different prayer passage or set of lines, with Team B going first. If a reader makes a mistake, ask him or her to read the word correctly before proceeding. (Alternative: When a word is read incorrectly, the word should be "passed along" to the next student who finishes the first student's word[s] and then continues with his or her own.)

Class

Announce a target time—a period of time for the class to beat while reading a particular prayer passage or set of lines. Ask each student to read one word in turn. If the class beats the target time, ask them to repeat the activity and try to beat the new time.

Tic-Tac-Toe

Draw a Tic-Tac-Toe diagram on the chalkboard. Divide students into two teams, X and O. Show a Word Card, then call on a student from Team X to read the Hebrew word. If the student reads correctly, ask him or her to place an X in one of the squares. Then it is Team O's turn; show another Word Card, and call on a student from Team O to read it.

Variations:

- Students must read the word on the Word Card and read the sentence (or line) in the prayer passage that contains the word before placing a mark in a square. (You can facilitate the game by telling the student which line contains the word.)

- Students must read the Hebrew and give the English meaning before placing an X or an O in a square.

- Students must answer questions about the prayer passage(s) in order to place an X or an O in a square.

- After drawing the Tic-Tac-Toe diagram, write the names of the prayer passages in the squares. Ask each student to choose a square and read the name of the prayer correctly in order to place an X or O in the square.

Beat the Clock

Draw the face of a clock on the chalkboard, but do *not* write the numbers. Draw the hands at the position of 12 o'clock. Think of a word that appears in one of the prayer passages (or ask a student to think of one) and draw horizontal lines on the board—one for each letter in the word. The lines should be next to each other. Then call on individual students to guess which letters are contained in the word. When a student guesses a letter correctly, write that letter over the line that corresponds to the place in the word where the letter appears. If the letter appears more than once, write it on multiple lines. If the student guesses a letter that is not in the word, then add an hour to the face of the clock on the chalkboard; first draw the 1, then the 2, the 3, etc. The object of the game is to guess the word before the clock "strikes 12."

Concentration

Place cards with Hebrew words and cards with the English translations in random order in a pocket chart or on the bottom edge of the chalkboard. Number the backs of the Hebrew words with even numbers and the English words with odd numbers. Then turn the cards over so only the numbers are showing. Ask students individually (or in teams) to try to match the Hebrew and English word pairs by calling out two numbers, one even (for the Hebrew) and one odd (for the English). Turn the two cards over. If they match, then the player scores a point and the matched pair of cards is removed. If they do not match, place the cards back in their original position and ask another student, or the other team, to go. The game continues until all sets have been matched and removed. The player or team with more sets of cards wins.

Hebrew Baseball

Divide the class into two teams. On the board, draw a baseball diamond and a score board. Appoint a student to keep score. Determine the number of words that must be read successfully in order for the reader to earn a "single," "double," "triple," and "home run." Then, as students on each team come "to bat," they can individually decide how many bases to try for—in order to get on base they must then read correctly that number of words from a prayer passage assigned by you. If a student reads incorrectly, he or she is "out" and the next team member goes. After three outs, change teams and repeat. Play for as many innings as you like.

Stop!

This reading game may be used for oral reading practice, review of English meanings, or recognition of prefixes, suffixes, and roots. Assign a student to read until a specific word is reached (for example, instruct the class: "Please read until you come to the Hebrew word for 'ruler.'"). Ask the class to call out "Stop!" when the reader reaches the designated word. Then continue with other students. This game may be played individually or in teams.

Hebrew Bingo

Select 16 Hebrew words or phrases. Prepare a Bingo board with 16 squares. In ten of the squares, chosen at random, write Hebrew words or phrases from among the 16 you selected, leaving the other six squares blank. On a separate piece of paper, draw six boxes (the same size as those on the Bingo board) and write in the remaining six Hebrew words or phrases. Call this card the Extra Word card.

Duplicate enough copies of both the Bingo board and the Extra Word card for every student in your class. Then, have your students cut up the six word boxes on the Extra Word card and paste or tape them at random in the empty boxes on the Bingo board. When the Bingo boards are ready, give each student small objects to use as markers. (The markers can be paper clips, pennies, or any other similar item.) To play, you should call out one of the 16 Hebrew words or phrases for the students to find and cover. The first student to cover four squares in a row (horizontally, vertically, or diagonally), and then read the covered words correctly, wins.

Variation: Instead of reading the 16 Hebrew words and phrases yourself, cut up one set of the words and phrases into individual words and phrases and place them in a container. Go around the class asking students individually to choose a word or phrase from the container and read it to the class in order to select the square to be covered.

Jeopardy

Create categories by (a) selecting Word Cards and (b) designing 3 x 5 Question Cards about prayers, blessings, rituals, values, etc. The first and easiest item in each category is worth 5 points. As point values increase, the Word Cards and Question Cards progress in difficulty. Write the number of points on the back of each card. Place cards in a pocket chart or on a bulletin board, with the backs facing the students. Label each category.

Divide the class into two or more teams. The first player chooses a category and the degree of difficulty, i.e., the number of points. If the player reads the Word Card correctly or answers the Question Card correctly, the team receives the number of points on the back of the card. The card is then removed from play. If the player's response is incorrect, the card remains in the game and is returned to its original position. Teams alternate. The game continues until all cards have been removed. The team with the most points wins the game.

Siddur Squares

This is a game for the whole class. It can be played using the questions from one of the lessons, or as a review of several lessons.

Select nine students to serve as the "siddur squares." (You might place nine chairs in a Tic-Tac-Toe board arrangement.) Divide the remaining students into two teams, X and O. You or a student can serve as moderator.

The first player on Team X will select one of the nine siddur squares, and the moderator will ask one of the prepared questions from the lesson being reviewed. The siddur square student should give an answer, and the Team X player must agree or disagree with the answer. If the Team X player is correct (that is, agrees with a correct answer or disagrees with an incorrect answer), then Team X should receive an X in that square. You may wish to draw a Tic-Tac-Toe board on the chalkboard to facilitate score keeping.

Continue in the same fashion with Team O. Continue, alternating teams, until one team has three squares in a row, diagonally, vertically, or horizontally.

Matching Questions with Answers

Write questions about the prayer passages on colored paper and put them in a box. Write answers to the questions on white paper and put them in a second box. Divide the class into Team A and Team B. Ask each student on Team A to take a question from the question box, and each student on Team B to take an answer from the answer box. Ask a player from Team A to read his or her question, and ask a student from Team B who thinks his or her card has the correct answer to read the card. Continue this way, asking another Team A member to read a question, and Team B to try to find the correct answer. After all the questions and answers have been correctly matched, collect and return them to their respective boxes and reverse the assignments so that members of Team B have the questions, and Team A the answers.

II. USING THE TEXTBOOK

INTRODUCING THE TEXTBOOK

Draw students' attention to the title of the book, "הִנֵּנִי."

Explain:

הִנֵּנִי means "Here I am" (הִנֵּה אֲנִי). The deep significance of the reply, הִנֵּנִי, is apparent from the first time it is used in the Torah. Abraham was the first person to answer הִנֵּנִי when God called upon him. His answer indicated his readiness to serve God (Genesis 22:1–3).

Generations later, God called to Moses from the burning bush. Again, the answer was הִנֵּנִי (Exodus 3:1–4), and Moses served God by leading the Children of Israel out of Egypt.

And yet generations later, Samuel expressed his readiness to serve God as a prophet when he said הִנֵּנִי (I Samuel 3).

The reply הִנֵּנִי indicates a readiness to listen and to serve God through action. You have heard your name and understand it to be a personal call. When we say הִנֵּנִי today, we indicate a willingness to step forward and continue in the tradition of our ancestors. With our faith in God, with God's faith in our abilities, and with assistance from others, we are ready to accomplish all that is before us.

LESSON 1 אָבוֹת

LEARNING OBJECTIVES
Prayer Reading Skills
- Terms for our ancestors
  אָבוֹת ("fathers," "patriarchs," or "ancestors")
  אִמָהוֹת ("mothers" or "matriarchs")
- Hebrew names
  Patriarchs: אַבְרָהָם יִצְחָק יַעֲקֹב
  Matriarchs: שָׂרָה רִבְקָה רָחֵל לֵאָה
- Hebrew names for God: אֵל אֱלֹהִים
- Hebrew for "God of": אֱלֹהֵי
- The prefix הַ ("the")
- The suffix נוּ ("our" or "us")

Prayer Concepts
- Related terms: עֲמִידָה תְּפִלָּה שְׁמוֹנֶה עֶשְׂרֵה
- The Amidah is the heart of every service
- Avot is the first blessing of the Amidah
- There are two versions of the Avot:
  (1) citing only the patriarchs (Abraham, Isaac, Jacob)
  (2) citing the patriarchs and the matriarchs (Sarah, Rebecca, Rachel, Leah)
- We should perform חֲסָדִים טוֹבִים ("acts of loving-kindness") as God does
- Ethical Echo: זְכוּת אָבוֹת ("merit of the ancestors")

BEYOND THE TEXTBOOK
- The term בְּרָכָה ("blessing")
- The phrase בָּרוּךְ אַתָּה יְיָ, indicating a blessing
- The root ברכ ("bless" or "praise")
- The root חסד ("goodness" or "kindness")
- The prefix וּ, וְ, וָ ("and")
- *Dagesh*: the dot in the middle of a letter

ABOUT THE PRAYER
The Avot blessing is the first blessing in the Amidah. It is part of every prayer service. The term Avot means "fathers" or "ancestors." It reminds us that our ancestors were the first people to believe in one God—Adonai. Each of our patriarchs understood God in his own way. We therefore distinguish each patriarch's relationship to God by reciting the phrases "God of Abraham, God of Isaac, and God of Jacob." In the version of the Avot that includes the matriarchs, we say "God of Sarah, God of Rebecca, God of Leah and Rachel" to distinguish each matriarch's relationship with God.

INSTRUCTIONAL MATERIALS
Text pages 4–15

Word Cards 1–21

Worksheet 1

Family Education: "As a Family: Family Tree" (at the back of this guide)

SET INDUCTION
Back to the Future
Tell students that actions in the past determine the future. The decisions made by our ancestors, both long ago and more recently, determine how we came to be who we are and where we are today. But it is *our* decisions that will affect future generations.

Visualizing the Concept
Draw a large circle on the chalkboard and divide it into three sections. Label one section "Past," the second section "Present," and the third, "Future." Ask the students to copy the diagram onto a piece of plain paper or a sheet of poster board and to label their diagrams "Back to the Future."

Assignment:
- Ask students to discuss with their parents the actions the students' grandparents and great-grandparents took that affected each generation that followed. Trigger questions can include: Where did they live? Where did they study? What were their occupations? How did history affect their lives? What were their Jewish connections?

- In the "Past" section, have them write key phrases describing the lives of their ancestors. In the section labeled "Present," have them write key phrases describing their family today by answering the same questions. In the "Future" section, have them write key phrases describing how they think their descendants will live.

- Have the students share their family responses. What common elements occur in families, such as their history (e.g., immigration), education, Jewish connections? Ask students how the decisions made by their ancestors affect them today. Ask if they think we can change the course of history by rejecting parts of what we've inherited from previous generations, and, if so, how.

> # אָבוֹת 1
>
> When someone asks who you are, you might answer with your name, or with something you like to do ("I'm a ballerina!"), or even by mentioning a relationship ("I'm a big brother!").
>
> The אָבוֹת is the first blessing of the Amidah—a group of blessings at the heart of every prayer service. It asks God to recognize us as descendants of our ancestors Abraham, Isaac, and Jacob, and it links each of us to the family of Abraham and Sarah. It asks God to watch over us, protect us, and bless us, just as God watched over our ancestors.
>
> In the Avot we recognize that God is mighty, powerful, and awesome, but also loving and protective. You can see this balance in your everyday life, too—your mom might be strict about you doing your homework, but she can also be loving and supportive when she helps you with it and praises you when you do well.
>
> Practice reading the אָבוֹת aloud.
>
> 1. בָּרוּךְ אַתָּה יְיָ, אֱלֹהֵינוּ וֵאלֹהֵי אֲבוֹתֵינוּ,
> 2. אֱלֹהֵי אַבְרָהָם, אֱלֹהֵי יִצְחָק, וֵאלֹהֵי יַעֲקֹב.
> 3. הָאֵל הַגָּדוֹל, הַגִּבּוֹר, וְהַנּוֹרָא, אֵל עֶלְיוֹן.
> 4. גּוֹמֵל חֲסָדִים טוֹבִים וְקוֹנֵה הַכֹּל, וְזוֹכֵר חַסְדֵי אָבוֹת,
> 5. וּמֵבִיא גוֹאֵל לִבְנֵי בְנֵיהֶם, לְמַעַן שְׁמוֹ, בְּאַהֲבָה.
> 6. מֶלֶךְ עוֹזֵר וּמוֹשִׁיעַ וּמָגֵן.
> 7. בָּרוּךְ אַתָּה יְיָ, מָגֵן אַבְרָהָם.
>
> *Praised are You, Adonai, our God and God of our fathers,*
> *God of Abraham, God of Isaac, and God of Jacob.*
> *The great, mighty, and awesome God, supreme God.*
> *You do acts of loving-kindness and create everything and remember the kindnesses of the fathers,*
> *and You will bring a redeemer to their children's children for the sake of Your name, and in love.*
> *Ruler, Helper, Rescuer, and Shield.*
> *Praised are You, Adonai, Shield of Abraham.*
>
> 4

Word Cards

Call on students to compare Word Cards 1 and 2.

Explain that the suffix נוּ means "our" or "us."

Ask students to translate each word. (1—"fathers"; 2—"our fathers")

Direct students to the Prayer Dictionary on page 6. Have them find and circle "fathers" and "our fathers" in the blessing on page 4. (*lines 1, 4*)

Display Word Cards 4–6. Have students read the Hebrew names aloud, then find and circle them in the blessing (*lines 2, 7*). Then have students find and circle them in the English translation of the blessing.

INTO THE TEXT

Tell the students that they will now study a prayer that links all of the generations of Jews together—from the very first Jews, Abraham and Sarah, to the students in the classroom today.

Display Word Card 1—אָבוֹת. Show the English meaning on the back of the Word Card ("fathers").

- Call on individual students to read aloud the first paragraph in the introduction on page 4.

- Ask students, "Who are *you*?" and have them answer by saying their names and a descriptive word, phrase, or sentence about themselves. (*Jonathan, and I'm a big hockey fan; Sarah, pianist; Mark, I'm going to sleep-away camp for the first time next summer*)

- Call on students to read the second and third paragraphs of the introduction aloud.

For Discussion

Why do you think the Amidah begins with the Avot blessing? (*connects us with our ancestors; reminds us how we began as a people; shows pride in our ancestry; shows that we are all part of the brit— the covenant—that God made with our ancestors Abraham [Genesis 12:2, 15:1–6, 17:1–8], Isaac [26:1–5], and Jacob [28:10-15, 35:12]*)

Ask students which lines in the English translation of the prayer reflect the following themes from the introduction on page 4.

- Adonai was the God of our ancestors. (*first two English lines*)

Call on students to read the corresponding Hebrew lines (1, 2).

- We hope for God's protection in the same way God protected our ancestors (*last two English lines*).

Call on students to read the corresponding Hebrew lines (6, 7).

Note: If it is the custom in your school to teach only the Avot, not the Avot V'imahot, you may choose to go directly to page 6 in the textbook.

Call on students to read the first paragraph of the introduction aloud. Ask them to share characteristics they have inherited from their mothers, grandmothers, and great-grandmothers. (*love to read, like to sleep late in the morning, play the piano well, can't draw very well*)

Call on students to read the second and third paragraphs of the introduction aloud.

Word Cards

Ask students to compare Word Cards 7 and 8.

Review the meaning of the suffix נוּ. (*"our" or "us"*)

Ask students to translate Word Cards 7 and 8. (*7—"mothers"; 8—"our mothers"*)

Direct students to find and circle "mothers" and "our mothers" in the blessing. (*lines 1, 5*)

Display Word Cards 9–12. Ask students to read each one aloud and circle the names in the blessing. (*lines 2, 3, and 7*) Then have students find and circle them in the English translation of the blessing.

A Blessing

Explain that בְּרָכָה means "blessing"—a prayer that praises and thanks God. Every בְּרָכָה contains the phrase בָּרוּךְ אַתָּה יְיָ ("Praised are You, Adonai").

Ask students why, according to the Avot, we praise and thank God. (*for being the God of our ancestors and creating the Jewish people; for God's acts of loving-kindness; for God's powers of creation; for God's remembering the kindnesses of our ancestors; for acting as Abraham's shield; for helping our matriarch Sarah*)

Note: Siddur Sim Shalom uses the phrase וּפֹקֵד שָׂרָה ("and Guardian of Sarah") instead of וְעֶזְרַת שָׂרָה ("and Help of Sarah").

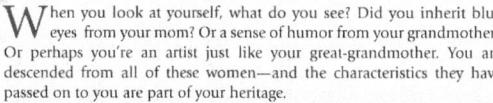

אָבוֹת וְאִמָּהוֹת

When you look at yourself, what do you see? Did you inherit blue eyes from your mom? Or a sense of humor from your grandmother? Or perhaps you're an artist just like your great-grandmother. You are descended from all of these women—and the characteristics they have passed on to you are part of your heritage.

Many congregations now include the אִמָּהוֹת in the Avot blessing. Adding the names of the Imahot links us directly to the matriarchs of the Jewish people—Sarah, Rebecca, Leah and Rachel. Just as we ask God to recognize us as descendants of the patriarchs Abraham, Isaac, and Jacob, we ask God to deal kindly with us because of the goodness of the matriarchs.

Whether the Amidah includes just the names of the Avot or also those of the Imahot, it reminds us that as Jews we have inherited God's favor because of our ancestors' goodness and faith.

Practice reading the אָבוֹת וְאִמָּהוֹת aloud.

1. בָּרוּךְ אַתָּה יְיָ, אֱלֹהֵינוּ וֵאלֹהֵי אֲבוֹתֵינוּ וְאִמּוֹתֵינוּ,
2. אֱלֹהֵי אַבְרָהָם, אֱלֹהֵי יִצְחָק, וֵאלֹהֵי יַעֲקֹב, אֱלֹהֵי שָׂרָה,
3. אֱלֹהֵי רִבְקָה, אֱלֹהֵי לֵאָה וְרָחֵל. הָאֵל הַגָּדוֹל, הַגִּבּוֹר,
4. וְהַנּוֹרָא, אֵל עֶלְיוֹן. גּוֹמֵל חֲסָדִים טוֹבִים וְקוֹנֵה הַכֹּל.
5. וְזוֹכֵר חַסְדֵי אָבוֹת וְאִמָּהוֹת, וּמֵבִיא גּוֹאֵל/גְּאֻלָּה לִבְנֵי בְנֵיהֶם,
6. לְמַעַן שְׁמוֹ, בְּאַהֲבָה. מֶלֶךְ עוֹזֵר וּמוֹשִׁיעַ וּמָגֵן.
7. בָּרוּךְ אַתָּה יְיָ, מָגֵן אַבְרָהָם וְעֶזְרַת שָׂרָה.

Praised are You, Adonai, our God and God of our fathers and mothers,
God of Abraham, God of Isaac, and God of Jacob, God of Sarah,
God of Rebecca, God of Leah and Rachel. The great, mighty, and awesome God, supreme God.
You do acts of loving-kindness and create everything and remember the kindnesses of the fathers
and mothers, and You will bring a redeemer/redemption to their children's children
for the sake of Your name, and in love. Ruler, Helper, Rescuer, and Shield.
Praised are You, Adonai, Shield of Abraham and Help of Sarah.

PRAYER VARIATIONS

Some congregations pray for God to bring a redeemer (גּוֹאֵל)—the Messiah—who will bring peace to the world, while other congregations pray for redemption (גְּאֻלָּה)—a state of peace and perfection in the world. But *all* Jews are alike in praying for a better and more peaceful world.

A Root

Write the root ברכ on the chalkboard. Below the root write the words בְּרָכָה and בָּרוּךְ. Explain to the students that these two words are built on the root ברכ, which means "praise" or "bless."

Ask them which three letters appear in both words. (ב, ר, כ/ךְ) Remind them that כ and ךְ are the same letter written differently. Ask if they can find two other related letters in the words you wrote.

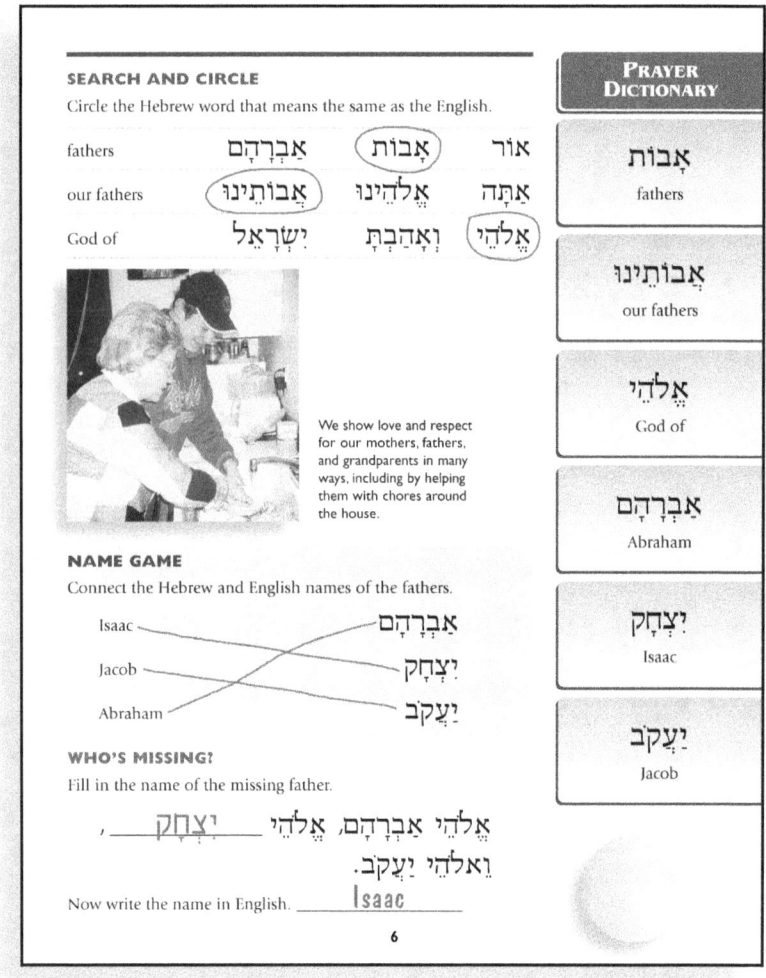

Photo Op

Note: "Photo Op" offers the teacher and students the opportunity to broaden class discussions using photographs that appear throughout the text.

The boy in the photo is helping in the kitchen. Ask students how they can show love and respect for their parents and grandparents.

PRAYER DICTIONARY

Display Word Card 3. In turn, hold up Word Cards 4–6 next to Word Card 3 and have students read and translate the three phrases: אֱלֹהֵי אַבְרָהָם ("God of Abraham"), אֱלֹהֵי יִצְחָק ("God of Isaac"), and אֱלֹהֵי יַעֲקֹב ("God of Jacob").

SEARCH AND CIRCLE

Direct students to complete the "Search and Circle" activity independently.

Option: Have students challenge themselves by covering the Prayer Dictionary while completing the exercise. They can then uncover it and check their own answers.

NAME GAME

Write the English names of our patriarchs—Abraham, Isaac, Jacob—on the chalkboard in random order.

Display Word Cards 4–6 in random order.

Call on a student to match each Hebrew Word Card with its English translation by placing the Word Card on the edge of the chalkboard under the correct English name.

WHO'S MISSING?

Have students complete the exercise.

Explain that the prefix וְ means "and." (וֵאלֹהֵי) Tell students they may see the Hebrew prefix meaning "and" in different forms. (וָ, וּ)

THE NEW HEBREW THROUGH PRAYER 2 • הִנֵּנִי

PRAYER DICTIONARY

Display Word Card 3. In turn, hold up Word Cards 9–12 next to Word Card 3 and have students read and translate the following phrases: אֱלֹהֵי שָׂרָה ("God of Sarah"), אֱלֹהֵי רִבְקָה ("God of Rebecca"), אֱלֹהֵי לֵאָה ("God of Leah"), אֱלֹהֵי רָחֵל ("God of Rachel").

SEARCH AND CIRCLE

Direct students to complete the "Search and Circle" activity independently.

NAME GAME

Write the English names of our matriarchs—Sarah, Rebecca, Leah, Rachel—on the chalkboard in random order.

Display Word Cards 9–12 in random order.

Call on a student to match each Hebrew Word Card with its English translation by placing the Word Card on the edge of the chalkboard under the correct English name.

WHO'S MISSING?

Have students complete the exercise.

Explain that the prefix וְ means "and." (וְרָחֵל)

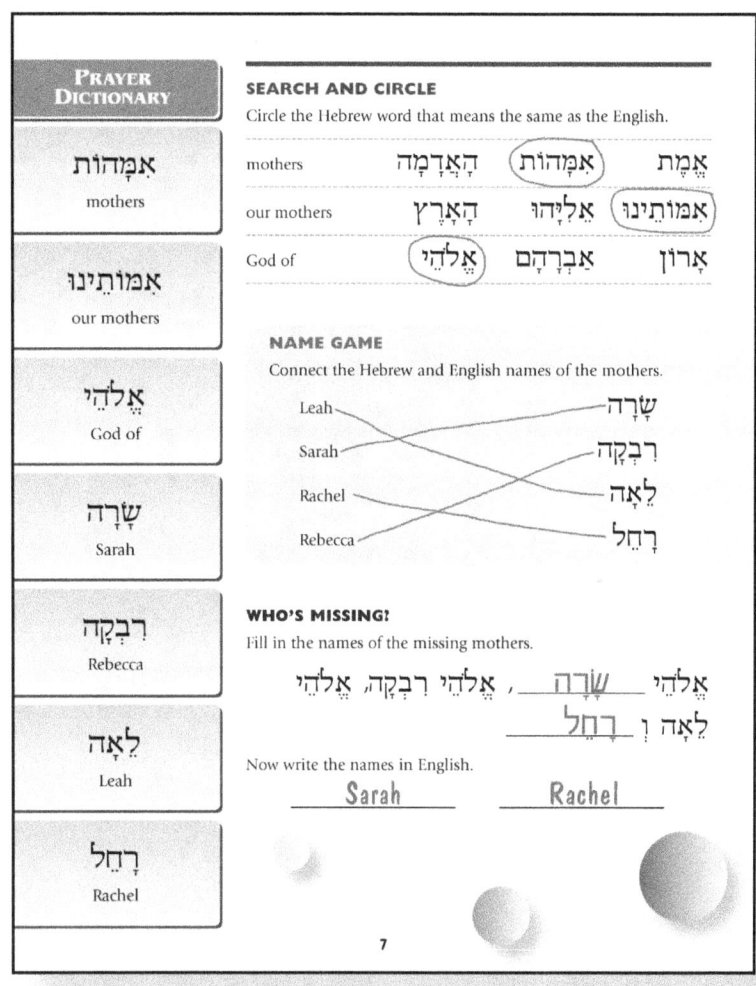

Patriarchs and Matriarchs

Display Word Cards 4–6 in random order. Call on students to place the names of the patriarchs in the correct order. Then have students give the English name for each one.

Display Word Cards 9–12 in random order. Call on students to place the names of the matriarchs in the correct order. Then have students give the English name for each one.

Challenge students to match the names of the husbands and wives. (*4 and 9; 5 and 10; 6 and 11, 12*)

Student Page

IN THE SYNAGOGUE

אָבוֹת is the first blessing in a very old and very important group of blessings called the עֲמִידָה. The עֲמִידָה is the heart or center of every synagogue service.

The עֲמִידָה has many names:

- The Hebrew name עֲמִידָה means "standing." We always stand when we say the עֲמִידָה. It is as if we are standing in front of God.

- It is sometimes called the "Silent Prayer" because many people say it in a very quiet voice. They are talking privately to God.

- Another name is שְׁמוֹנֶה עֶשְׂרֵה (the Hebrew word for "eighteen"). Originally, the עֲמִידָה contained eighteen blessings. Now it consists of nineteen blessings (when it is said on a weekday) or seven blessings (when it is said on Shabbat and holidays). The first three blessings and the last three blessings of every עֲמִידָה are always the same. Only the middle section changes.

- The עֲמִידָה is so important that many congregations simply call it the "Prayer" (תְּפִלָּה).

▶	אָבוֹת
	גְּבוּרוֹת
	קְדוּשָׁה
	קְדוּשַׁת הַיּוֹם
	עֲבוֹדָה
	הוֹדָאָה
	בִּרְכַּת שָׁלוֹם

TRUE OR FALSE

Put a ✓ next to each sentence that is true.

✓ The אָבוֹת refers to our relationship with our ancestors.

___ The אָבוֹת is the last part of the עֲמִידָה.

✓ The עֲמִידָה is said at every synagogue service.

✓ Another name for the עֲמִידָה is שְׁמוֹנֶה עֶשְׂרֵה.

___ The עֲמִידָה always contains 18 blessings.

✓ When we say the "Prayer," we are referring to the עֲמִידָה.

8

IN THE SYNAGOGUE

Read the section aloud with the students.

Take your students to visit the sanctuary in your synagogue. Have them open siddurim and help them locate the seven blessings in the Shabbat morning Amidah. Read the final sentence of each blessing. Each final sentence concludes with the words בָּרוּךְ אַתָּה יְיָ...

TRUE OR FALSE

When reviewing the answers, call on students to correct the two statements that were not checked, by changing one word in each statement. (*statement 2:* <u>first</u> part; *statement 5:* <u>seven</u> or <u>nineteen</u> blessings)

THE NEW HEBREW THROUGH PRAYER 2 • הִנְנִי

PRAYER DICTIONARY

Word Cards 13–16

Display Word Cards 13–16 and ask students to read them. Review the meaning of the prefix וְ. ("and") Explain that the prefix הַ means "the."

Read aloud the corresponding English translation on the back of each Word Card.

Extending the Lesson

Display the Hebrew side of Word Cards 13–16 and place them on the edge of the chalkboard in the order in which the words appear in the prayer. Read the words chorally with the class several times.

Ask the students to close their eyes. Remove one card. Have students open their eyes. Call on a student to recite all four words including the missing word. Return the card to the set in its correct place. Repeat the activity three more times, removing a different card each time.

For other activities of this kind, see "Reinforcing Word Order" on page 7 at the front of this guide.

You may wish to repeat the activity with the English sides of Word Cards 13–16.

GOD'S GREATNESS

Direct students to complete the <u>first part</u> of "God's Greatness" on the top of page 9 in their textbooks. Have students cover the Prayer Dictionary while working on the exercise. They can then uncover it and check their own answers.

Word Cards 17–21

Display Word Cards 17–21 and ask students to read them. Remind students that the prefix וְ means "and."

Read the corresponding English translation on the back of each Word Card.

Extending the Lesson

Follow the same activities described above in "Extending the Lesson."

GOD'S GREATNESS

Direct students to complete the <u>second part</u> of "God's Greatness."

Have students follow the procedure described for the <u>first part</u>.

Photo Op

The children in this photo are standing while they pray.

In what other ways do we show respect for God during a service? (*by not talking; in many congregations, by covering our heads and/or wearing a tallit; by participating fully in the service; by treating the siddur with respect*)

PRAYER BUILDING BLOCKS

"Prayer Building Blocks" are found throughout the textbook. This activity highlights specific words and phrases from the prayer. It often focuses on roots to help students understand the meaning of prayer words.

Direct students' attention to the logo at the top of the page—the open siddur and the roots קדש ("holy"), חיה ("life"), and שלמ ("peace").

For Discussion

Why do you think these three roots might have been selected as part of the logo? (קדש—*the siddur is holy; God is holy; we are a holy people;* חיה—*we pray that the life of the Jewish people continues; we pray for a good life; we pray for long life;* שלמ—*we pray for peace; peace is important for the world*)

אֱלֹהֵי "God of"

Read the first Building Block with the students.

Direct students to page 4, line 2, or page 5, lines 2–3. Read the line(s) in unison with the students.

Discuss possible answers before students complete the question in the box.

הַגָּדוֹל, הַגִּבּוֹר, וְהַנּוֹרָא "the great, the mighty, and the awesome"

Read the second Building Block with the students.

Discuss possible answers before students complete the question in the box.

Bring in a *Tanach*—a Bible—and show students the source of the biblical phrase: Nehemiah 9:32.

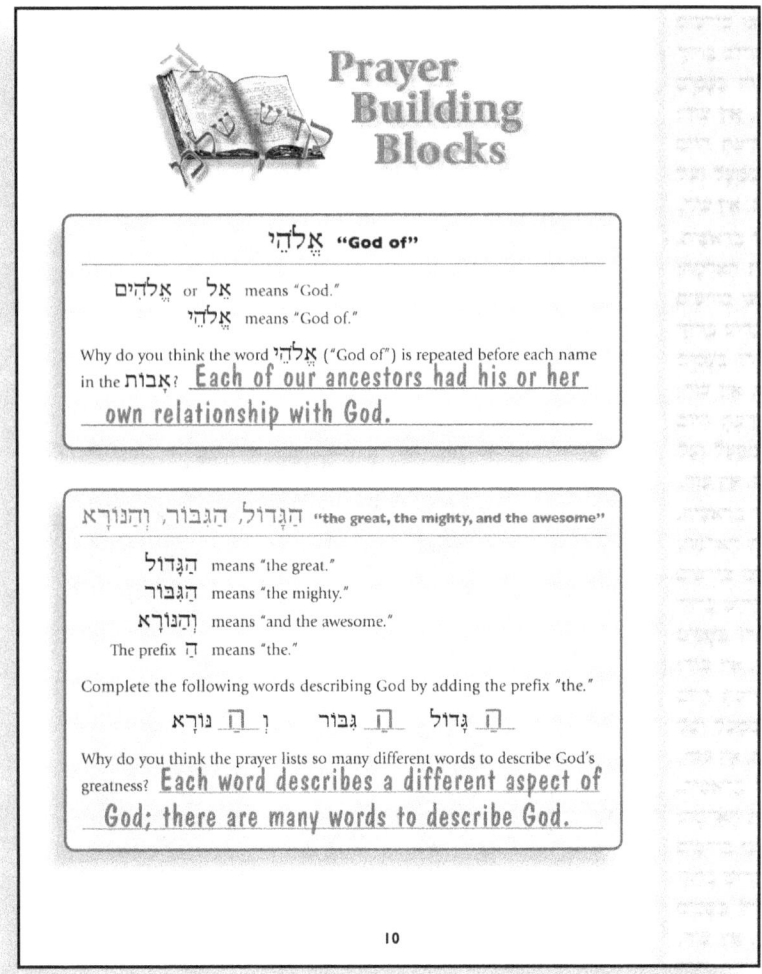

Review the *dagesh* (דָּגֵשׁ)—the dot in the middle of a letter.

Write the following pairs of letters on the chalkboard: בּב כּכ פּפ. Ask students how the *dagesh* affects the sound of each letter in which it appears.

Write the following letters on the chalkboard: ג צ י ל ד נ

Ask what sound each letter makes.

Now add the *dagesh* to each one: גּ צּ יּ לּ דּ נּ

Ask students what sound each letter now makes. Did the sound change? (*no*)

Tell them that in most Hebrew letters, when the *dagesh* appears, it does not change the sound of the letter.

TORAH CONNECTION

Ask students to read the four underlined words aloud together.

Follow the directions in the middle of the page.

Call on students to read lines 1–4 aloud together and then individually.

Direct students to write the name of the prayer and the meaning of the underlined words on the blank lines.

Read the question at the bottom of the page aloud to students.

Discuss possible responses with students before they write their answers.

TORAH CONNECTION

Read this verse from the Torah (Deuteronomy 10:17).

1. כִּי יְיָ אֱלֹהֵיכֶם הוּא אֱלֹהֵי הָאֱלֹהִים
2. וַאֲדֹנֵי הָאֲדֹנִים הָאֵל הַגָּדֹל הַגִּבֹּר וְהַנּוֹרָא

Do you recognize the underlined words?

Underline the same four words as they appear in the following lines from the siddur.
(Hint: Some of the words may look slightly different.)

1. בָּרוּךְ אַתָּה יְיָ, אֱלֹהֵינוּ וֵאלֹהֵי אֲבוֹתֵינוּ,
2. אֱלֹהֵי אַבְרָהָם, אֱלֹהֵי יִצְחָק, וֵאלֹהֵי יַעֲקֹב.
3. הָאֵל הַגָּדוֹל, הַגִּבּוֹר, וְהַנּוֹרָא, אֵל עֶלְיוֹן.
4. גּוֹמֵל חֲסָדִים טוֹבִים וְקוֹנֵה הַכֹּל ...

What is the name of this prayer? ___אָבוֹת___

Write the English meaning of the words you underlined.
___the great, the mighty, and the awesome God___

Why do you think the words הָאֵל הַגָּדוֹל הַגִּבּוֹר וְהַנּוֹרָא are written in the Torah and then repeated in the עֲמִידָה?
___They have great importance because they come from the Torah; we are quoting words from the Torah.___

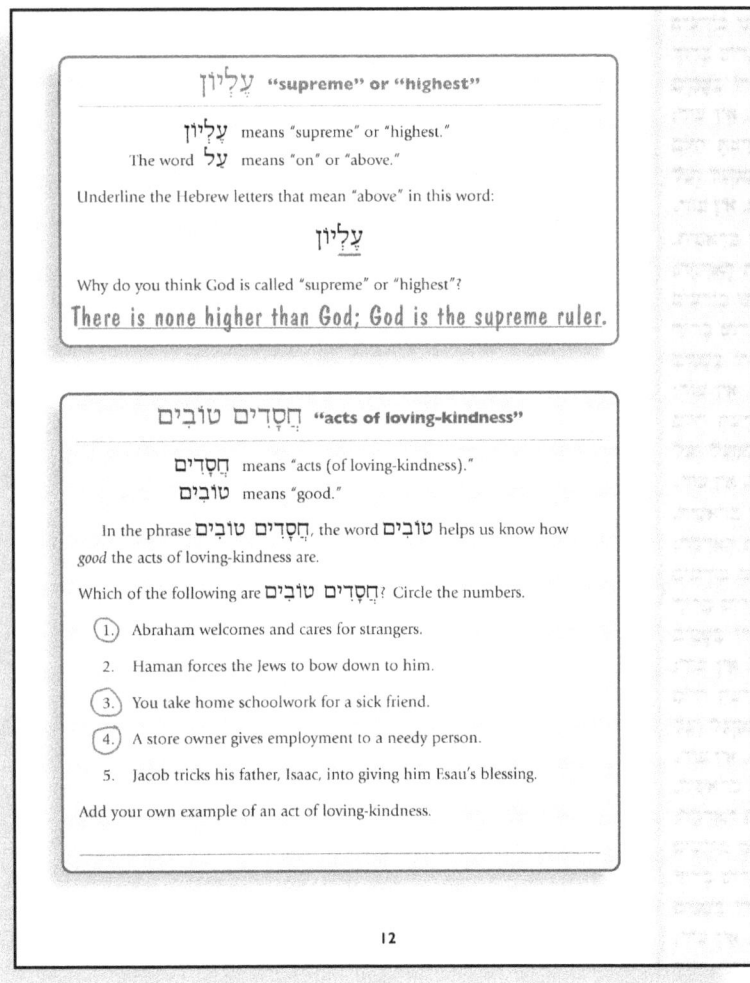

עֶלְיוֹן "supreme" or "highest"

Read the Building Block aloud with students.

To help students respond to the question, discuss other ways "supreme" is used (Supreme Court, the Supremes).

Double Challenge

Display Word Cards 13–16 in random order. Ask students to place the words in the order in which they are found in the Avot and to give the English meaning for each word.

Direct students to page 4, line 3, or page 5, line 3, sixth word to line 4, third word.

Read the sentence in unison with the students. Then call on individual students to read.

חֲסָדִים טוֹבִים "acts of loving-kindness"

Write the following words on the chalkboard:

חֲסָדִים חַסְדֵי חַסְדוֹ חֶסֶד

Call on students to determine the root of all four words. (חסד)

Explain that the root חסד means "kindness" or "goodness."

Have students complete the Building Block.

Explain that another term for acts of loving-kindness is גְּמִילוּת חֲסָדִים.

Read page 4, line 4; or page 5, line 4, fourth word through line 5, fourth word.

Which two words mean "kindness"? (חַסְדֵי, חֲסָדִים)

Ask students to find and read the English translation of the line(s).

Torah Study

Bring in ḥumashim to class. Help students find examples of Abraham's acts of loving-kindness (Genesis 13:5–12; 18:1–8, 20–33). Together read about Rebecca's kindness to animals (Genesis 24:10–20).

A Weekly Diary

Have students keep a weekly diary of their own acts of loving-kindness. Explain that just as our ancestors' acts of loving-kindness helped build a stronger, more just nation, so will *their* acts of loving-kindness be passed on to the next generation and contribute to the goodness of our people.

מֶלֶךְ עוֹזֵר וּמוֹשִׁיעַ וּמָגֵן
"ruler, helper, and rescuer and shield"

Ask if students remember the meaning of the prefix וּ. ("and")

Call on students to read the four Hebrew words at the top of page 13 aloud.

Point out that there are other ways to translate the phrase. ("a helpful Ruler and a Rescuer and a Shield"; "a helpful and saving Ruler and a Shield")

Direct students to complete the Building Block exercise and to read the completed sentences aloud.

Allow students time to think about the final question and to write down their insights.

Call on students to share their ideas.

Games . . . Games . . . Games

Look at the "Classroom Games" section at the front of this guide. Select one or more to reinforce reading and concepts. Suggestions are: "Word Search," "Stop!" "Beat the Clock," or "Jeopardy."

Reading and Chanting Practice

Direct students to page 4 or 5 in the text.

- Read the blessing aloud in unison.
- Call on individual students to read parts of the blessing aloud.
- Teach students to chant the blessing with the melody used in your synagogue.

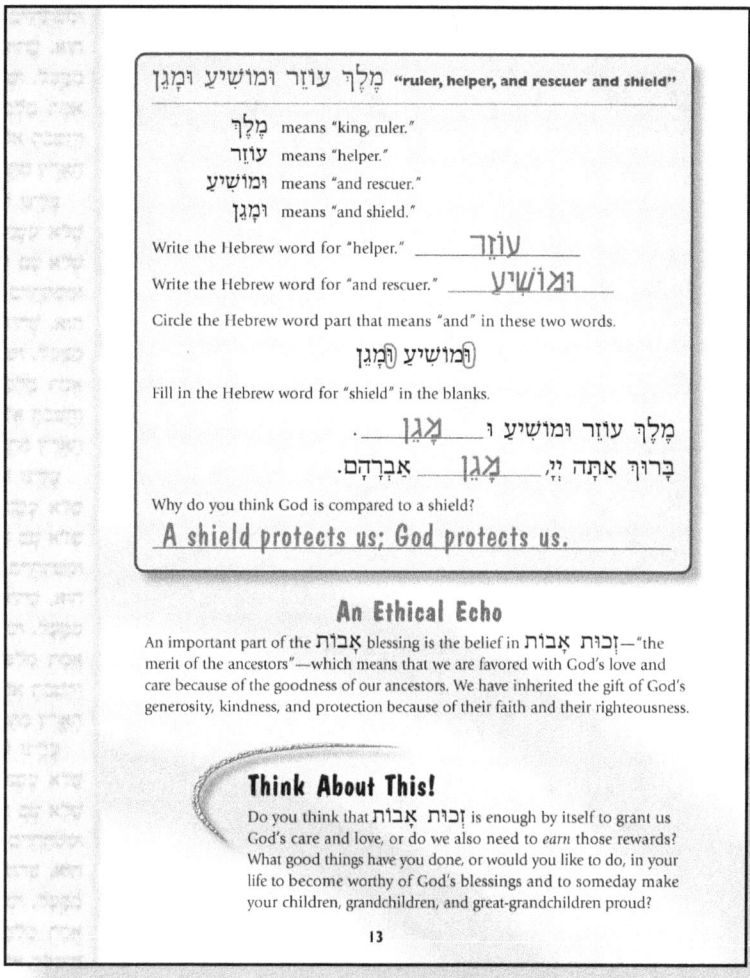

AN ETHICAL ECHO

Read the paragraph aloud with the students.

Ask them if there have been occasions when someone was particularly kind to them because of the merit of their parents. Did their parents' good name and reputation "automatically" bring kindness and honor to the students? Have them explain their answers.

THINK ABOUT THIS!

Pause after each question and discuss it with the students.

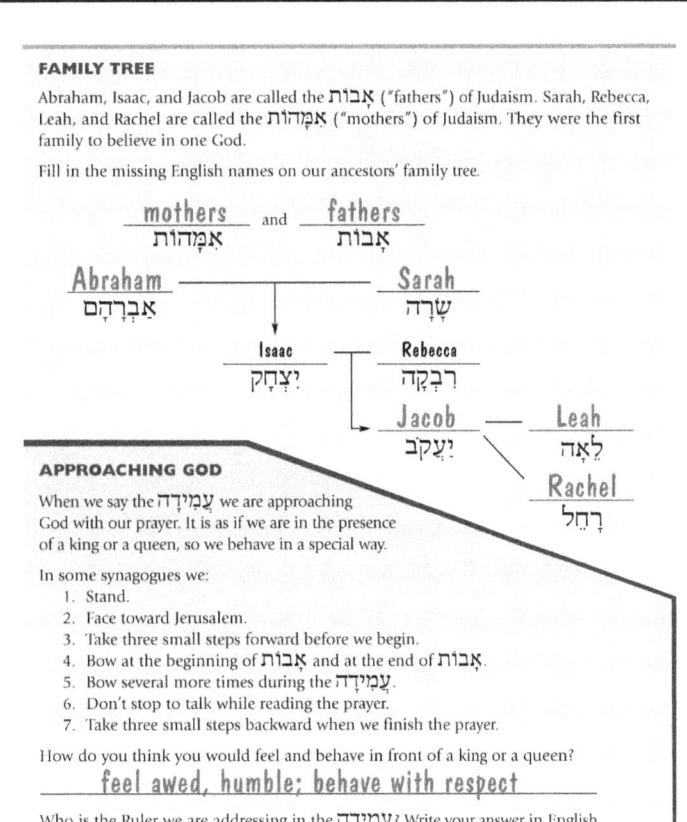

FAMILY TREE

Explain to the students the concept of a family tree. Tell them to listen to the discussion closely because each student's family will be asked to create their own unique family tree. (See "As a Family: Family Tree" at the back of this guide.)

Ask students to complete our ancestors' family tree at the top of page 14.

Explain that Jacob had twelve sons and one daughter. The Jewish people are descendants of Jacob's twelve sons (Genesis 35:22–26). Because the leaders of the Twelve Tribes of Israel bore the names of Jacob's sons, we imagine that the members of each tribe were the descendants of each son.

What's In a Name?

What was Abraham's original name? Read Genesis 17:1–6.

Who was once known as Sarai? Read Genesis 17:15–16.

Which patriarch was renamed Israel? Read Genesis 32:25–29.

APPROACHING GOD

Read and complete the activity with your students.

Have students follow the procedure described on page 14 (or the procedure that is customary in your own synagogue) while reciting or chanting the Avot aloud.

FLUENT READING

Word Search

Call on students to search for the following words. In each case, they should read the word and then the line containing the word.

Read each word:

- with a prefix meaning "the" or "and" (*lines 1, 3, 4, 5, 7, 8, 10*)
- built on the root חסד (*lines 7, 9, 10*)
- that is the name of a patriarch (*line 2*)
- related to God's name אֵל (*lines 2, 3, 4*)
- derived from the word אָב (*lines 1, 6, 8*)
- meaning "the great, the mighty, and the awesome" (*lines 3, 8*)
- meaning "the great, the mighty" (*line 4*); "the great and the awesome" (*line 5*)

Stop!

Play the game "Stop!" found on page 10 in the front of this guide. Assign a student to read up to a specific word on a line. For example: "Read line 1 until you read the Hebrew word meaning 'shield.'" Or, "Read line 10 until you read the Hebrew word built on the root meaning 'kindness.'" The class should follow the reading and when the designated reader reaches the word you have specified, the class should call out "Stop!" Another reader then continues.

WORKSHEET

Duplicate and hand out copies of the worksheet for Lesson 1 to review skills and concepts.

FAMILY EDUCATION

Duplicate and send home copies of "As a Family: Family Tree" (at the back of this guide).

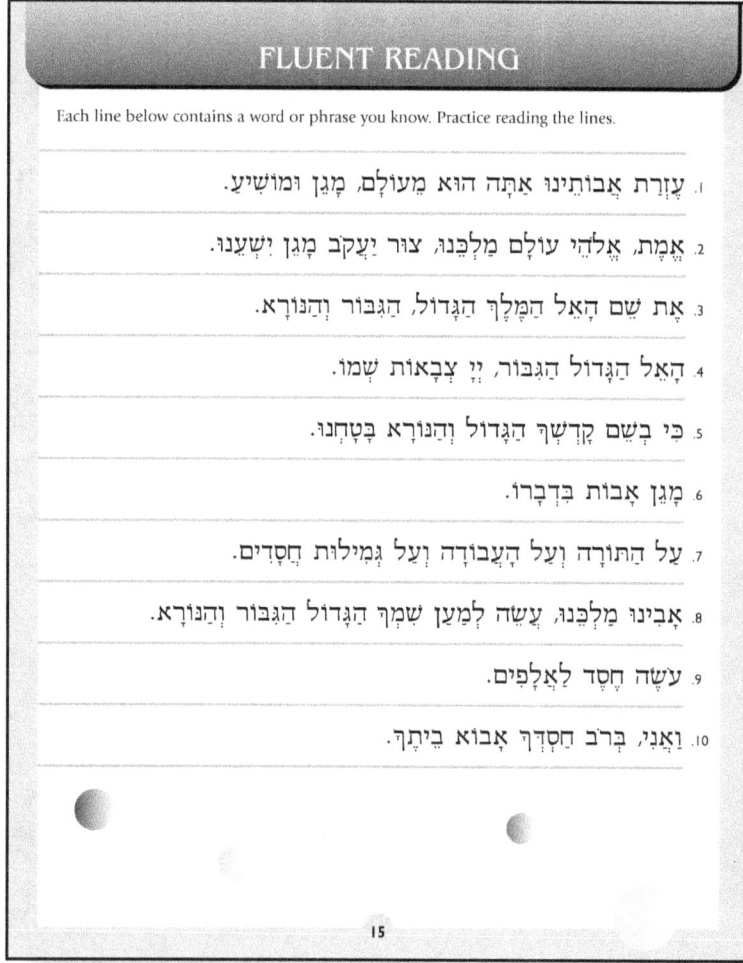

LESSON 1
Worksheet

Name: _____

אָבוֹת וְאִמָּהוֹת

1. Write the English translation for each term below.

    עֲמִידָה　　　　שְׁמוֹנֶה עֶשְׂרֵה　　　　תְּפִלָּה

    _____　　_____　　_____

2. Circle the suffix in each word below.

    אֲבוֹתֵינוּ　　　　אִמּוֹתֵינוּ

    What does this suffix mean? _____ _____

3. Write the English name below each Hebrew name.

    אַבְרָהָם　רִבְקָה　יַעֲקֹב　שָׂרָה　לֵאָה　יִצְחָק　רָחֵל

    _____ _____ _____ _____ _____ _____ _____

    Write the Hebrew names of the patriarchs in the order in which they appear in אָבוֹת.

    אֱלֹהֵי _____ אֱלֹהֵי _____ וֵאלֹהֵי _____

    Write the Hebrew names of the matriarchs in the order in which they appear in אָבוֹת וְאִמָּהוֹת.

    אֱלֹהֵי _____ אֱלֹהֵי _____ אֱלֹהֵי _____ וְ _____

    What is the English meaning of אֱלֹהֵי? _____

4. Connect each Hebrew word to its English meaning.

    helper　　　　מֶלֶךְ
    ruler　　　　מוֹשִׁיעַ
    shield　　　　עוֹזֵר
    rescuer　　　　מָגֵן

5. In many synagogues we follow several steps when we say the עֲמִידָה.
   Write three of the steps here.

   _____
   _____
   _____

6. Give one example of what your generation can do to ensure that Judaism continues in the next generation.

   _____

LESSON 2
גְּבוּרוֹת

LEARNING OBJECTIVES
Prayer Reading Skills
- The prefix בְּ ("with")
- The suffix ךָ ("your")
- The roots חיה ("live"); רחמ ("compassion" or "mercy")

Prayer Concepts
- Structure of the Amidah: the first three blessings and last three blessings are always the same
- Different versions of גְּבוּרוֹת: Reform, Reconstructionist, Conservative, and Orthodox
- God's powers: create life, save life, sustain life, help those who have fallen, heal the sick, free the captive, take care of the souls of those who have died
- Our souls live on forever
- Ethical Echoes:
  רוֹפֵא חוֹלִים ("healing the sick")
  בִּקוּר חוֹלִים ("visiting the sick")

BEYOND THE TEXTBOOK
The root חסד ("kindness")

ABOUT THE PRAYER
The blessing speaks of God's powers to help us when we are in need. While God's powers are many, this blessing speaks of God's power to create, to save, and to sustain life. God also helps the falling, heals the sick, frees the captive, and takes care of the souls of those who have died.

INSTRUCTIONAL MATERIALS
Text pages 16–27

Word Cards 22–29

Worksheet 2

Family Education: "As a Family: My Hero" (at the back of this guide)

SET INDUCTION
Your Reflection
Bring a mirror to class. Ask what its purpose is. (*reflects our image; shows how we look*)

Discuss the meaning of the terms "reflection" and "image." (*reflection is your exact physical likeness; image often indicates more than your reflection—image can indicate who you are: your values, the way you conduct yourself, the decisions you make*)

Call on students to describe people who have a positive image and those who have a negative image. What have these people done to create that image?

In God's Image בְּצֶלֶם אֱלֹהִים
Jewish tradition teaches that each of us is made in God's image—בְּצֶלֶם אֱלֹהִים. Our actions can reflect God's characteristics of power, love, and loving-kindness.

The Prayer: גְּבוּרוֹת
In the גְּבוּרוֹת we read of God's powers.

List the following four powers on the chalkboard:
- helps the falling
- heals the sick
- frees the captive
- keeps faith with (takes care of) the souls of those who have died

Divide the class into four groups. Assign one of God's powers to each group. Ask students in each group to discuss the actions they can take that would reflect the image of God. Designate one student per group to record the group's ideas; then, have each group share its ideas with the class. (<u>helps the falling</u>: *assist students struggling to achieve in school, in sports, with making friends; help those with disabilities; help those in need of food or clothing;* <u>heals the sick</u>: *call or visit sick friends and relatives; send get-well cards; contribute to funds seeking to find cures;* <u>frees the captive</u>: *write letters to seek political solutions; have a drive for supplies—such as school supplies, toys, food, and clothing—needed by those who are captive to poverty, war, oppression;* <u>keeps faith with the souls of those who have died</u>: *perform acts of loving-kindness in their memory; mourners recite the Kaddish; light a yahrzeit candle; plant a tree in Israel in their memory*)

You and Your

Direct students to find and circle the words "You" and "Your" each time they appear in the English translation.

Ask them why these words are written with a capital Y. ("*You*" *and* "*Your*" *refer to God and we always capitalize God's name; a capital letter indicates respect for God*)

Ask them in what other ways we show respect for God's name. (*we do not use God's name in vain; we do not throw away books with God's name; we kiss the siddur when prayers are completed or if we drop it*)

INTO THE TEXT

Call on students to read the first paragraph of the introduction on page 16.

Ask them to describe the powers in nature that most impress or inspire them.

Call on students to read the second paragraph.

Ask them to describe times when they acted to make the world a better place for their parents, grandparents, siblings, friends, or even strangers.

Word Study

Direct students to the English translation of the prayer.

Note the parentheses around the words "powerful" and "mercy." These indicate an alternate English translation for the Hebrew words גִּבּוֹר ("mighty"—line 1) and רַחֲמִים ("compassion"—line 2).

Write the Hebrew and English phrases מְחַיֵּה הַכֹּל ("You give life to all") and מְחַיֵּה מֵתִים ("You give life to the dead") on the chalkboard. Explain that some synagogues use the first phrase while others use the second. Direct students to the four times the alternate choices הַכֹּל/מֵתִים appear in the Hebrew and in the English. Bring in your synagogue prayer book and show them which phrase appears there.

Note: Students will read more about these terms on page 17 in their text.

A First Reading

The English translation is divided into four sections.

Call on students to count off 1-2, 1-2, and so on, around the room to form reading partners. Direct Partner 1 to read each English section aloud and Partner 2 to read the corresponding Hebrew. When they have completed all four sections, the partners should switch so that Partner 2 reads the English and Partner 1 reads the corresponding Hebrew.

Corresponding sections: English section 1 ("You are eternally mighty [powerful] . . .") corresponds to Hebrew line 1; English section 2 ("With kindness . . .") corresponds to Hebrew lines 2–3; English section 3 ("Who is like You . . .") corresponds to Hebrew lines 4–5; English section 4 ("You are faithful . . .") corresponds to Hebrew lines 6–7.

PRAYER DICTIONARY

Word Pass

Distribute Word Cards 22–29 among eight students.

Call out the following categories, one at a time, and have students holding a Word Card in that category stand and read it aloud in Hebrew and English:

- a "final letter"
- the letter ה
- one of the sound-alike letters, ך כ ח
- a "silent letter" (א, ע, or ה at the end of a word without a vowel)
- the letter *yud*
- a letter with a *dagesh*

Some of the words fit into more than one category, so play the game again with different students (e.g., the word מְחַיֵּה is in the category with the letter ה, sound-alike letters, and silent letters).

WHAT'S MISSING?

Display Word Cards 23, 26, 27, 29 in random order on the edge of the chalkboard or in a pocket chart. Have students complete the exercise by selecting their answers from the Word Cards on display.

PRAYER VARIATIONS

Read the complete explanation aloud with your students.

Practice reading the prayer in your synagogue prayer book.

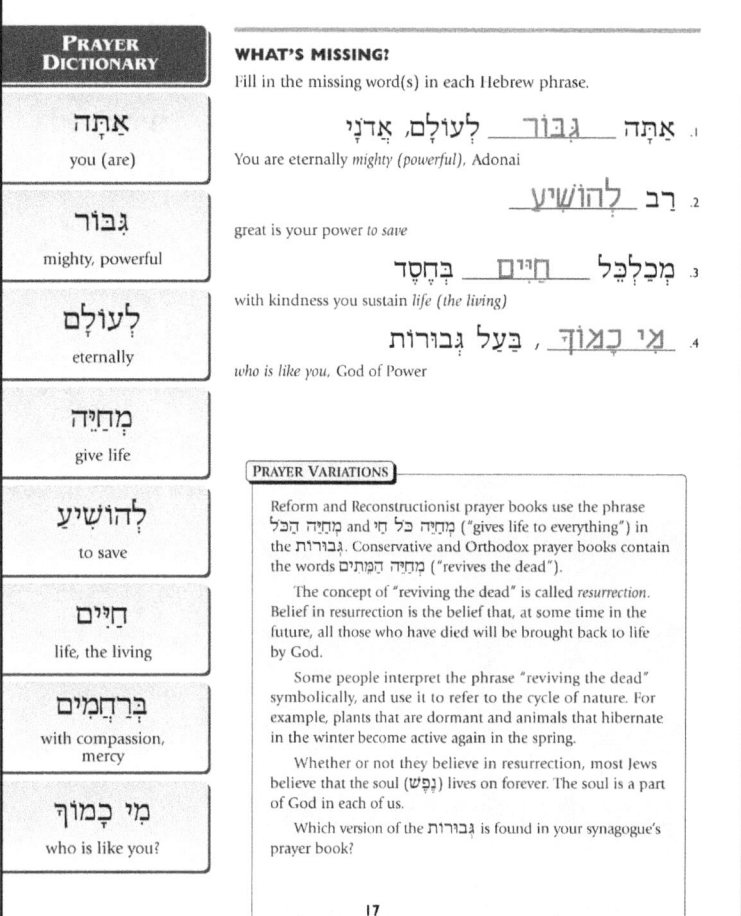

29 LESSON 2

POWERFUL WORDS

Have students complete the exercise using the Prayer Dictionary for reference.

Call on students to read aloud all the choices in each row and then to read the correct answer.

Vocabulary Review

Have the students close their textbooks. Display Word Cards 22–29 on the edge of the chalkboard. Call out English meanings in random order and have individual students select and read the matching Hebrew Word Card.

Note: Refer to "General Word Card Techniques and Games" on page 6 of this guide for other ideas.

IT'S A MATCH!

Instruct students to complete the activity individually, then review it together.

THEME OF גְּבוּרוֹת

Read the introductory sentence to the class.

Call on six students to each read one of God's powers listed at the top of the page.

Read aloud the sentences that follow the list of God's powers.

Divide the students into discussion groups of two to four students each. Direct each group to choose three of God's powers and to discuss what we can do to emulate God. Encourage students to draw upon previous class discussions for their ideas. Have the group members write down one or more of their shared ideas in their textbooks. Then ask students to share their responses with the class.

Reading Skills

Refer students back to the prayer on page 16.

Unison Reading: Call on students to read the English lines that reflect God's powers, as listed on page 19. (*first three English sentences: "You are eternally . . . sleep in the dust"*)

Call on the class to read the corresponding Hebrew lines in unison. (*page 16, lines 1–3*)

Phrase by Phrase: Have half the class read the same English lines, pausing at each comma or period. Have the other half of the class read the corresponding Hebrew phrases. When students read the phrases with the choice of הַכֹּל or מֵתִים, have them use the word found in your synagogue's prayer book.

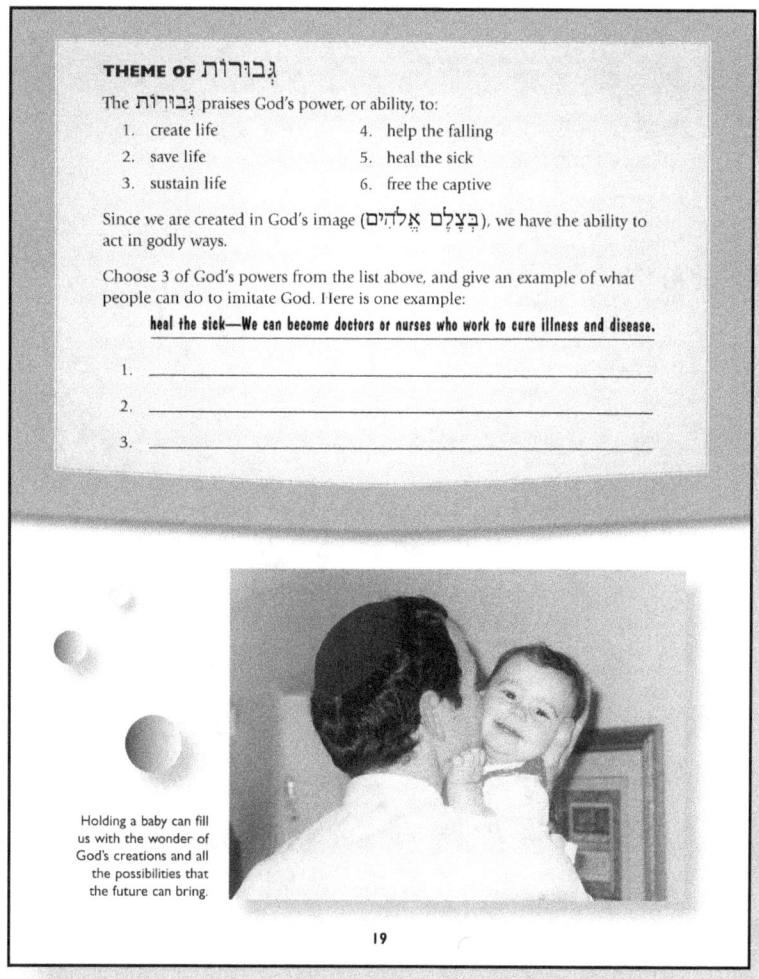

Photo Op

Which of God's powers is represented by the birth of a baby? (*creates or gives life*)

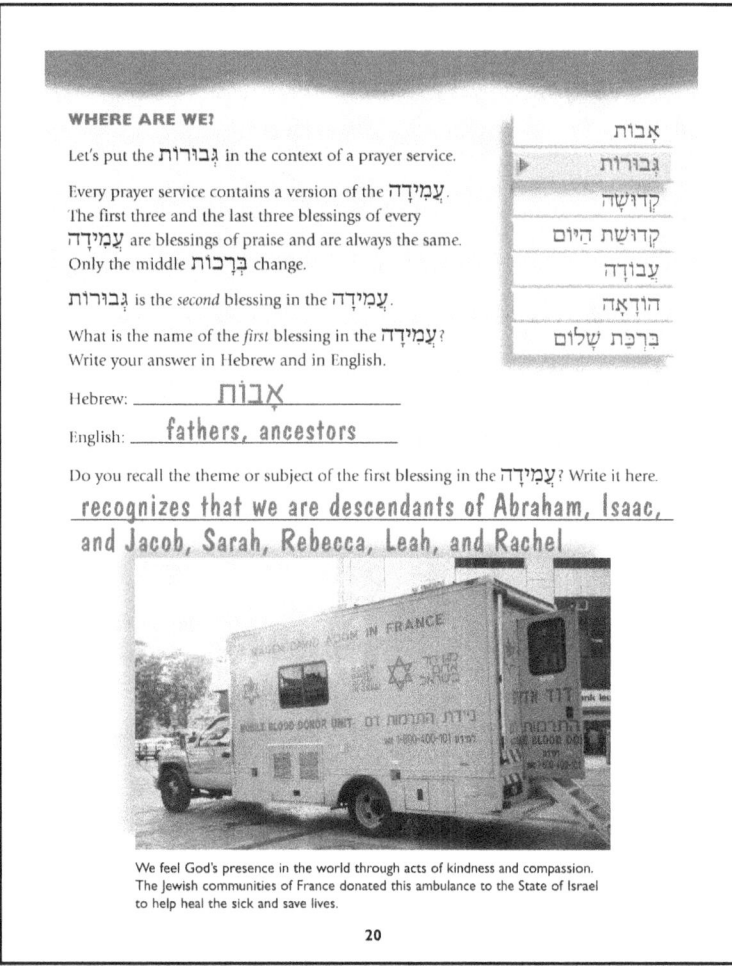

WHERE ARE WE?

Read the activity aloud to the students.

Direct their attention to the list of the seven blessings in the Shabbat morning Amidah that appears in the top right corner of the page, and to the arrow pointing to the second blessing, גְבוּרוֹת.

Ask them to read the names of the seven blessings in unison.

Siddur Geography

Enlarge and photocopy the list of seven blessings.

Cut the sheet into the names of the seven blessings and number them 1–7 on the back.

Place the names of the blessings on a bulletin board in random order. Call on individual students to arrange the blessings in the correct order either from top to bottom or right to left.

Students can correct a newly placed random arrangement each class session.

Photo Op

Direct students to the name printed across the top of the ambulance. (*Magen David Adom in France*)

Ask them to read the name next to the Jewish Star, either on the left in English or on the right in Hebrew. (*Magen David Adom in Israel*)

Ask them what the Hebrew phrase is for Jewish Star. (מָגֵן דָוִד—*Shield of David*)

Explain that the word אָדוֹם means "red."

Ask them to translate "Magen David Adom in Israel." (*Red Shield of David in Israel*).

Explain that "Magen David Adom in Israel" is the name for Israel's "Red Cross."

PRAYER BUILDING BLOCKS

אַתָּה גִבּוֹר לְעוֹלָם

"you are eternally mighty (powerful)"

Read and complete the Building Block together.

Have students read the first line in the blessing on page 16 in unison.

Then have them complete the exercises on page 21.

Computer Whiz

Ask students to describe the function of "spell check" on a computer. (*checks and corrects spelling errors*)

Introduce a variation of spell check—"reading check," in which students check the reading of six other students who read lines 1–6 in turn. Alternatively, have partners check one another.

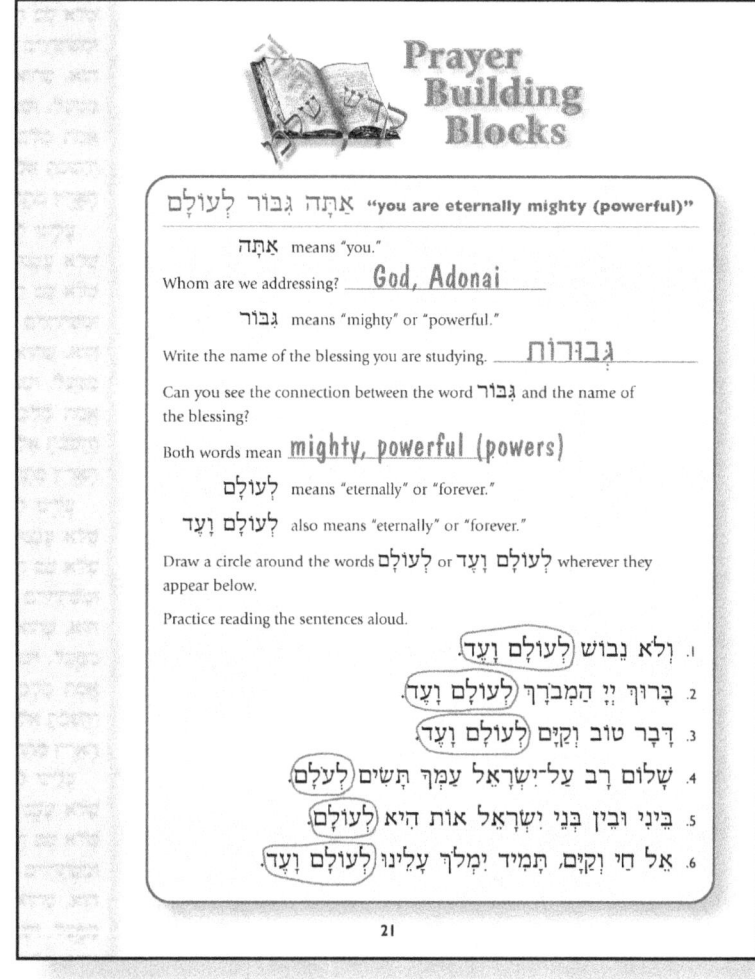

33 LESSON 2

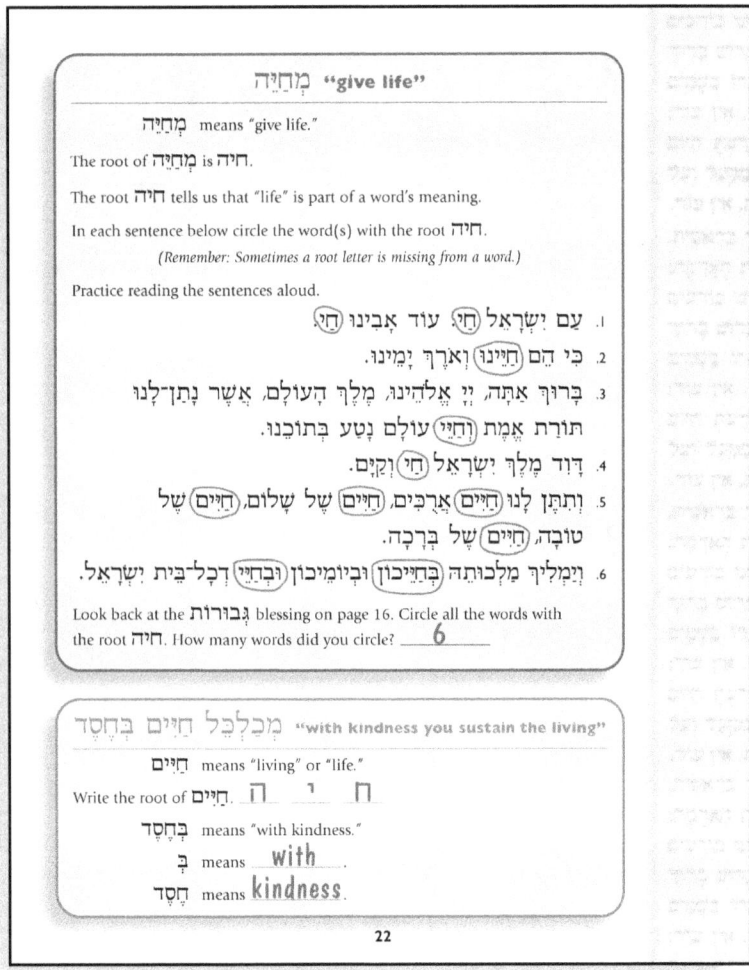

מְחַיֶּה "give life"

Read the first part of the Building Block together. Ask students if they or any family members have the Hebrew name חַיִּים ("life"). Remind them that sometimes a root letter does not appear in a word built on that root.

Reading Skill

Have students circle and read aloud the words built on the root חיה in sentences 1–6.

Call on individual students to read each line. Direct the reader to pause before each circled word in the line. The class should then read the circled word aloud in unison. The reader can then continue reading.

The Fruit of the Tree

Start "planting an orchard" in your classroom. Create a "tree" with three roots from oaktag, poster board, or construction paper. On each of the roots of the tree, write one letter: חיה. Write the word "life" on the trunk.

Let students choose the kind of fruit they would like to grow on their חיה tree and cut out the shapes of the fruit. (*orange tree—orange paper; banana tree—yellow paper; apple tree—red or green paper*).

On each "fruit," write a different Hebrew word that grows from the root חיה. You might wish to have individual students write the words.

Begin with the Building Block word מְחַיֶּה. Add the words students circled in sentences 1–6 and the words they circled in גְבוּרוֹת on page 16.

Each time new words built on this root are introduced, add them to the tree.

Each time a new root is introduced in the textbook, add a new fruit tree to the orchard. There will be eighteen fruit trees in all.

A Tasty Treat

Students might enjoy a treat of the fruit they have chosen for their orchard; for example, bring in oranges or apples.

Sing-Along

Line 1 on page 22 is a well-known Hebrew song. Sing the song together with the class.

מְכַלְכֵּל חַיִּים בְּחֶסֶד
"with kindness you sustain the living"

Call on students to read the Building Block phrase aloud.

Have them complete the activity independently and then review the answers together.

The Fruit of the Tree

Create a fruit tree with the root חסד ("kindness").

Place a fruit on the tree with the word from the Building Block. (בְּחֶסֶד)

Add words from אָבוֹת, the first blessing of the Amidah, on page 4. (חֲסָדִים, חַסְדֵּי)

Extending the Concept

Challenge students to write words or phrases indicating acts of kindness. Add those fruit to the tree. (*give tzedakah; create peace; show friendship; feed the hungry; hold a clothing drive; volunteer in a service organization*)

"LIVELY" TIDBITS

Read this section aloud with your students.

Discuss responses to the question at the end of the section.

Encourage the class to make a tzedakah donation of $18 to an organization of their choice.

> ### "LIVELY" TIDBITS
>
> - Did you ever see grownups clink glasses and toast each other with the word "לְחַיִּים"—"To Life!"?
> - Is there someone in your class wearing a חַי necklace? We know that חַי means "life."
> - Did you know that each Hebrew letter also has a numerical value? There's even a system—called *gematria*—of interpreting a Hebrew word by adding up the value of its letters. For example, the letter ח has the value 8 and the letter י has the value 10. Together they add up to 18—and they spell the word חַי! That's why we often give monetary gifts at Jewish celebrations in multiples of $18.
>
> Why do you think it is appropriate to give gifts in multiples of $18?
>
> *It's as if we're saying, "I wish you a long and good life"; it's symbolic of our wishes for a long life.*
>
> *People often give gifts in multiples of $18 in celebration of weddings and other lifecycle events.*

Photo Op

Review the symbolism of the number 18.

Ask why a gift in multiples of $18 is especially appropriate as a wedding gift. (*the couple is beginning a new life together; we wish them a happy new life as a married couple; we hope they have a long life together*)

Talk about other life-cycle events that we might acknowledge with gifts in multiples of $18. (*Baby: new life; long life; good life; Bar/Bat Mitzvah: beginning a new stage in life; new Jewish responsibilities in life; Confirmation: confirming a commitment to a Jewish life; Death and mourning: in memory of the life that was lived; a reminder of the good the person did in life*)

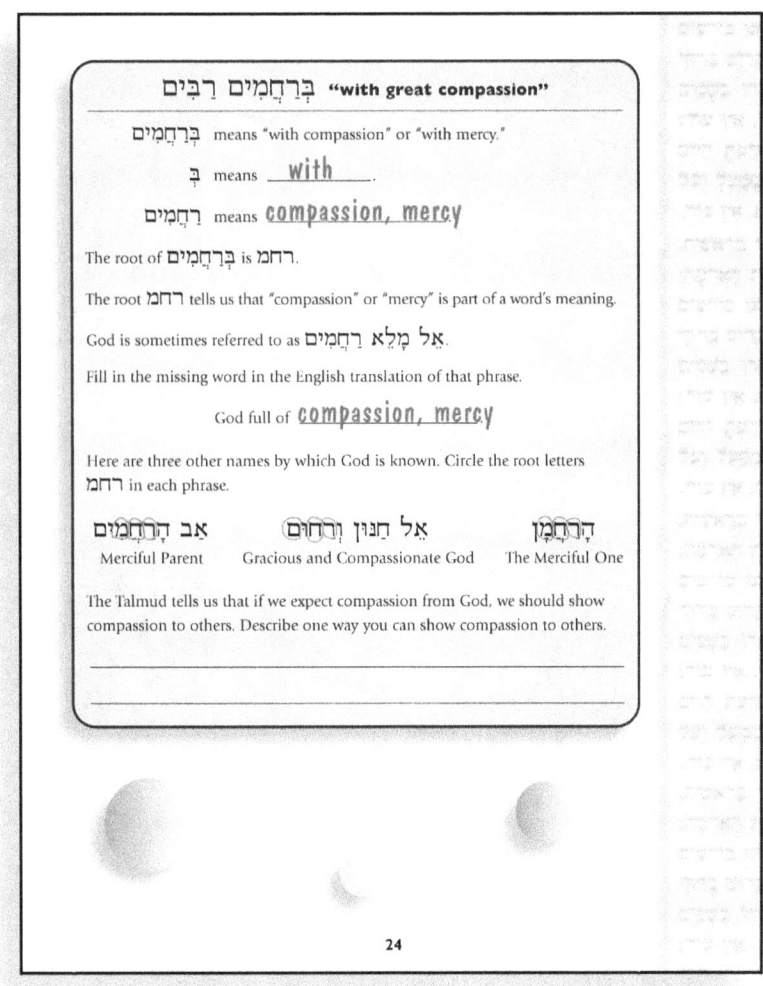

בְּרַחֲמִים רַבִּים
"with great compassion"

Have students read the Building Block phrase aloud.

Complete the first five lines of the Building Block with the students. Call on students to read in unison line 2 in the blessing on page 16, followed by its English meaning. ("*With kindness . . .*")

The Fruit of the Tree

Create a fruit tree with the root רחמ. Write "compassion" and "mercy" on the trunk. Write בְּרַחֲמִים on a fruit for the tree.

Read the remaining section of the page together. Add the four names for God to the fruit of the tree.

Ask students to complete the bottom of the page independently and to share their answers.

The Crown of a Good Name

Rabbi Shimon in Pirke Avot ("Sayings of the Fathers") 4:13 says, "There are three crowns: the crown of Torah (teaching and learning), the crown of priesthood (Temple service), and the crown of royalty (power). But the crown of a good name exceeds them all."

Creating a Crown

Have the students cut out paper in the shape of a crown and write their names and שֵׁם טוֹב ("a good name") on it. Each time students perform an act of loving-kindness, they should add a Jewish Star to a point on their crowns and write the type of act they performed. Create a bulletin board with the crowns.

For Discussion

Discuss the choice of a crown metaphor. (*a crown is a symbol of power and glory*) Why is the crown of a good name more important than all the other crowns? (*it reflects kind deeds you may have done, how others benefit because of you; being a mensch is more important than being learned or powerful*)

How does performing acts of loving-kindness —גְּמִילוּת חֲסָדִים—create a perfect "fit" for the crown of your good name? (*your good deeds earn you the right to wear the crown*)

מִי כָמוֹךָ "who is like you?"

Read the Building Block together. After students complete the activity, have them read each circled word aloud before reading each line aloud.

CHALLENGE QUESTION

Have students read and then sing lines 2 and 3 in unison.

AN ETHICAL ECHO

Read "An Ethical Echo" together with students. Challenge them to locate and circle the Hebrew phrase meaning "and heals the sick" on page 16, line 3. (וְרוֹפֵא חוֹלִים)

Call on students to read the complete sentence. (line 2, last word through line 3)

THINK ABOUT THIS!

Read "Think About This!" together.

Discuss with students how we can cheer the sick.

An Act of Loving-Kindness

Have the class decide on a project to help those who are sick. (*volunteer to visit a local hospital; send cards to patients in a hospital ward; direct a fundraising drive for money to be donated to a medical cause; direct a toy drive for a children's ward*)

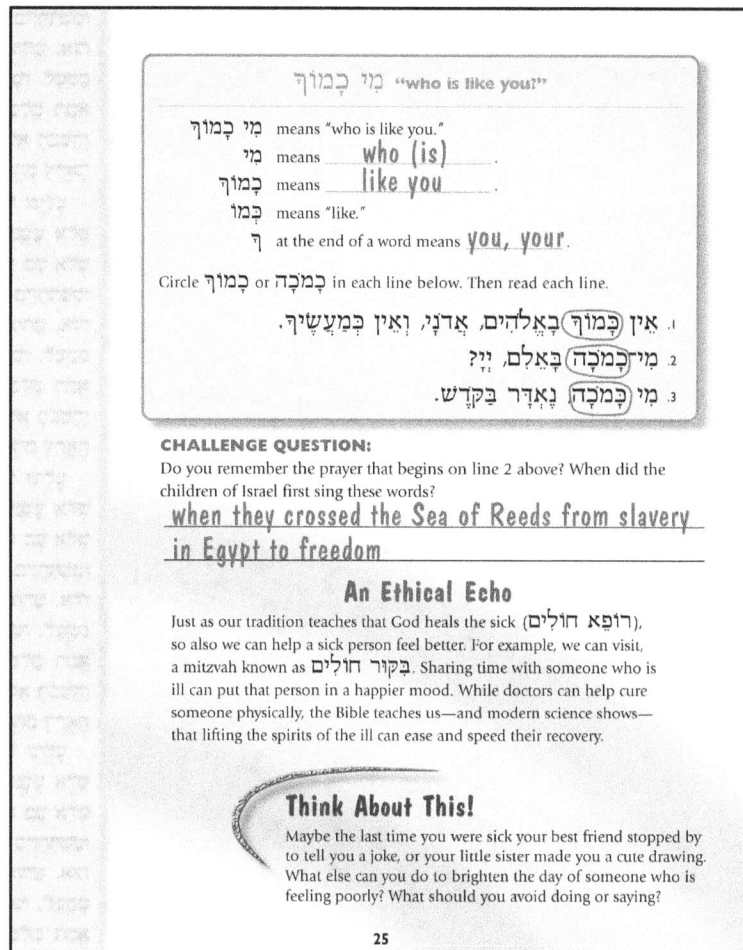

37 LESSON 2

> **WHO'S YOUR HERO?**
>
> The word גִבּוֹר means "mighty," "powerful," or "hero." A hero is somebody who does something brave, like climbing Mt. Everest, or who helps make the world a better place, like a doctor who discovers the cure for a disease. You too can be a hero by doing something brave or by helping others.
>
> 1. Name a hero from Jewish history who acted bravely *and* helped the Jewish people. Describe what he or she did.
>
>   _____
>   _____
>   _____
>
> 2. Describe something brave that *you* have done. Did it help to make your home, school, or even the world a better place? Explain your answer.
>
>   _____
>   _____
>   _____
>
>
>
> A hero isn't just someone who climbs mountains or saves lives. For example, Israeli scouts such as these are heroes when they help feed those in need.
>
> 26

Photo Op

Read the photo caption aloud.

Ask students if anyone in the class belongs to a group, such as the scouts, that helps others. Encourage students to share their experiences.

WHO'S YOUR HERO?

Display Word Card 23 (גִבּוֹר). Ask students to read the word and give the English meaning. (*"mighty," "powerful"*)

Tell students there is a third meaning for גִבּוֹר— "hero."

Read the introduction on page 26 with them.

Ask the students:

- who they consider to be heroes (*firefighters; soldiers; people who find joy in the world despite adversity such as a serious illness; people who work very hard to support their families*)

- if they personally know someone they would call a גִבּוֹר—a "hero."

Direct students to the first question.

Brainstorm a list of men and women from Jewish history whom they consider to be heroes. Write the names on the chalkboard with one or two phrases describing what the person did.

Have each student select the name of the person he or she wishes to salute and write about that person in response to question 1.

Direct students to the second question.

Allow students time to write about themselves in response to question 2. Encourage students to share their responses.

THE NEW HEBREW THROUGH PRAYER 2 • הִנְנִי

FLUENT READING

Read the introductory paragraph aloud.

In ancient times, the family of Aaron, Moses' brother, served as the priests in Israel. They offered sacrifices to God in the Tabernacle when the Israelites wandered in the desert and in the Holy Temple after it was built by King Solomon in Jerusalem. Today, their descendants are still called "kohanim" ("priests"), but their role in Jewish life is strictly ceremonial.

Reading Rules
Double Sh'va

When a *sh'va* appears in the middle of a word under two adjacent letters (קָדְשְׁךָ), the first *sh'va* is silent (קָדְ) and the second *sh'va* is sounded (שְׁךָ).

Ask students which word in the Priestly Blessing has a double *sh'va*. (*line 1*—וְיִשְׁמְרֶךָ)

Have the class read line 1 of the Priestly Blessing in unison. Then call on individual students to read line 1.

The Dagesh

When the final letter ך has a *dagesh* (ךּ), it has the sound "k" just like the letter כ.

The letter-vowel combination ךָ has the sound "kah."

Ask students which word in the Priestly Blessing ends with ךָ. (*line 2*—וִיחֻנֶּךָּ)

Have the class read the last two words in line 2 of the Priestly Blessing. Highlight the difference between ךָ (אֵלֶיךָ) and ךָּ (וִיחֻנֶּךָּ).

Call on individual students to read the two words.

Have the class read lines 1–3 of the Priestly Blessing in unison. Call on individual students to read lines 1–3.

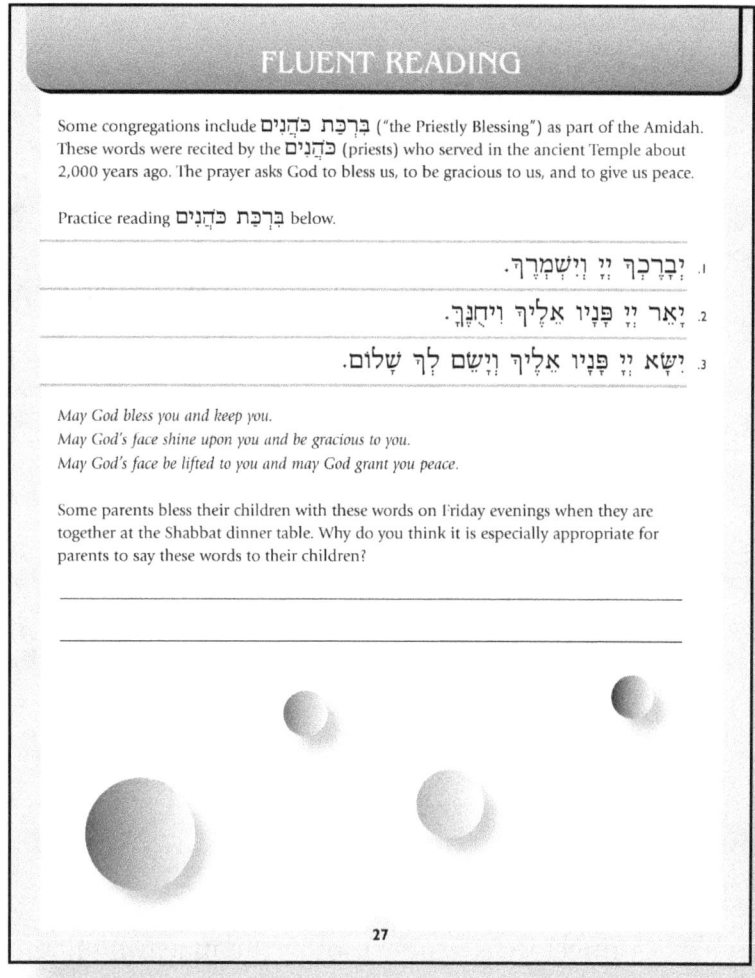

WORKSHEET

Duplicate and hand out copies of the worksheet for Lesson 2 to review skills and concepts.

FAMILY EDUCATION

Duplicate and send home copies of "As a Family: My Hero" (at the back of this guide).

LESSON 2
Worksheet

Name: _____

גְּבוּרוֹת

1. How many blessings are there in the Shabbat morning עֲמִידָה? _____

   Unscramble the letters to spell the name of the first blessing: בוֹאָת _____

   What is the English meaning of the name? _____

   Unscramble the letters to spell the name of the second blessing: רוֹגְבוּת _____

   What is the English meaning of the name? _____

2. Write the English meaning next to each Hebrew word or phrase below.

   רוֹפֵא חוֹלִים _____   בִּקוּר חוֹלִים _____

   גִּבּוֹר _____   עֲמִידָה _____

   כֹּהֲנִים _____   בִּרְכַּת כֹּהֲנִים _____

3. Connect the Hebrew root to the matching English.

   bless, praise   רחמ

   kindness   חיה

   compassion, mercy   ברכ

   life   חסד

4. Using your knowledge of roots, connect each Hebrew word or phrase below to its English meaning.

   the Merciful One   תּוֹרַת חַיִּים

   Blessing after Meals   גְּמִילוּת חֲסָדִים

   acts of loving-kindness הָרַחֲמָן

   Torah of life   בִּרְכַּת הַמָּזוֹן

HINENI—THE NEW HEBREW THROUGH PRAYER 2 © Behrman House Publishers

LESSON 3 — קְדוּשָׁה

LEARNING OBJECTIVES

Prayer Reading Skills
- The suffixes ךָ ("your"); וֹ "his"
- The prefixes בַּ ("in the"); הָ ("the")
- The roots קדש ("holy," "sanctify"); מלכ ("rule")

Prayer Concepts
- The Kedushah is the third blessing in the Amidah
- The Kedushah proclaims God's holiness
- Verses in the Kedushah come from the section of the Bible called "Prophets"
- We imitate the angels in the prophet Isaiah's visions when we recite the prayer
- Reciting the Kedushah requires a minyan

ABOUT THE PRAYER

To be holy is to be separate and special. The blessing speaks of the holiness of God. When we recite the Kedushah, we publicly proclaim God's holiness.

INSTRUCTIONAL MATERIALS

Text pages 28–35

Word Cards 30–36

Worksheet 3

Family Education: "As a Family: Holy Times" (at the back of this guide)

SET INDUCTION

To Be Holy

Discuss the meaning of the term *"kadosh"* ("holy"). (*separate and special, unlike anything or anyone else*) Discuss the things that are holy. (*God; objects, such as the Torah, siddur, Ark; places, such as Jerusalem, the Western Wall; time, such as Shabbat, holy days*)

Extend the discussion to events that may be seen as holy experiences. (*creation, marriage, birth of a baby, seeing a beautiful sunset*)

To Be a Holy People

In the Torah we are told to be a holy people ("You shall be holy for I, Adonai, your God, am holy" [Leviticus 19:2]).

Since we are made in the image of God, we strive to fulfill this commandment by acting in holy ways. Ask students what actions they think are expected from a holy people. (*kindness, caring, repairing the world, respect for God and for others, praying, studying the Torah*)

קְדוּשָׁה 3

Have you ever imagined that you were someone else? Perhaps you had the role of a princess in a school play and you spoke and walked regally. Or maybe you and your buddies pretended to be pro-basketball stars. The קְדוּשָׁה, the third blessing in the Amidah, helps us stretch our imaginations so we can picture angels as they praise God.

The Torah tells us in the Book of Isaiah that winged angels praised God with the words of the Kedushah (*kadosh, kadosh, kadosh*). We are like angels when we say these words—we rise up on our toes three times and we imagine that we are elevating ourselves in the same way that the angels are elevated in God's eyes. *Kedushah* means "holy," and in this—the central blessing in the Amidah—we express our awe at God's holiness.

When we say these words, we try to focus on being kinder and more patient, more helpful and more thoughtful. In this way, the Kedushah helps us concentrate on becoming better people.

Practice reading these excerpts from the קְדוּשָׁה aloud.

1. נְקַדֵּשׁ אֶת שִׁמְךָ בָּעוֹלָם, כְּשֵׁם שֶׁמַּקְדִּישִׁים אוֹתוֹ בִּשְׁמֵי מָרוֹם,
2. כַּכָּתוּב עַל יַד נְבִיאֶךָ: וְקָרָא זֶה אֶל־זֶה וְאָמַר:
3. קָדוֹשׁ קָדוֹשׁ קָדוֹשׁ יְיָ צְבָאוֹת, מְלֹא כָל־הָאָרֶץ כְּבוֹדוֹ.
4. בָּרוּךְ כְּבוֹד־יְיָ מִמְּקוֹמוֹ.
5. יִמְלֹךְ יְיָ לְעוֹלָם, אֱלֹהַיִךְ צִיּוֹן, לְדֹר וָדֹר. הַלְלוּיָהּ!
6. לְדוֹר וָדוֹר נַגִּיד גָּדְלֶךָ, וּלְנֵצַח נְצָחִים קְדֻשָּׁתְךָ נַקְדִּישׁ.
7. וְשִׁבְחֲךָ, אֱלֹהֵינוּ, מִפִּינוּ לֹא יָמוּשׁ לְעוֹלָם וָעֶד.
8. בָּרוּךְ אַתָּה, יְיָ, הָאֵל הַקָּדוֹשׁ.

Let us sanctify Your name in the world, as they sanctify it in the highest heavens, as it is written by Your prophet, and one called to another and said:

"Holy, Holy, Holy is Adonai of the heavenly legions, the whole earth is full of God's glory."

Praised is the glory of God from God's heavenly place.

Adonai will rule forever; your God, O Zion, from generation to generation. Halleluyah! From generation to generation we will tell of Your greatness, and for all eternity we will proclaim Your holiness. And our praise of You, O God, will not depart from our mouths forever and ever. Praised are You, Adonai, the holy God.

28

INTO THE TEXT

Read the introduction with your students.

Ask students to stand and read the blessing in unison. Explain that they should rise up on their toes three times when they say "*kadosh, kadosh, kadosh*" in line 3.

Then have them read the English meaning of line 3 in unison. ("*Holy, holy, holy . . . glory*")

Parallel Prayers

Explain that we recite the Kedushah during the morning, afternoon, and evening services. During the evening service we recite a shorter version of the blessing aloud. Both versions conclude with the same sentence.

Ask the students to read the concluding Hebrew and English sentences in unison. (*Hebrew—line 8; English—last line on the page*)

A Blessing Note

The phrase בָּרוּךְ אַתָּה יְיָ ("Praised are You, Adonai") indicates that this is a blessing.

The words following בָּרוּךְ אַתָּה יְיָ highlight the theme of the blessing.

PRAYER DICTIONARY

Word Cards

Display Word Cards 30–36. Call on students to read:

- the words with a final ךּ (31, 33, 36)
- the word built on the root for "holy" (30)
- all the words in unison

Call on individual students to read each of the Word Cards.

Password

Distribute Word Cards 30–36 among seven students. Tell them to look for their word or phrase in the prayer on page 28 in their textbooks and have them lightly circle it in the prayer passage.

Note: Word Card 34 appears twice (lines 5 and 6).

Next, have the seven students pass their Word Cards to seven classmates. Follow the same procedure until all students in the class have had a turn.

Allow students a minute or two to practice reading the complete line that contains their circled word. Call on students to read their lines aloud.

Note: In each round, students may read the same lines more than once; for example, line 6 will be read three times, since it contains words found on Word Cards 34, 35, and 36.

After each student has had a chance to circle a word or phrase and read the corresponding lines, ask the students who circled the same word to stand and read their lines in unison. For example, those who circled the word נְקַדֵּשׁ (Word Card 30) should read line 1 together, and those who circled the word נַגִּיד (Word Card 35) should read line 6 together.

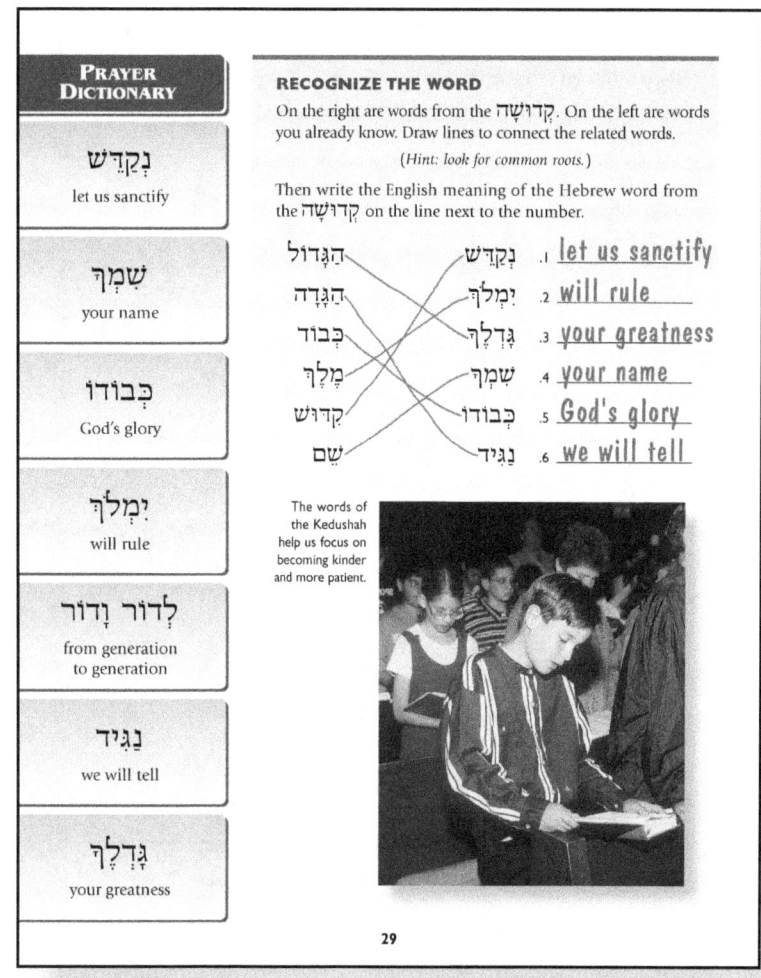

RECOGNIZE THE WORD

Read the instructions on page 29 with the students and have them complete the exercise independently.

Call on students to read aloud the connected word pairs and their corresponding English meanings.

43 LESSON 3

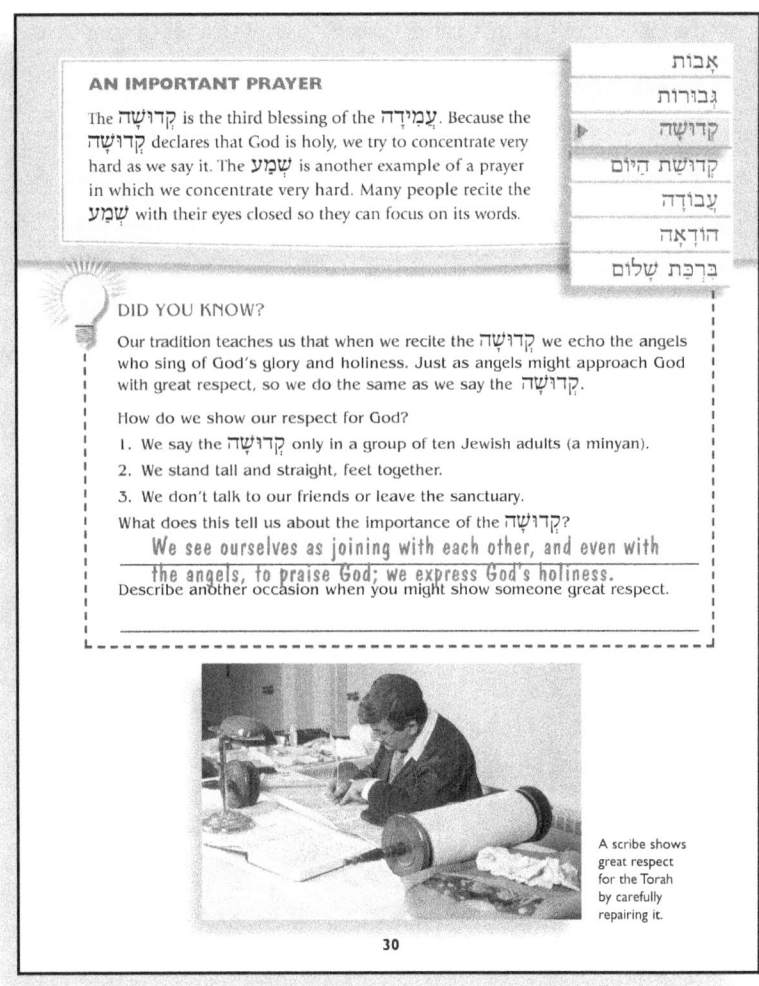

AN IMPORTANT PRAYER

Direct students' attention to the list of the seven blessings in the Shabbat morning Amidah that appears in the top right corner of the page, and to the arrow pointing to the third blessing, קְדוּשָׁה.

Ask students to read the names of the first three blessings of the Amidah. (*Avot, G'vurot, Kedushah*)

Ask them to read the names of the seven blessings in unison.

Call on a student to read "An Important Prayer" aloud.

Have the class recite the Sh'ma with their eyes closed.

DID YOU KNOW?

Call on a student to read aloud the introductory paragraph.

Together discuss items 1–3 in "Did You Know?":

1. A minyan consists of at least ten adults over the age of bar or bat mitzvah. Many prayers are recited only in the presence of a minyan, which represents the Jewish community.

2. Posture reflects attitude and awareness. When we recite the Kedushah we indicate our respect for God.

3. Quiet attentiveness shows respect for God and for our fellow congregants.

Have students complete the "Did You Know?" questions and share their responses.

Photo Op

Call on a student to read the caption.

Write the Hebrew word for "scribe" on the chalkboard (סוֹפֵר). A *sofer* does the holy work of writing or repairing a *Sefer Torah* or other sacred texts, such as the parchment inside a mezuzah. A *sofer* must follow specific rules; for example, the *sofer*:

- must recite a blessing before beginning work and before writing God's name.

- must copy the Torah text with a feather pen dipped in a special black ink.

- may not write from memory, but instead must copy the text from another scroll.

- must pronounce each word before writing it.

Ask students why they think a *sofer* must follow such specific rules. (*show respect for the Torah; be sure the work is done correctly; show how important the work is*)

PRAYER BUILDING BLOCKS

נְקַדֵּשׁ אֶת־שִׁמְךָ בָּעוֹלָם
"let us sanctify your name in the world"

נְקַדֵּשׁ — Have students complete the section individually. Review answers.

Have students read page 28, line 1 to first comma in unison.

שִׁמְךָ — Have students complete the section individually. Review answers.

Have students read page 28, line 1 in unison.

בָּעוֹלָם — Have students complete the section individually. Review answers.

Have students read page 28, lines 1–2 in unison.

Direct students to complete the exercise at the bottom of page 31.

Have them read in unison the six words built on the root קדשׁ.

Call on each student to read the six words twice for a "personal best."

Call on students to read aloud lines 1, 3, 6, and 8 on page 28:

- first reading—in unison
- second reading—individual students

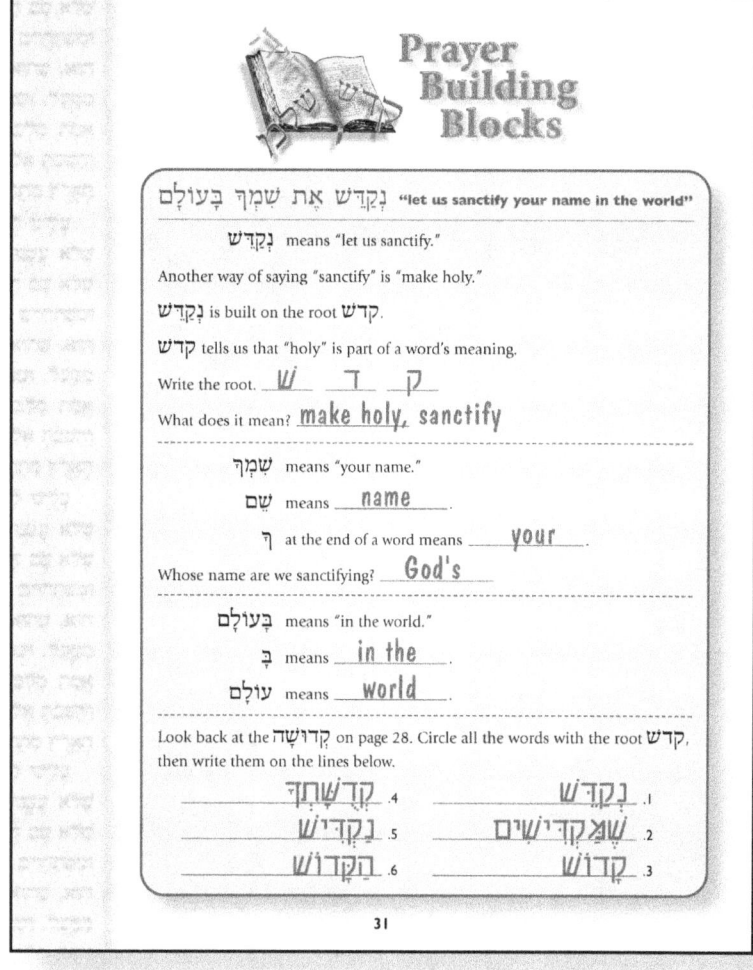

45 LESSON 3

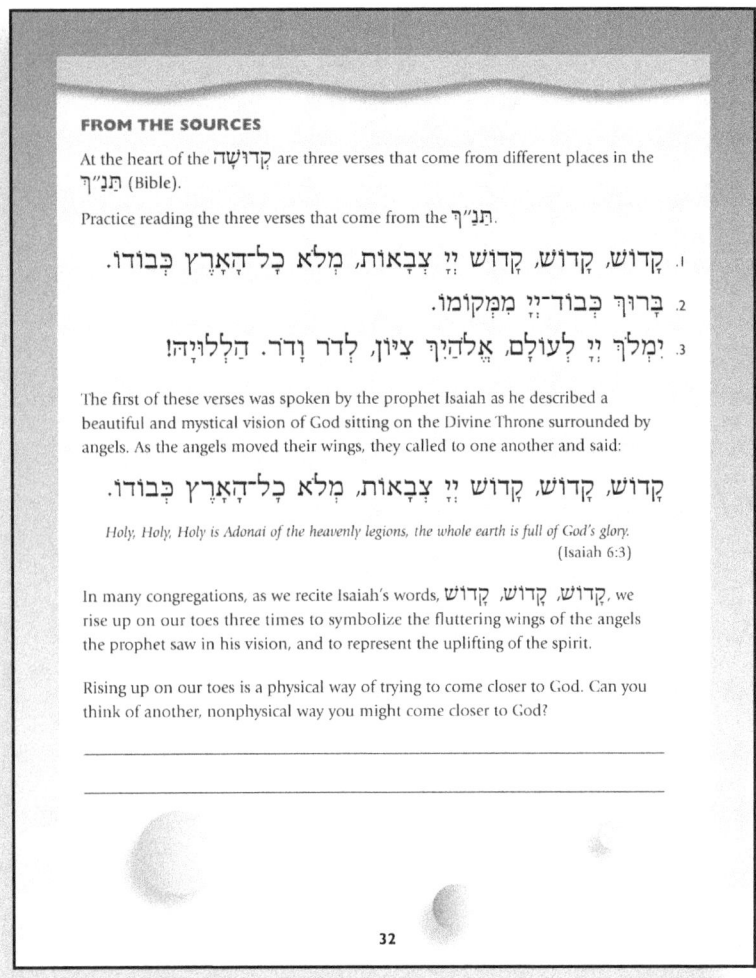

Reading Practice

Call on students to read page 28, lines 1–5.

Remind them of the "choreography" of the prayer—to rise on their toes three times when reciting "*kadosh, kadosh, kadosh*" (line 3).

The Book of Isaiah

Bring a *Tanach*—a Bible—to class. Read aloud the description of the angels in Isaiah's visions (Isaiah 6:1–3). **Note:** Verse 2 is from Ezekiel 3:12 and verse 3 is from Psalms 146:10.

FROM THE SOURCES

Read the first sentence of "From the Sources" aloud with students.

Reading Review

Have the class read the three Hebrew lines in unison several times. Call on individual students to read aloud all three lines or one line each.

Note: In some synagogues the reader chants the Kedushah alone and the congregation reads these three Hebrew sentences as a community response. In other synagogues the congregation chants the entire Kedushah together.

Tell the students the tradition in your synagogue.

Place papers with the numbers 1, 2, and 3 in a brown bag. Include a paper for each student. Students should reach into the bag and select a number. All those with the number 1 should stand in a designated section of the classroom. All those with the number 2 should stand in a second section, and those with the number 3 in a third section. Group 1 should read line 1 together, group 2 should read line 2, and group 3 should read line 3.

Then, have all the 1s read line 2, the 2s read line 3, and so on.

Continue reading "From the Sources" with students.

Call on students to stand and recite the sentence in the middle of the page. Remind them to rise up on their toes to symbolize the wings of angels.

מְלֹא כָל־הָאָרֶץ כְּבוֹדוֹ
"the whole earth is full of God's glory"

- Call on the students to read the Building Block aloud.

  Allow students a few moments to complete the first part of the Building Block.

- Explain that the seventh day—שַׁבָּת—and the word שָׁבַת in the selection are built on the same root (שבת). Words built on the root שבת have "rest" as part of their meaning.

- Call on individual students to read the five words with a שׁ in the selection.
  (שֵׁשֶׁת, הַשָּׁמַיִם, הַשְּׁבִיעִי, שָׁבַת, וַיִּנָּפַשׁ)

  Ask them to read the one word with a שׂ.
  (עָשָׂה)

- Read the selection in unison with the students. Call on individual students to read it aloud.

Read and complete the second part of the Building Block exercise with students.

יִמְלֹךְ יְיָ לְעוֹלָם
"Adonai will rule forever"

Call on students to read the Building Block aloud and then have the class answer the question independently.

Bring a *Tanach* to class and show students the source of the verse: Psalms 146:10.

Have them read page 28, lines 3–5 in unison and individually.

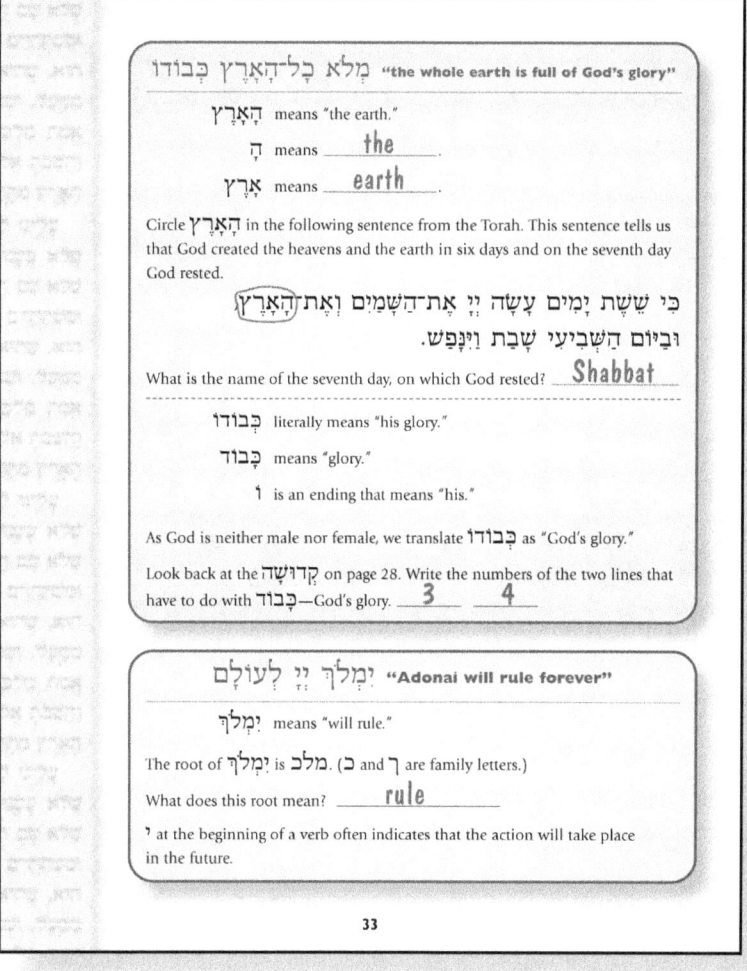

Classroom Games

Students might enjoy playing one or more of the "Speed Reading" games on page 9 in the front of this guide.

47 LESSON 3

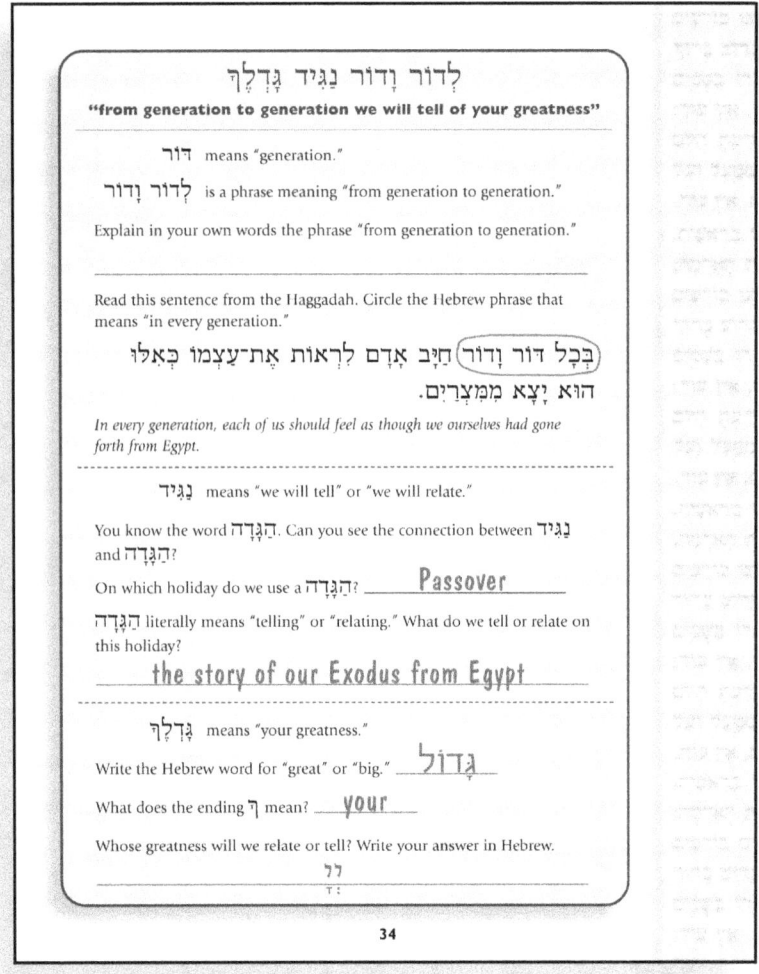

Reading Practice

Direct students to page 28.

For line 6:

Practice reading the phrase וּלְנֵצַח נְצָחִים.

Challenge students to see how fast they can read the phrase.

Practice reading the two words built on the root קדש.
(קִדַּשְׁתָּֿ נַקְדִּישׁ)

Challenge students to see how fast they can read the two words.

Read line 6 in unison.

For lines 7–8:

Practice reading the first two words. (וְשִׁבְחֲךָ אֱלֹהֵינוּ)

Challenge students to see how fast they can read these words.

לְדוֹר וָדוֹר נַגִּיד גָּדְלֶךָ
"from generation to generation we will tell of your greatness"

Call on students to read the Building Block aloud.

Explain that the prefix לְ usually means "to," but in this phrase we translate לְ as "from" ("from generation to generation").

Have students complete the activity individually and share their responses.

From Generation to Generation

Encourage students to talk about the generations in their own families. Remind them of the discussions the class had when they were learning about generations in the Avot. Ask how far back they can trace family members.

How does each generation pass along our Jewish heritage to the next generation? (*study, ritual practice, Shabbat and holiday observance, attending services, Hebrew names, Jewish books in the home*)

Complete the three Building Block activities with students.

The Haggadah

Ask students why each generation should relate the story of Passover at the seder. Why should each generation "feel as though we ourselves had gone forth from Egypt"? (*to remember in each generation that God redeemed us from slavery; to appreciate our freedom; to remind ourselves that it is our obligation to work for others to be free*)

FLUENT READING

Remind students that the first three blessings and the last three blessings are the same in every Amidah. During the week there are 13 middle blessings. On Shabbat there is only one middle blessing.

Read the introduction on page 35 with students.

Challenge students to determine the English meaning of the phrase *"Kedushat Hayom."*

Hint: *"Yom"* means *"day."* (*"Holiness"* or *"Sanctification of the Day"*)

Classroom Game: Odds and Evens

Have students count off 1-2, 1-2 around the room. All the 1s should read the odd-numbered lines in unison (1, 3, 5, 7). All the 2s should read the even-numbered lines in unison (2, 4, 6).

Then have the two groups alternate to read the entire prayer.

Have the groups switch roles and read through the prayer once again.

Have students complete the questions below the prayer and review together.

Review, too, "Prayer Variations" at the bottom of the page.

WORKSHEET

Duplicate and hand out copies of the worksheet for Lesson 3 to review skills and concepts.

FAMILY EDUCATION

Duplicate and send home copies of "As a Family: Holy Times" (at the back of this guide).

LESSON 3
Worksheet

Name: _____

קְדוּשָׁה

1. Write the root of each Hebrew word on the first line below the word.

   Write the English for the root on the second line below the word.

קְדוּשָׁה	בָּרוּךְ	נְקַדֵּשׁ	יִמְלֹךְ
_____	_____	_____	_____
_____	_____	_____	_____

2. Complete each word by adding the root letters for "holy."

   4. ‎_ _ _ תְךָ   1. נְ _ _ _

   5. ‎_ _ _ ‎יִ _ נַ   2. שְׁמַ _ _ _ ‎יִ _ יִם

   6. ‎_ _ _ הַ _ וֹ _   3. _ וֹ _ _

3. Why do you think the קְדוּשָׁה contains so many words with the root קדשׁ?

   _____

4. Word Match!

   Write the number of the Hebrew word or phrase next to the matching English.

   _____ we will tell (or relate)   1. הָאָרֶץ

   _____ the earth   2. תַּנַ"ךְ

   _____ God's glory   3. לְדוֹר וָדוֹר

   _____ the Bible   4. נַגִּיד

   _____ your greatness   5. כְּבוֹדוֹ

   _____ from generation to generation   6. גָּדְלְךָ

5. Why do we rise up on our toes when we recite the words קָדוֹשׁ, קָדוֹשׁ, קָדוֹשׁ?

   _____

LESSON 4
הוֹדָאָה

LEARNING OBJECTIVES
Prayer Reading Skills
- The suffix ךָ ("you")
- The prefix בְּ ("in")
- The word אֲנַחְנוּ ("we")
- The root הלל ("praise")

Prayer Concepts
- Hoda'ah is the sixth blessing of the Shabbat Amidah
- Hoda'ah is a blessing of thanksgiving for all the good God has created
- We thank God for our lives, our souls, miracles in the world, and wonders and great gifts
- We bow at the beginning and conclusion of the blessing as a sign of respect to God

BEYOND THE TEXTBOOK
The sounded *sh'va* with a double letter: לְלוּ

The suffix נוּ ("us," "our")

The prefix וּ, וְ ("and")

The *dagesh*

The יו ending

The double-duty dot

The double *sh'va*

ABOUT THE PRAYER
The Hoda'ah ("thanksgiving") is the second-to-last blessing in the Shabbat Amidah. Before we conclude the Amidah, we say a prayer of thanksgiving to God. We acknowledge that God alone created the blessings and the good in our lives. We bow at the beginning and end of the blessing to show respect and gratitude.

INSTRUCTIONAL MATERIALS
Text pages 36–45

Word Cards 31, 37–43

Worksheet 4

Family Education: "As a Family: A Family Thanksgiving" (at the back of this guide)

SET INDUCTION
Thank You
Give students two sheets of paper each.

Ask them to think of something special they received from someone else (an object, a trip, a special experience).

Have students fold the first sheet of paper in half. On one half, have them write what they received, and list the reasons that this gift or experience was so special to them.

On the other half, have them list words of appreciation. (*thank you, grateful, appreciative, flattered, honored, awed, overwhelmed, moved, wowed*)

On the second sheet of paper, have them write a thank-you note to the person who gave them their special gift. They should include the words of appreciation they wrote on the first sheet of paper.

Ask students who feel comfortable doing so to share their thank-you notes with the class.

Pose the Questions
Why is it important to say "thank you"? (*not to take the good in life for granted; to let others know they made a difference in your life*)

Why is it important to use appropriate words? (*to convey thoughts and feelings in concrete terms*)

הוֹדָאָה — 4

How many times in a day do you say "thank you"? Probably more than you can count. You might thank your best friend for bringing his soccer ball to the game. Or maybe your sister agrees to let you borrow her sweater for the dance and you give her a hug of thanks. Not only are you thanking them, but you are also recognizing and acknowledging their kindness.

The הוֹדָאָה ("thanksgiving") blessing is the next-to-last blessing of the Amidah. In it, we thank God for our many blessings, and we recognize and acknowledge that God is One alone in creating and making possible life's goodness. Because we are expressing our gratitude to God, in many congregations we bow respectfully both at the start and at the end of the Hoda'ah blessing.

Practice reading these excerpts from the הוֹדָאָה aloud.

1. מוֹדִים אֲנַחְנוּ לָךְ, שָׁאַתָּה הוּא יְיָ אֱלֹהֵינוּ וֵאלֹהֵי אֲבוֹתֵינוּ/וְאִמּוֹתֵינוּ
2. לְעוֹלָם וָעֶד. צוּר חַיֵּינוּ, מָגֵן יִשְׁעֵנוּ, אַתָּה הוּא לְדוֹר וָדוֹר.
3. נוֹדֶה לְךָ וּנְסַפֵּר תְּהִלָּתֶךָ...
4. וְעַל כֻּלָּם יִתְבָּרַךְ וְיִתְרוֹמַם שִׁמְךָ, מַלְכֵּנוּ, תָּמִיד לְעוֹלָם וָעֶד.
5. וְכֹל הַחַיִּים יוֹדוּךָ סֶּלָה, וִיהַלְלוּ אֶת שִׁמְךָ בֶּאֱמֶת,
6. הָאֵל יְשׁוּעָתֵנוּ וְעֶזְרָתֵנוּ סֶלָה.
7. בָּרוּךְ אַתָּה, יְיָ, הַטּוֹב שִׁמְךָ וּלְךָ נָאֶה לְהוֹדוֹת.

We give thanks to You, that You are Adonai our God and the God of our fathers/and mothers forever and ever. You are the Rock of our lives, the Shield who saves us, from generation to generation. We will give thanks to You and tell of Your praises . . .

And for all this Your name will be praised and exalted, our Ruler, always and forever.

And all living things will acknowledge and praise Your name in truth, the God who is our Rescuer and our Helper. Praised are You, Adonai, whose name is good and to whom we give thanks.

36

Into the Prayer

Ask students to circle the word "thanks" wherever it appears in the English translation of the blessing. (*first line, third line, last line*) Call on students to read each English line aloud.

Direct them to Hebrew lines 1, 3, and 7. Explain that the first word in line 1 (מוֹדִים) and in line 3 (נוֹדֶה) and the last word in line 7 (לְהוֹדוֹת) are all related to "thank."

Have students read and circle the three words.

Read Hebrew lines 1, 3, and 7 in unison with students.

INTO THE TEXT

Ask students to read the first paragraph of the introduction on page 36 aloud.

Pose the following questions:

- Do you always remember to say "thank you" when you should?
- What are some of the ways we can thank people?
- How do you feel when others thank you for something you have done?

Call on students to read the second paragraph of the introduction aloud.

Pose the following questions:

- What are the good things in your life?
- How can you show appreciation for the good things in your life? (*doing loving acts for members of your family; donating food, clothing, and toys to the needy; showing true friendship to your friends*)
- Traditionally, we bow in appreciation at the beginning and conclusion of the blessing. What physical gestures can we make when we thank people? (*hugs, handshakes, kisses, patting on the back or on the head, hand over the heart, hands clasped together*)

PRAYER DICTIONARY

Word Cards

Display Word Cards 37, 39, and 43. Tell students that each word is related to "thank."

Call on students to read the three words.

Reading Rule

Sometimes a double letter appears in a word: לל מִמ. If the first letter has a *sh'va* (ְ) under it, the *sh'va* is sounded ("a" as in "alone").

Write לְלוּ on the chalkboard.

Write the following words on the chalkboard in this way:

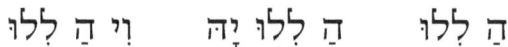

Display Word Card 41. Call on students to read the word and the English meaning on the back.

Display Word Card 40. Explain that this word is related to Word Card 41. Call on students to read both sides of Word Card 41.

Show students that the English word in common on both Word Cards is "praise."

Word Challenge: What does the word הַלְלוּיָהּ mean? **Hint:** The word יָהּ is a name for God. (הַלְלוּיָהּ — *"praise God"*)

FAMILY WORDS

Allow a few minutes for students to complete the exercise.

Display Word Cards 31, 37–43 in random order.

- Ask three students to select and read the words related to "thank you." (37, 39, 43)
- Ask two students to select and read the words related to "praise." (40, 41)
- Have the class read the words in each set in unison.
- Have the class read all eight words in unison.

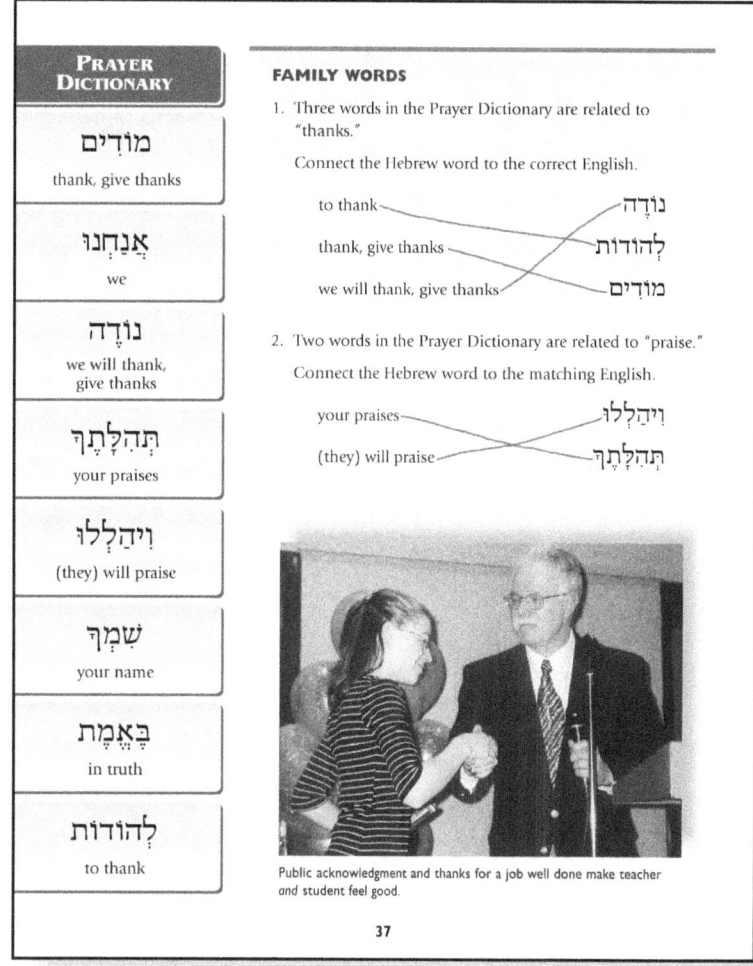

Tic-Tac-Toe

Draw an oversized tic-tac-toe grid on the chalkboard. Write הוֹדָאָה in the middle square. Place a different Word Card (31, 37–43) in each of the other eight boxes using a sticky, removable putty, or tape.

Game 1:

If a player reads the Hebrew word in a square correctly, remove the Word Card and write an X or an O instead. If a player reads the word in the middle square (הוֹדָאָה), erase it and write an X or an O instead.

Game 2:

A player must read the Hebrew word *and* know the English meaning to score.

Note: הוֹדָאָה means "thanksgiving."

Photo Op

Ask students if they have been publicly acknowledged for a job well done. (*music, sports, academics, art*)

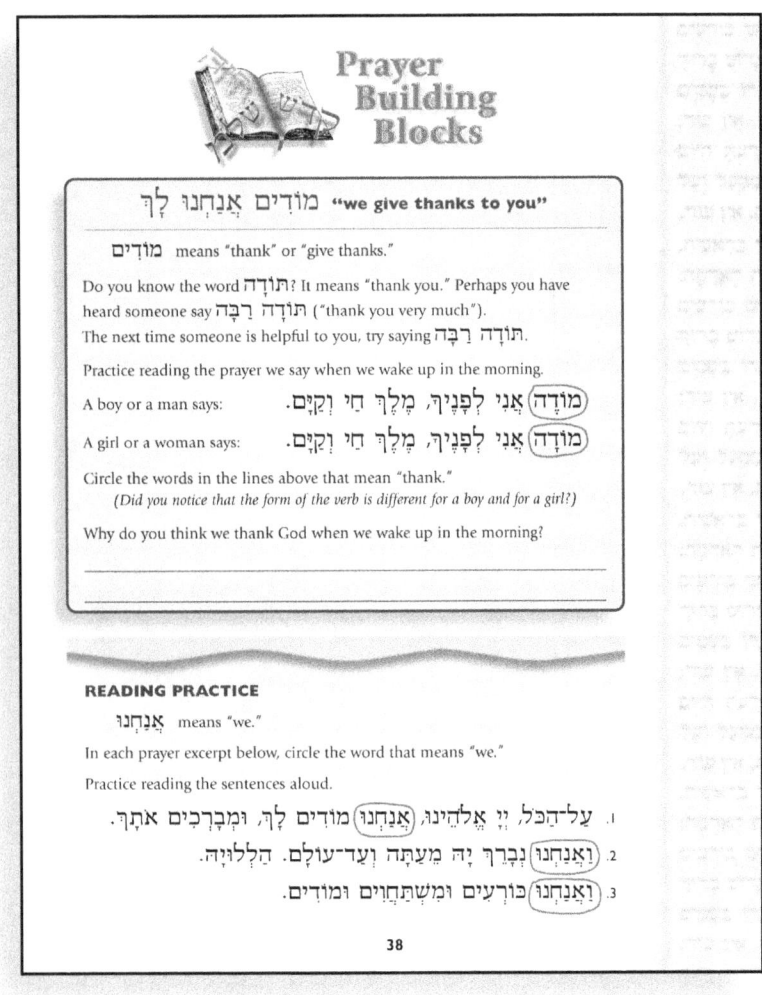

Reading Rounds

Call on student A to read line 1.

Call on student A to read line 1 and student B to read line 2.

Call on student A to read line 1, student B to read line 2, and student C to read line 3.

Call on the class to read all three lines in unison.

Alternative

Do the same with three groups. Instead of individuals reading, have each group read in unison.

PRAYER BUILDING BLOCKS

מוֹדִים אֲנַחְנוּ לָךְ

"we give thanks to you"

Call on students to read the Building Block phrase and the explanation aloud.

You might wish to incorporate the Hebrew phrase תּוֹדָה רַבָּה ("thank you very much") in your classroom interactions with students.

Suggest to students that they say מוֹדֶה/מוֹדָה אֲנִי לְפָנֶיךָ מֶלֶךְ חַי וְקַיָּם when they awake in the morning. Explain that this is the introductory sentence for the morning prayer, מוֹדֶה/מוֹדָה אֲנִי. It means: "I am grateful to You, living and enduring Ruler. . . ." Encourage students to complete this sentence themselves each morning. (*for giving me life, for a new day, for a good night's rest*)

Note: The מוֹדֶה/מוֹדָה אֲנִי prayer concludes with the words "for restoring my soul to me in compassion. You are faithful beyond measure."

Have the class read page 36, lines 1–2, in unison and individually.

READING PRACTICE

Call on students to read the explanation aloud.

Have students circle the word אֲנַחְנוּ as directed. Ask the following questions:

- Which word has a prefix? (וַאֲנַחְנוּ)

  What is the meaning of the prefix וַ? (*and*)

- Which words in lines 1 and 3 mean "thanks"? (וּמוֹדִים, מוֹדִים)

  What is the meaning of the prefix וּ? (*and*)

- What word in line 2 means "praise God"? (הַלְלוּיָהּ)

THE ROCKS IN YOUR LIFE

Read the introduction with the students.

Discuss the meaning of the question, "Who are the 'rocks' in your life?" (*those who are strong, who do not bend in adversity, who are always there for you, on whom you can rely, who offer support*)

Allow students time to list the "rocks" in their lives and the reasons they included these people.

Then have them answer the concluding question.

Encourage students to share their responses.

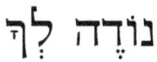
"we will give thanks to you"

Call on students to read the Building Block phrase aloud.

Complete the Building Block together.

THE ROCKS IN YOUR LIFE

צוּר means "rock."

Who is the "rock" in the הוֹדָאָה? __God, Adonai__

Who are the "rocks" in your life? List them and explain why you included each one on the list.

My "Rocks"	Reason
1. _____	_____
2. _____	_____
3. _____	_____
4. _____	_____
5. **Adonai**	_____

What are the common characteristics of all the "rocks" on your list?

_____
_____

נוֹדֶה לְךָ "we will give thanks to you"

נוֹדֶה means "we will give thanks."

לְךָ means "to you."

לְ means __to__.

ךָ means __you__.

To whom will we give thanks? __God, Adonai__

39

---

55 LESSON 4

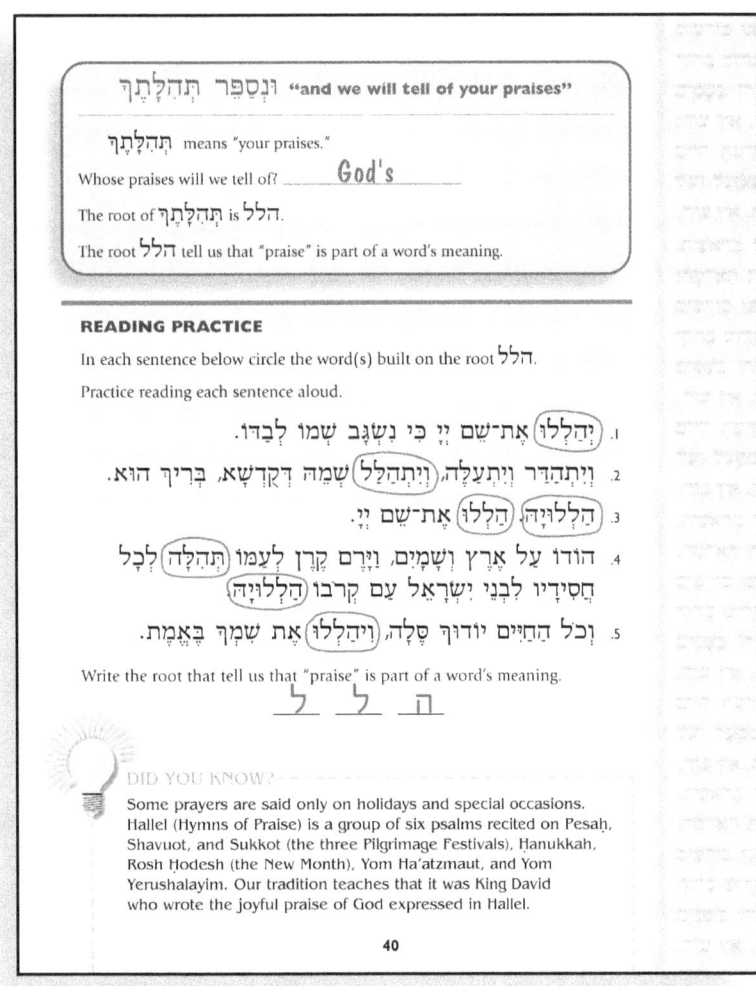

וּנְסַפֵּר תְּהִלָּתֶךָ
"and we will tell of your praises"

Call on students to read the Building Block phrase aloud.

Complete the Building Block with students.

Call on students to read page 36, line 3, in unison and individually, and then lines 1–3 in unison and individually.

The Fruit of the Tree

From oaktag create a fruit tree with three roots.

Write the letters הלל, one letter on each root.

Write "praise" on the trunk of the tree.

Create a fruit for the word in the Building Block built on the root הלל. (תְּהִלָּתֶךָ)

READING PRACTICE

Call on students to read aloud each word they circled.

Add the words in sentences 1–5 built on the root הלל to the fruit tree.

A Designated Reader

Designate a different reader for each of sentences 1–5.

The reader should read the line, pausing before each word built on the root הלל. The class should then read that word in unison. If a line begins with a word built on the root הלל, then the class should begin the reading for that sentence (sentences 1 and 3), and the reader should continue alone.

DID YOU KNOW?

Note: Excerpts from the six psalms in Hallel appear on page 22 in the workbook that is available for this textbook.

וִיהַלְלוּ אֶת שִׁמְךָ בֶּאֱמֶת
"and will praise your name in truth"

Have the students read the Building Block phrase aloud.

Complete the Building Block with students.

Call on students to read the following on page 36:

- line 5 in unison and individually
- lines 1–5 in unison and individually
- lines 1–7 in unison and individually

Show students how to bow when reciting line 1, the first two words ("We give thanks to You") and line 7, the first two words ("Praised are You").

Note: If the congregation is seated during the blessing, congregants bow by lifting themselves forward slightly in their seats.

READING PRACTICE

After students have circled אֱמֶת in each sentence, have them read specific words in each of the sentences, as described in the corresponding lines below.

1. the words with a *yud*

   the words with a *dagesh* that does not affect the sound of the letter (הַנֶּאֱמָרִים, אַתָּה)

2. the word with the "ahv" ending (דְּבָרָיו)

   the words with a *dagesh* that does not affect the sound of the letter (דְּבָרָיו, וּמְקַיֵּם, הַנֶּאֱמָן)

3. the word with a double-duty dot—a dot for שׁ and for the "oh" vowel preceding שׁ (שְׁלֹשָׁה)

   the words with a *dagesh* that does not affect the sound of the letter (הַשָּׁלוֹם, הַדִּין, קַיָּם)

4. the words with the sound-alike letters ת ט

   the words with a *dagesh* that does not affect the sound of the letter (וְחַיֵּי, תּוֹרַת, אַתָּה)

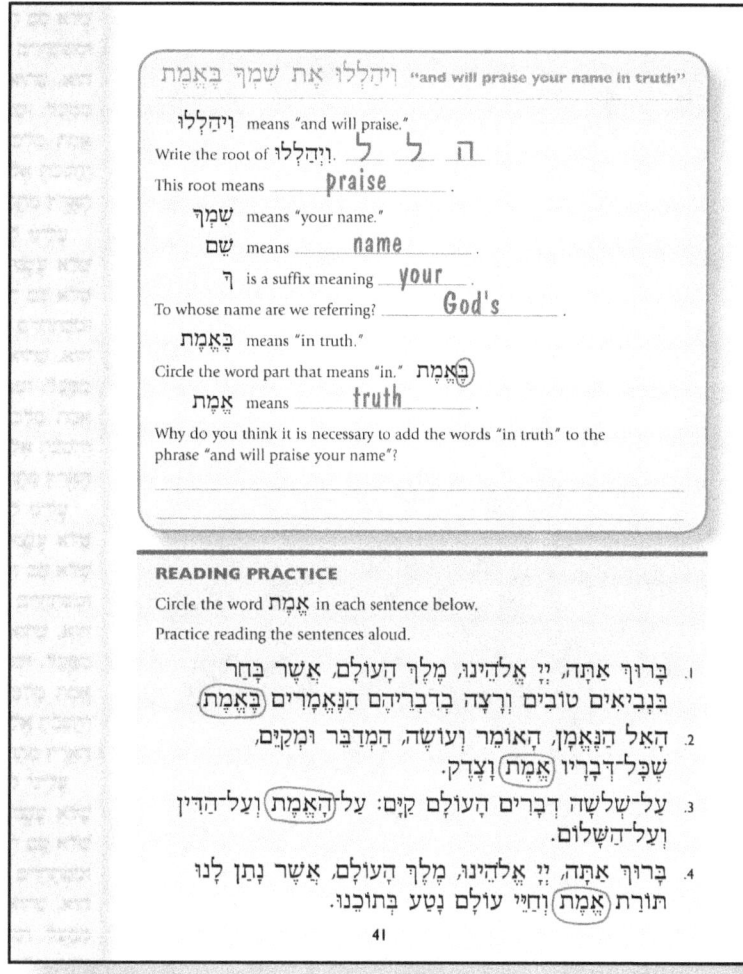

57 LESSON 4

SAYING "THANK YOU"

After students have read the introduction and circled the words that mean "thank," call on them to read aloud:

- each circled word
- the three lines that appear in the הוֹדָאָה (lines 1, 3, 7)
- the remaining lines (2, 4, 5, 6, and 8)

See "Classroom Games" in the front of this guide for reading reinforcement activities.

Photo Op

Encourage students to answer the question below the photo and explain their answers.

WHERE ARE WE?

Direct students' attention to the list of the seven blessings in the Shabbat Morning Amidah that appears in the top right corner of the page, and to the arrow pointing to the sixth blessing, הוֹדָאָה.

Have students read the names of the blessings of the Amidah in unison.

THEME OF THE PRAYER

Read the section aloud with students.

Allow time for them to respond to the exercise with an example on each line.

Call on students to share their responses.

Students might wish to create two bulletin board displays—"Miracles in the World Around Us" and "Miracles in Our Own Lives"—to illustrate their written examples. They may use drawings, poems, newspaper cuttings, and photographs.

DID YOU KNOW?

Bring a dictionary to class. Call on two students to look up the meaning of "thank" and "acknowledge." Compare the definitions.

Ask students to complete the exercise.

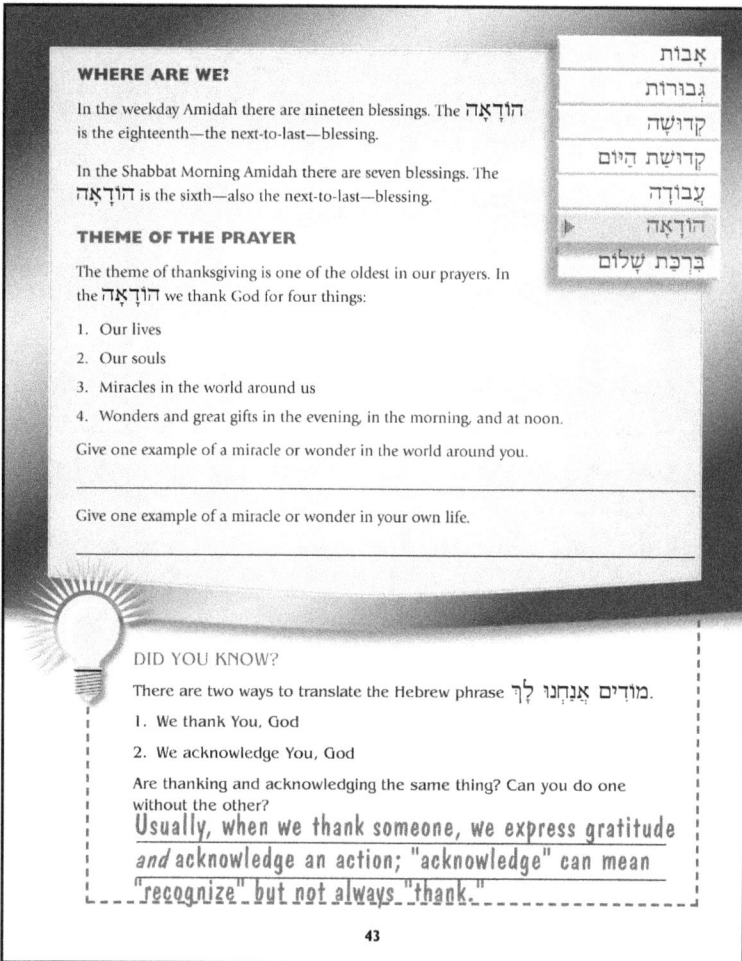

YOUR PERSONAL THANKS

YOUR PERSONAL THANKS

When you are grateful for something, you can *say* thank you ("Thanks for helping me fix my computer") or you can *show* your thanks (by doing a favor in return).

Name one thing for which you are grateful to God.

_____

The הוֹדָאָה prayer is a way to *say* thank you to God.

Now list 3 things you can do to *show* your thanks to God.

1. _____
2. _____
3. _____

Name one thing for which you are grateful to another person.

_____

Now list 3 things you can do to *show* your thanks to that person.

1. _____
2. _____
3. _____

What is the difference between the way you thank God and the way you thank other people?

44

YOUR PERSONAL THANKS

Read the introduction together with students.

Allow them time to name one or more things for which they are grateful to God.

Brainstorm the ways people can show thanks to God. List their ideas on the chalkboard.

Have students select three ways that they think are meaningful and write them next to numbers 1–3 in the textbook.

Allow time for students to name something for which they are grateful to another person.

Brainstorm the ways we can show thanks to other people. Again, you might list the various ways on the chalkboard.

Have students select three ways that they think are meaningful and write them next to numbers 1–3 in the textbook.

Read the concluding question aloud. (*we thank God indirectly by appreciating and caring for the world around us, by praying; we thank people through direct contact; we may get a direct response from the other person when we express our thanks*)

THE NEW HEBREW THROUGH PRAYER 2 • הִנְנִי

FLUENT READING

Matching Lines

Challenge students to match the lines on page 36 with the complete blessing on page 45. (*page 36: lines 1–3 match page 45: lines 1–3, fourth word; page 36: lines 4–7 match page 45: lines 8–11*)

Tell students to circle the matching line numbers on page 45. (*lines 1–3, 8–11*)

Read lines 1–3, 8–11 in unison with students. Call on individual students to read individual lines.

Reading Rules Lines 4-7

Line 5 (נִפְלְאוֹתֶיךָ): Double *sh'va*— the first *sh'va* is silent and blended with the letter-vowel combination that precedes it (נִפְ); the second *sh'va* is sounded ("a" as in "alone").

Line 7 (קִוִּינוּ): *Vav* with a *dagesh*—the *vav* is a letter with a *dagesh* (וּ) and not the vowel "oo" if the letter preceding it already has a vowel (קִ).

Call on individual students to read phrases from lines 4–7 aloud.

Remind students that we bow when we recite the first two words in the first sentence and the first two words in the last sentence.

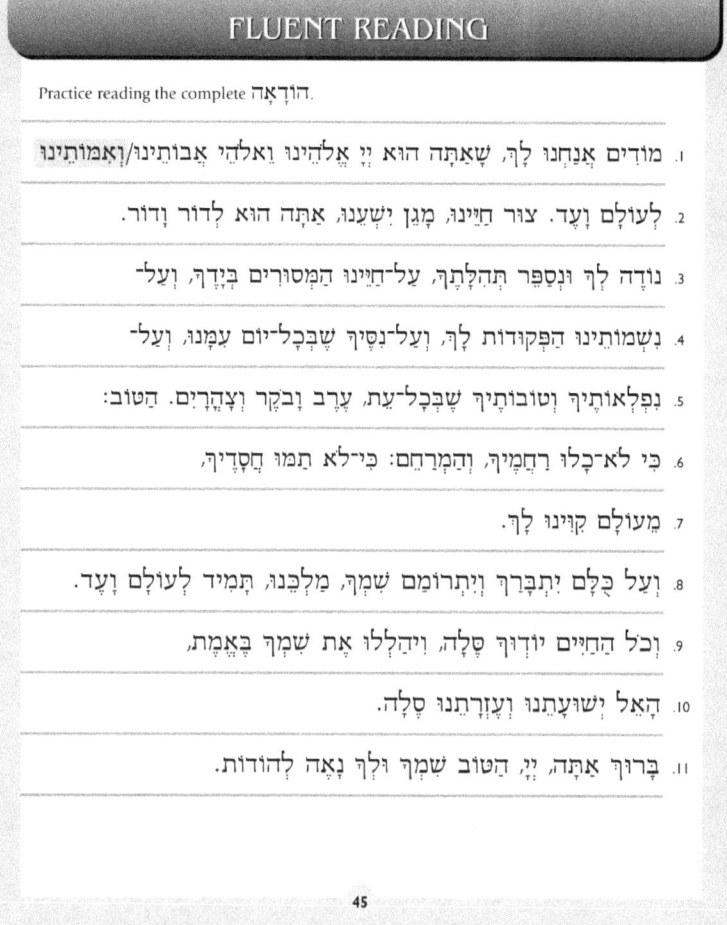

WORKSHEET

Duplicate and hand out copies of the worksheet for Lesson 4 to review skills and concepts.

FAMILY EDUCATION

Duplicate and send home copies of "As a Family: A Family Thanksgiving" (at the back of this guide).

LESSON 4
Worksheet

Name: _____

הוֹדָאָה

1. What is the common meaning for the words below? _____

    מוֹדָה   לְהוֹדוֹת   נוֹדֶה   מוֹדִים   הוֹדָאָה   מוֹדֶה

    Select and write the correct word from the list above to complete the introductory phrase in the הוֹדָאָה blessing.

    _____ אֲנַחְנוּ לָךְ

    Select and write the correct word from the list above to complete the final sentence in the הוֹדָאָה blessing.

    בָּרוּךְ אַתָּה, יְיָ, הַטּוֹב שִׁמְךָ וּלְךָ נָאֶה _____ .

2. What is the common meaning for the words below? _____

    וִיהַלְלוּ   תְּהִלָּתֶךָ   הַלְלוּיָהּ   יְהַלְלוּ

    What root do these words share? ____ ____ ____

3. What is the English meaning of the suffix ךָ? _____

    Add the suffix ךָ to complete each of the following words from the הוֹדָאָה blessing.

    וּלְ___   יוֹדוּ___   שִׁמְ___   תְּהִלָּתֶ___   לְ___

4. What is the English meaning of the word אֲנַחְנוּ? _____

    What is the English meaning of the suffix נוּ? _____

    Add the suffix נוּ to complete each of these words from the הוֹדָאָה blessing.

    יִשְׁעֵ___   חַיֵּי___   וְאִמּוֹתֵי___   אֲבוֹתֵי___   אֱלֹהֵי___

    וְעֶזְרַת___   יְשׁוּעָת___   מַלְכֵּ___

5. Complete the English phrase with your own words of appreciation:

    I give thanks to You, God, for _____

    _____

LESSON 5

בִּרְכַּת שָׁלוֹם:
שָׁלוֹם רָב/שִׂים שָׁלוֹם

LEARNING OBJECTIVES

Prayer Reading Skills

- The suffixes ךָ ("your"); נוּ ("us," "our")
- The prefixes בְּ, בָּ ("with"); כְּ ("as"); וְ ("and")
- The roots שלמ ("peace," "harmony," "completeness," "wholeness"); ברכ ("bless"); שימ ("put"); נתנ ("give"); אהב ("love")

Prayer Concepts

- The final blessing of the Amidah is a prayer for peace
- Peace is the most important blessing for the Jewish people
- There is an evening version and a morning version of the prayer for peace
- Ethical Echo: רוֹדֵף שָׁלוֹם ("seeking peace")

BEYOND THE TEXTBOOK

Reading Rules: "vo," "eye," and "ahv" endings

ABOUT THE PRAYER

The Amidah culminates with a prayer for peace, which we recite as a community. In the version of the blessing recited during the evening service—שָׁלוֹם רָב—we ask God for peace for our people and for all people. In the version of the blessing recited during the morning service—שִׂים שָׁלוֹם—we ask that God inspire us to make peace and lead us to actions that help bring peace.

INSTRUCTIONAL MATERIALS

Text pages 46–57

Word Cards 44–59

Worksheet 5

Family Education: "As a Family: Words of Peace" (at the back of this guide)

SET INDUCTION

For Discussion

Tell students that since we are made in the image of God, we reflect God's image in the ways we work to create peace. Ask them to think of ways we can work to create peace. (*treat our family and friends with respect; act as a mediator when friends are fighting; attend solidarity meetings for peace in Israel; contribute money to peace-seeking organizations*)

Tell students that many of the prayers in the siddur reflect our wish for peace. Ask them why they think the Amidah concludes with a prayer for peace. (*we will remember it; it is the most important quest for the Jewish people*)

Signs of Peace

Together with students, create a list of Jewish peace symbols, terms, songs, and prayers. Examples:

יוֹנָה—"dove"; קֶשֶׁת—"rainbow"; שָׁלוֹם—"peace"; יְרוּשָׁלַיִם—"city of peace"; שַׁבַּת שָׁלוֹם—"Sabbath peace"; שָׁלוֹם רָב—"great peace"; שִׂים שָׁלוֹם—"grant peace"; עֹשֶׂה שָׁלוֹם—"makes peace"; שָׁלוֹם עֲלֵיכֶם—"peace upon you"

Prayers for Peace

Encourage students to write prayers for peace. The entire class can contribute ideas, or students can work in small groups. Each group should read its prayer to the class. Post the prayers on a bulletin board entitled "Prayers for Peace."

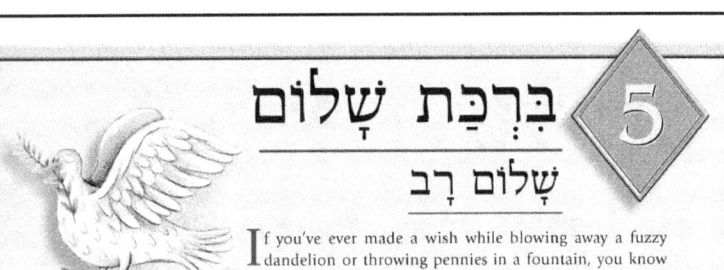

INTO THE TEXT

Read the first paragraph of the introduction to your students.

Ask students: If you had one wish, what would it be?

Call on students to read aloud the second paragraph of the introduction.

For Discussion

Think about conversations you have had with a parent before you leave the house to go out.

- What kind of statements does your parent make? (*be careful where you go with your friends; remember to be home by a specified time; call home if you will be late; put on a sweater*)

- Why does your parent save these statements for when you are about to leave? (*this is the most important idea for you to remember and take with you; you will remember the last thing you hear*)

- Why do you think the final blessing of the Amidah is a prayer for peace? (*it is our final word to God; we highlight the importance of this wish before we step back at the end of the Amidah and leave God's presence*)

Call on students to read aloud the third paragraph of the introduction.

Read the prayer in Hebrew and in English with the class.

Recognizing Words

Ask students which words they read that:

- have ברכ ("bless") as their root (לְבָרֵךְ, בָּרוּךְ, הַמְבָרֵךְ)

- relate to peace (שָׁלוֹם, הַשָּׁלוֹם, בִּשְׁלוֹמֶךָ, בַּשָּׁלוֹם)

- refer to the Jewish people (עַמְּךָ, עַמּוֹ, יִשְׂרָאֵל)

PRAYER DICTIONARY

Word Cards

Display Word Cards 44–51 in random order.

Ask students to read aloud the Hebrew words that match the following descriptions. As each word is read, turn the card over to show the English meaning. Have them find:

- words meaning "peace" (44, 51)
- words ending with the suffix meaning "your" (47, 49, 51)
- words referring to the Jewish people and to the Jewish homeland (46, 47)

PHRASE MATCH

Have students cover the Prayer Dictionary and complete the exercise. Remind them to look for words or roots they know when making a match.

Word Card Match

Display Word Cards 44–51 in random order.

Call on a student to read aloud an English phrase from "Phrase Match." (*Example: "Israel your people"*)

Challenge students to select the correct Word Cards to form the matching Hebrew phrase. (*Example: Word Cards 46, 47*)

Repeat until students have made Word Card matches with all four English phrases.

Note: There is no Word Card for אֶת since it has no English translation.

Personal Best

Ask each student to read the four Hebrew phrases aloud twice for a personal best reading.

PICK-OUT-PEACE

Have students complete the exercise independently.

Call on individual students to read a sentence in the blessing that contains one of the circled words.

Note: Sentence 1 will have two circled words and should be read twice.

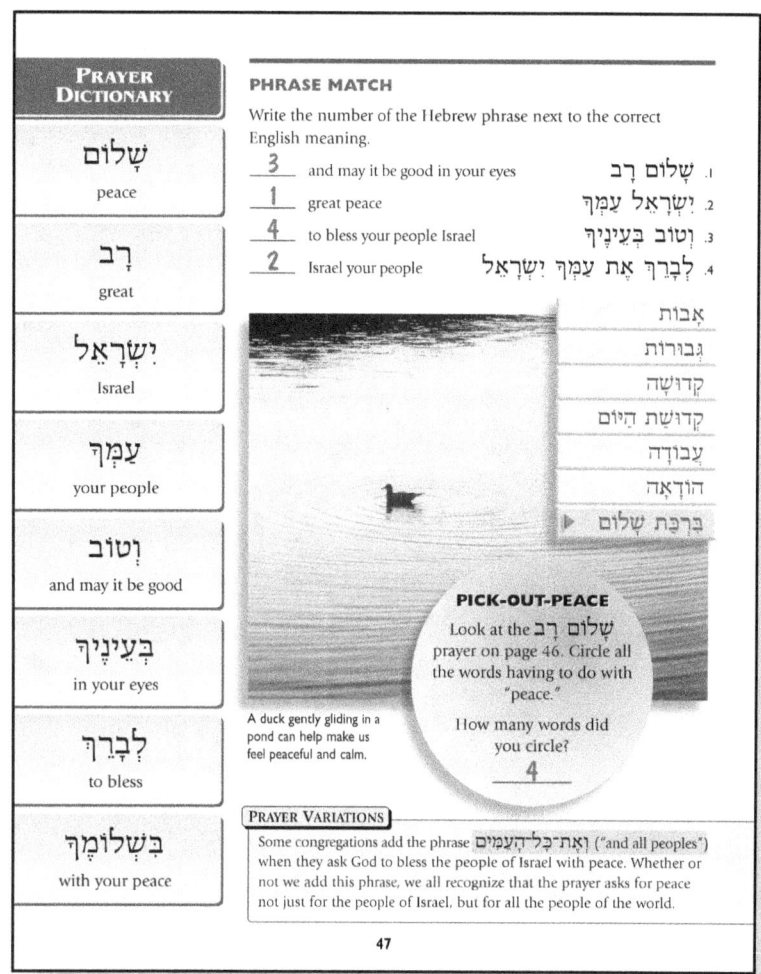

Siddur Geography

Direct students' attention to the list of seven blessings in the Shabbat Morning Amidah that appears in the middle of page 47, and to the arrow pointing to the final blessing, בִּרְכַּת שָׁלוֹם.

Ask them to read the names of the seven blessings in unison.

Photo Op

Read the caption.

Ask: What other scenes might help us feel peaceful and calm? (*sky; setting sun; meadow; boat gliding in the water; trees swaying in the breeze; a baby sleeping*)

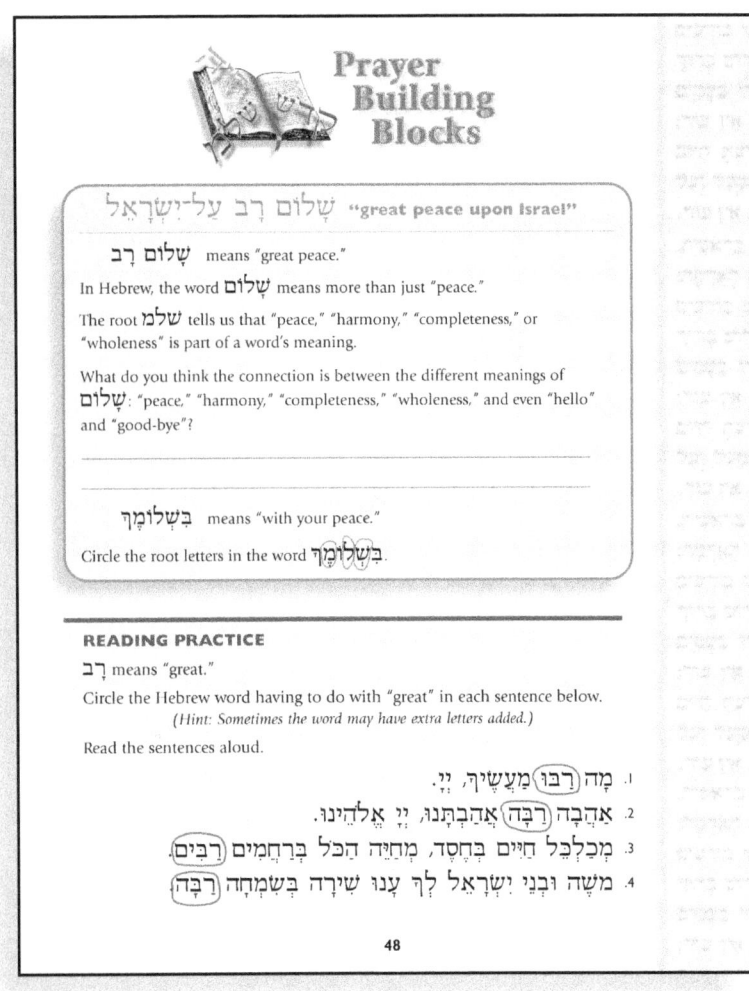

PRAYER BUILDING BLOCKS

שָׁלוֹם רָב עַל־יִשְׂרָאֵל
"great peace upon Israel"

Call on students to read the Building Block phrase aloud.

Read the section aloud with students.

Create "study partners" to discuss the question in the middle of the Building Block.

Direct each set of partners to write down their ideas on the blank lines.

Call on each set of partners to share their ideas with the class.

The Fruit of the Tree

Create a new fruit tree for the root שׁלמ.

Write "peace," "harmony," "completeness," and "wholeness" on the trunk of the tree.

Write the words in the blessing built on שׁלמ and the phrases שָׁלוֹם רָב and בִּרְכַּת שָׁלוֹם on fruit for the tree.

Creating Peace

As a demonstration that we can help create peace in our own lives, ask the students to keep individual logs for a week noting occasions on which peace in their lives is disrupted.

Next to each entry they should note if they changed the situation to create peace. What could they have done differently?

At the end of the week, have students share the insights in their logs with the class.

READING PRACTICE

Have students complete the exercise. Have individual students read the four lines aloud.

עַל־יִשְׂרָאֵל עַמֶּךָ
"upon Israel your people"

Call on students to read the Building Block phrase aloud.

Complete the Building Block with students.

Call on students to read the words with a star on page 46.

וְטוֹב בְּעֵינֶיךָ לְבָרֵךְ אֶת־עַמְּךָ יִשְׂרָאֵל
"and may it be good in your eyes to bless your people Israel"

Call on students to read the Building Block phrase aloud.

Complete the first part of the Building Block together.

Discuss answers to the question in the middle of the Building Block with students. (*the Jewish people want to live in peace; we do not want anti-Semitism; we want Israel to grow strong in peace; we want to live our lives without fear of hatred or war*)

Have students complete the Building Block.

The Fruit of the Tree

Create a new fruit tree with the root ברכ.

Write "bless" and "praise" on the trunk of the tree.

Write the words in Shalom Rav built on the root ברכ on fruit for the tree.

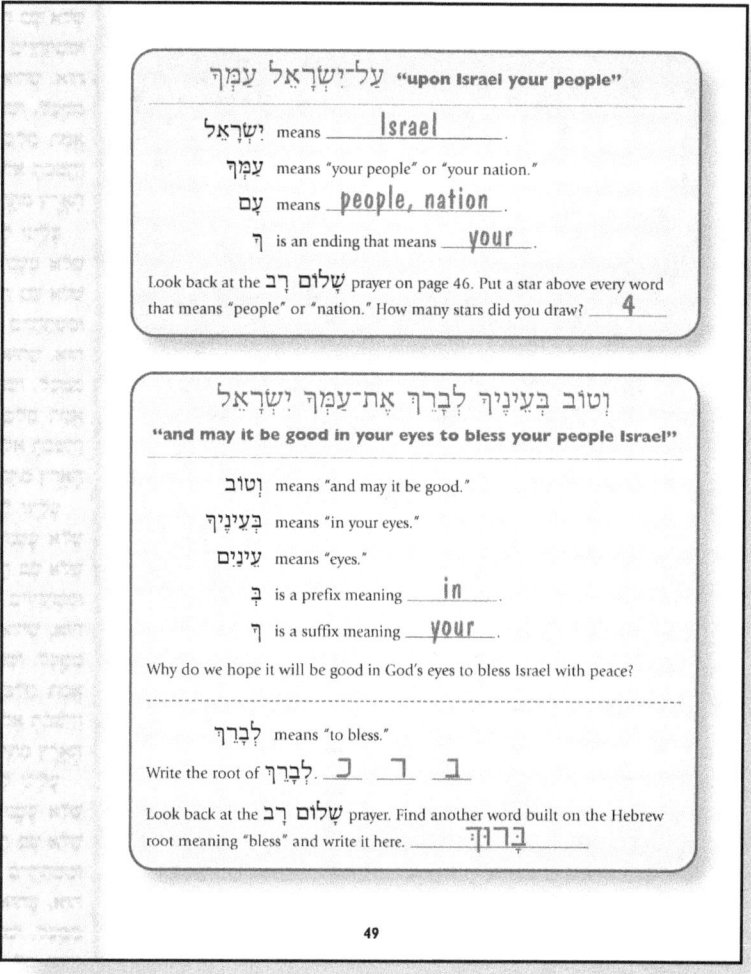

Reading Rotation

There are three sentences in Shalom Rav on page 46: lines 1–2, lines 2–3, line 4.

Form three reading rows of students in the classsroom.

1st rotation:
Row 1 reads sentence 1. Row 2 reads sentence 2. Row 3 reads sentence 3.

2nd rotation:
Row 2 reads sentence 1. Row 3 reads sentence 2. Row 1 reads sentence 3.

3rd rotation:
Row 3 reads sentence 1. Row 1 reads sentence 2. Row 2 reads sentence 3.

Variation

Select three students to read instead of an entire row of students.

INTRODUCING שִׂים שָׁלוֹם

שִׂים שָׁלוֹם and שָׁלוֹם רָב are two versions of the same prayer; the first appears in the evening service and the second in the morning service. In this case, the prayers have the same theme (peace) and end with the same words. In other prayers—for example, מַעֲרִיב עֲרָבִים and יוֹצֵר אוֹר—the prayers have the same theme (creation), but have very different words.

INTO THE TEXT

Read the introductory paragraph on page 50 together with the students.

Parallel Prayers

Ask one half of the class to open their textbooks to page 46, Shalom Rav. The other half of the class should remain on page 50, Sim Shalom.

Ask each half of the class to read the following identical sentences, at the same time, from the two versions of the blessing: Shalom Rav—line 2, fifth word, through line 4; Sim Shalom—lines 6–8. Lead the reading to pace the students.

Have the groups switch pages and read the sentences once again.

Everyone should then read the English translation of the sentences: "And may it be good in your eyes . . . Israel with peace."

PRAYER DICTIONARY

Word Cards

Display Word Cards 52–59 in random order. Call on individual students to read the phrases on cards 56, 58, and 59. Ask students if they recognize words within the phrases. Show the English meaning on the back of each Word Card.

Call on students to read Word Cards 52–55 and 57 in turn. Before turning the Word Card over to see the English meaning, ask if they recognize the word or a part of the word.

Word Match

Instruct the students to cover the Prayer Dictionary and complete the exercise, and then to uncover it to check their answers.

Word Card Games

Review all Word Cards (44–59) utilizing "General Word Card Techniques and Games" found at the front of this guide.

Photo Op

Ask students in what ways the boy looks peaceful. (*not speaking; chin resting on hand; eyes downcast; looks introspective*)

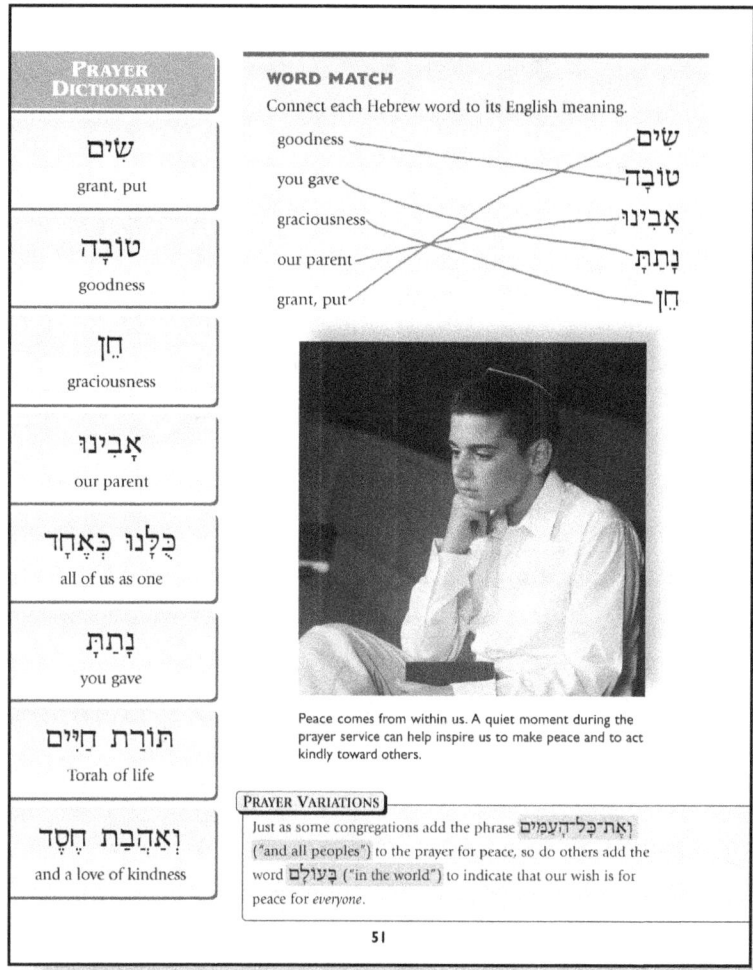

PRAYER VARIATIONS

Read the explanation with students.

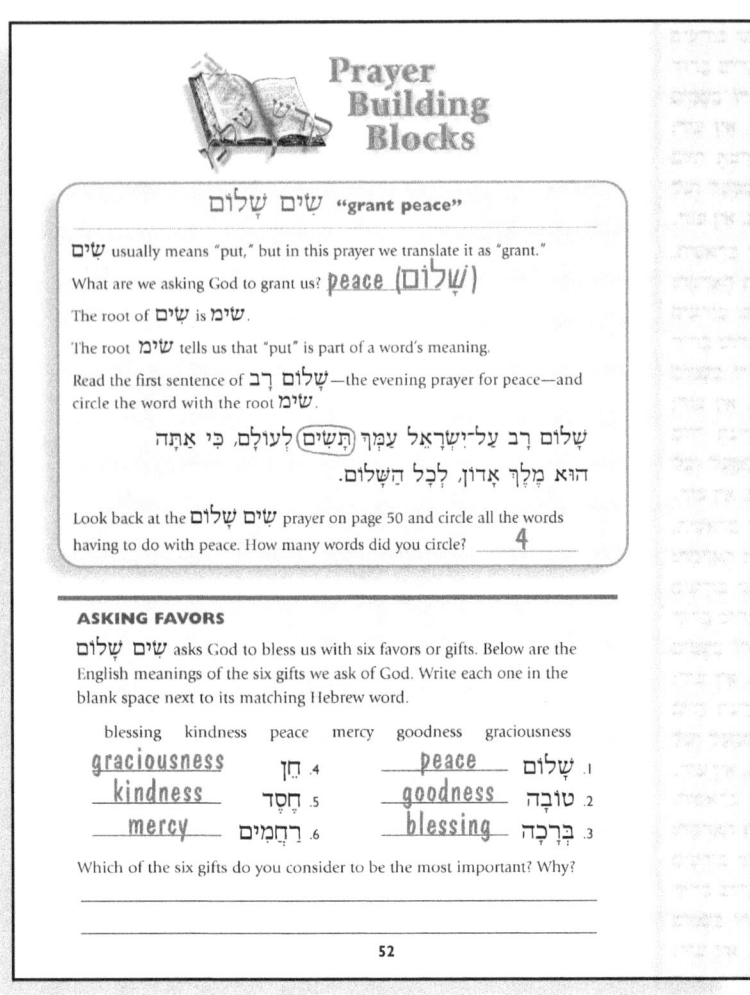

שִׂים שָׁלוֹם "grant peace"

Call on students to read the Building Block phrase aloud.

Complete the first part of the Building Block together.

The Fruit of the Tree

Create a new fruit tree for the root שׂימ.

Write "put" and "grant" on the trunk of the tree.

Place fruit with the words שִׂים and תָּשִׂים on the tree. Add the phrase שִׂים שָׁלוֹם.

ASKING FAVORS

Read the introduction with students.

Ask a student to read the six English terms.

Ask another student to read the six Hebrew terms.

Direct students to complete the exercise.

Student Hint: Look for roots you know (רחמ, שלמ, חסד, ברכ) and words you have learned in the Prayer Dictionary.

Allow time for students to write responses to the questions at the bottom of the page.

Ask each student who selected שָׁלוֹם as the most important gift to explain his or her choice.

Follow this procedure for each of the remaining five gifts.

Responsive Reading

Tell students to look at page 50, lines 1–2, in their textbooks.

Read each English phrase to the class and have the students respond with the corresponding Hebrew phrase as follows:

Teacher	Students
Grant peace (in the world)	שִׂים שָׁלוֹם (בָּעוֹלָם)
goodness and blessing	טוֹבָה וּבְרָכָה
graciousness and kindness	חֵן וָחֶסֶד
and mercy	וְרַחֲמִים
upon us and upon all	עָלֵינוּ וְעַל כָּל
Israel Your people	יִשְׂרָאֵל עַמֶּךָ

Together read lines 1–2 and 6–8.

בָּרְכֵנוּ, אָבִינוּ, כֻּלָּנוּ כְּאֶחָד
"bless us, our parent, all of us as one"

Call on students to read the Building Block phrase aloud.

Complete the first part of the Building Block, בָּרְכֵנוּ אָבִינוּ, together.

Recognizing Roots

Ask students to find the word in line 1 that means "our ruler." (מַלְכֵּנוּ)

Ask students to find the words in line 2 having to do with "mercy" or "compassion." (הָרַחֲמָן, הַמְרַחֵם, רַחֵם)

Complete the second part of the Building Block, כֻּלָּנוּ כְּאֶחָד, together.

Insight

Ask: Why do we ask God to bless "all of us as one"? (*we are one people; we believe in one God; we are praying together; we are a community*)

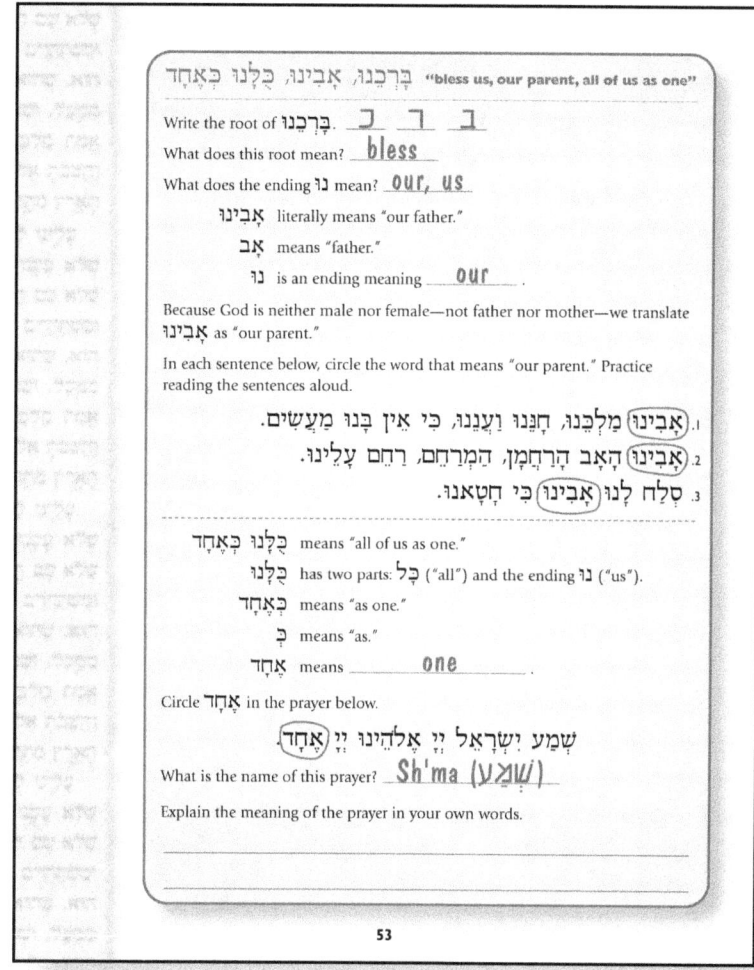

LESSON 5

> ### An Ethical Echo
> Read these words from Psalm 34:15 in Hebrew and in English.
>
> סוּר מֵרָע וַעֲשֵׂה־טוֹב בַּקֵּשׁ שָׁלוֹם וְרָדְפֵהוּ.
>
> *Turn aside from the bad and do good; seek peace and pursue it.*
>
> Jewish tradition teaches us that רוֹדֵף שָׁלוֹם—seeking peace—is a holy act. The mitzvah of רוֹדֵף שָׁלוֹם is the act of pursuing peace in our homes, in our communities, and in the world.
>
> The two prayers you are studying in this chapter ask for peace. So do many other prayers, including בִּרְכַּת הַמָּזוֹן—Grace After Meals—where we ask that God "cause peace to dwell among us."
>
> **Think About This!**
> Why do you think we need prayers to help us achieve peace in our homes, in our communities, and in the world?
>
> **MAKE PEACE**
> An ancient rabbi said: "Those who make peace in their homes are as if they made peace in all Israel."
>
> List 4 things you can do to help make your home a more peaceful and loving place.
>
> 1. ___
> 2. ___
> 3. ___
> 4. ___

AN ETHICAL ECHO

Read the top half of the page with students.

THINK ABOUT THIS!

Discuss the question with students. (*prayers remind us of our goals; when we pray for peace as a community, we recognize that we have a common interest and goal; prayers help sustain us in our efforts toward peace*)

Expanding the Concept

Why do we begin making peace first in our homes, then in our communities, and then in our world? (*we begin making peace among those we know and care about; we take the peace-making techniques from our home and apply them to our community—our schools, teams, clubs, and then to people outside our community; we start small and move on to bigger goals*)

MAKE PEACE

Read the introduction and discuss ways students can make their homes a more peaceful and loving place. Direct students to write down the four ways that are best for them.

Consider sending home the "As a Family: Words of Peace" page at the back of this guide. Ask each student to bring the completed page back to class. Call on students to share their family's ideas.

נָתַתָּ לָנוּ "you gave to us"

Call on students to read the Building Block phrase aloud.

Complete the Building Block together.

Reading Game: Stop and Go

Direct students to page 50, line 3.

Call on a student to be the reader. The reader should select a word on the line and, without telling the class which word it is, should read the line and stop before the selected word.

When the reader stops, it is a signal for the class to "go"—to read the word in unison. The reader then continues reading the rest of the line.

Repeat several times, each time with a new reader.

Variation: Expand the game to include lines 3–5.

TORAH BLESSINGS

Call on students to read the explanation on page 55 and to underline the words as directed.

Student Challenge

- Read each line with a word built on the root נתן. (*first blessing: lines 4, 5; second blessing: lines 1, 3*)

- Call on students to read the last sentence in each blessing.

  Ask them what they noticed about the last sentence in each. (*they are the same*)

  Comprehension: What do you think the sentence means in English? (*"Praised are You, Adonai, who gives us the Torah"*)

- Call on students to read lines 1–2 in the "Blessing before the Torah Reading."

  Ask students if they recognize the lines. (*Bar'chu*) Ask: Why do you think the Bar'chu introduces the Blessing before the Torah Reading?

  (*The Bar'chu is the Call to Worship. It is a signal that the prayer service is about to start; in this case, the Bar'chu is a signal that the Torah Reading is about to start; it calls the congregation to attention.*)

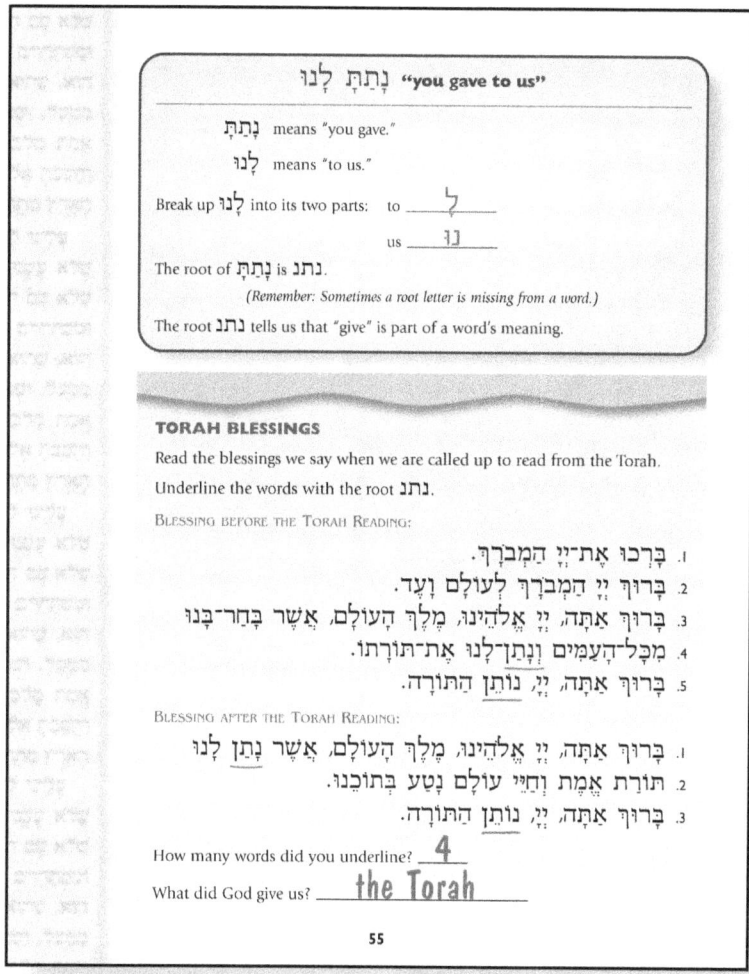

The Blessing before the Torah Reading

The person honored with an *aliyah* to the Torah chants line 1. The congregation chants line 2. The person honored with an *aliyah* repeats line 2 and then chants the remaining lines (3–5). Each person honored with an *aliyah* repeats this ritual.

The Blessing after the Torah Reading

Each person honored with an *aliyah* to the Torah chants the blessing after the *aliyah*.

Reading and Chanting Practice

Read the Torah Blessings with students.

Call on individual students to read each blessing.

You might wish to teach students how to chant the blessings.

The Fruit of the Tree

Create a new fruit tree with the root נתן.

Write "give" on the trunk of the tree.

Place fruit on the tree with the words and phrases in the Building Block and the Torah Blessings (נָתַתָּ, וְנָתַן, נוֹתֵן, נָתַן). Remind students that sometimes a root letter does not appear in a word built on that root.

תּוֹרַת חַיִּים, וְאַהֲבַת חֶסֶד
"the Torah of life, and a love of kindness"

Call on students to read the Building Block phrase aloud.

Complete the first part of the Building Block exercise, תּוֹרַת חַיִּים, together.

Allow students several minutes to respond to the question in the middle of the Building Block.

Complete the second part of the Building Block, וְאַהֲבַת חֶסֶד, together.

The Fruit of the Tree

Create a tree with the root אהב. Write "love" on the trunk of the tree.

Add fruit to the tree: וְאַהֲבַת חֶסֶד, אַהֲבַת

READING PRACTICE

Direct students to read the explanation and follow the directions.

Call on individual students to read each line aloud.

Ask:

- Which line is found in Birkat Shalom? (*line 3*)
- What is the English translation of the line? (*"Grant peace, goodness and blessing, graciousness and kindness and mercy [compassion]"*)

Quarters and Quartets

Call on a student to read the last English sentence on page 56.

There are four phrases in the last Hebrew sentence.

- Divide the class into quarters, i.e., four groups. Each group should read one phrase in turn. Rotate the reading four times in the class. A different group should begin each time.
- Divide the students into "quartets," i.e., sets of four students each. Each member of a quartet should read one phrase in turn to their group. Rotate the reading four times within the quartet. A different member of the quartet should begin each time.

Read the complete Hebrew sentence in unison with students.

A Prayer Ending

Divide the class in half.

First one half of the class should read page 46, line 1 through line 2, fourth word.

Then the other half of the class should read page 50, lines 1–5.

Finally, the entire class should read the prayer ending, which is the same in both prayers: page 46, line 2, fifth word through line 4; page 50, lines 6–8.

A Musical Note

Teach students to chant the evening blessing (page 46) and the morning blessing (page 50) with the melody used in your synagogue.

FLUENT READING

Read the introduction together with students.

For Discussion

Ask: Why do you think the personal prayer asks God to help us choose our words carefully? (*what we say to others is important in building relationships; our choice of words reflects our image and we reflect God's image; we can cause harm with the wrong words; we can make someone happy with the right words*)

Reading Rules
"Vo"

Sometimes וֹ looks like the vowel "oh." The symbol וֹ has the sound "vo" if the letter before it already has a vowel (צְוֹ).

Call on students to read the first word in line 3.

Call on students to read the complete line aloud.

"Eye" Ending

When *yud* follows the vowel ַ or ָ at the end of a word, the vowel has the sound "eye."

Call on students to read each word in line 1 ending with the "eye" sound.
(אֱלֹהַי, וּשְׂפָתַי, וְלִמְקַלְלַי)

Call on students to read the complete line aloud.

"Ahv" Ending

When the letter *vav* follows an "eye" vowel, ָיו, the vowel has the sound "ahv" (the *yud* is not pronounced).

Call on students to read the third word in line 5 correctly.

Call on students to read lines 5 and 6 aloud.

Read the complete prayer aloud with students.

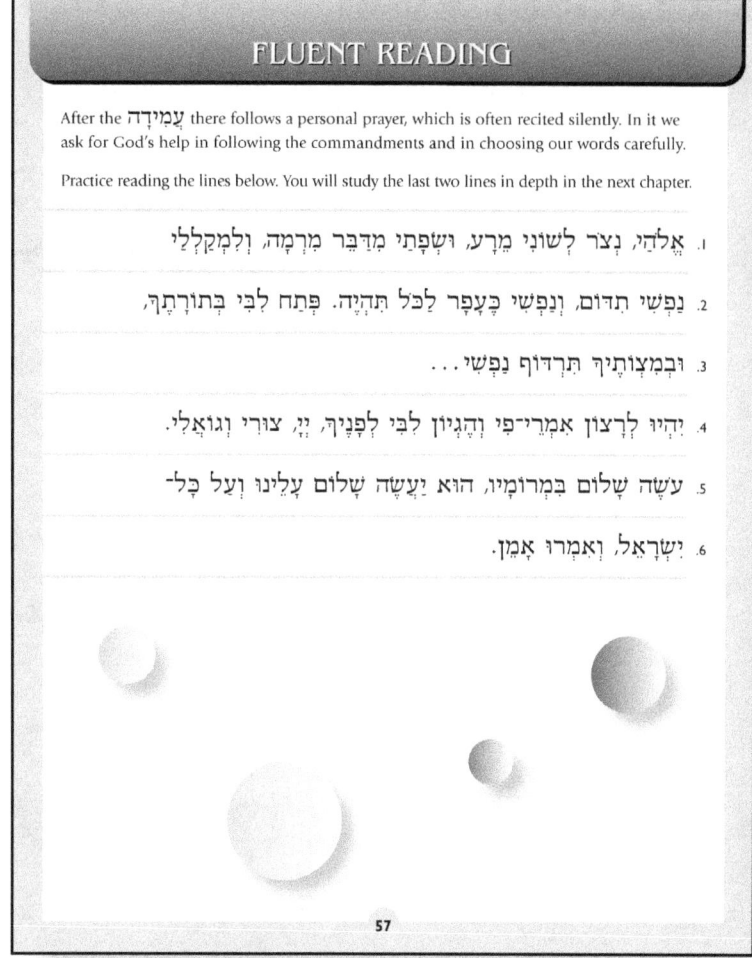

WORKSHEET

Duplicate and hand out copies of the worksheet for Lesson 5 to review skills and concepts.

FAMILY EDUCATION

Duplicate and send home copies of "As a Family: Words of Peace" (at the back of this guide) if you did not do so when you were teaching page 54 in the textbook.

LESSON 5
Worksheet

Name: _____

בִּרְכַּת שָׁלוֹם:
שָׁלוֹם רָב/שִׂים שָׁלוֹם

1. Which version of בִּרְכַּת שָׁלוֹם do we say in the evening service and which do we say in the morning service? Write your answers below.

   שִׂים שָׁלוֹם   שָׁלוֹם רָב

   Evening _____   Morning _____

2. Draw lines to connect the Hebrew words to their roots.

   Set 1

רַחֲמִים	ברכ
הַמְבָרֵךְ	חיה
בִּשְׁלוֹמֶךָ	רחמ
חַיִּים	שלמ

   Set 2

אַהֲבַת	נתנ
לְבָרֵךְ	שימ
נָתַתָּ	אהב
שִׂים	ברכ

3. The English phrases below are in the order in which we recite them in שִׂים שָׁלוֹם. Number the Hebrew phrases in the correct order to match the English.

   1. grant peace   ____ עָלֵינוּ וְעַל כָּל יִשְׂרָאֵל עַמֶּךָ
   2. goodness and blessing   ____ חֵן וָחֶסֶד וְרַחֲמִים
   3. graciousness and kindness and mercy (compassion)   ____ שִׂים שָׁלוֹם
   4. upon us and upon all Israel Your people   ____ טוֹבָה וּבְרָכָה

4. Write the following English words and phrases under the matching Hebrew words and phrases from שִׂים שָׁלוֹם:

   and a love of kindness   and life   Torah of life   and blessing
   and righteousness   and mercy/compassion   and peace

   וּצְדָקָה   וְאַהֲבַת חֶסֶד   תּוֹרַת חַיִּים

   _____   _____   _____

   וְשָׁלוֹם   וְחַיִּים   וְרַחֲמִים   וּבְרָכָה

   _____   _____   _____   _____

HINENI—The New Hebrew Through Prayer 2 © Behrman House Publishers

LESSON 6

עֹשֶׂה שָׁלוֹם

LEARNING OBJECTIVES
Prayer Reading Skills
- The prefix וְ ("and")
- The suffix יִ ("my")
- The roots עשה ("make"); עלה ("go up"); שלמ ("peace"); אמר ("say")

Prayer Concepts
- Understanding the meaning of *shalom* to the Jewish people
- Jerusalem: City of Peace
- David and Solomon: kings and leaders of our people
- Teachings from the *Tanach*—the Bible—are reflected in our siddur
- Ethical Echo: שָׁלוֹם בַּיִת (*"peace in the home"*)

BEYOND THE TEXTBOOK
- The endings יִ , יָ ("eye"); יו ("ahv")
- The root אמנ ("faith")
- Why we say "Amen"

ABOUT THE PRAYER
We say Oseh Shalom immediately after the Amidah. *Shalom* is translated as "peace" but it means much more than that. *Shalom* comes from the Hebrew word *shalem* which means "complete" or "perfect." When we create peace, we are complete and are helping to create a perfect world.

INSTRUCTIONAL MATERIALS
Text pages 58-67

Word Cards 44, 46, 60–66

Worksheet 6

Family Education: "As a Family: Sh'lom Bayit" (at the back of this guide)

SET INDUCTION
For Discussion
Tell students that God created a world at peace. When God completed creation, God "blessed the seventh day and made it holy" (Genesis 2:3). We, who are made in the image of God, have the obligation to "make peace" each day of the week.

A Recipe for Peace
Together with the class, create a recipe to make a "Peace Pie."

On one half of the chalkboard or on a piece of butcher paper, draw up with students a list of incidents in their lives that were the *opposite* of peace. (*arguments over a game or TV show, school-yard disagreements, sports team conflicts, family disputes, name calling*)

On the second half of the chalkboard or butcher paper write a recipe for peace by brainstorming a list of "ingredients" that would go into making the "Peace Pie." (*smiles, handshakes, kind words, acts of loving-kindness, sharing, discussing, friendship, love, hugs, laughter, understanding*)

Make a large circular "Peace Pie" out of poster board and divide the circle into seven segments to symbolize the seven days of creation. Entitle the circle "Peace Pie."

Have the students select seven "ingredients" from the list for the pie. Write a different ingredient on each of the seven segments of the pie. Choose seven students to illustrate the ingredient on each segment. They can work on it upon completion of class work. Display the pie in the classroom.

Variation
Each student can create a "Peace Pie" to take home. Call on students to share their recipe choices.

A First Reading

Read lines 1 and 2 aloud with students.

Ask a student to read the English translation aloud.

INTO THE TEXT

Direct students to read the first paragraph quietly.

Pose the Questions

- What kinds of peace are described in the paragraph? (*between countries, between family members, between friends; peace of mind*)

- Why is peace better than conflict? (*people progress in life with a happy, positive state of mind; working, playing, and living together in peace allows for cooperation; people do not get hurt physically or emotionally*)

Call on students to read the second and third paragraphs aloud.

- Why is it significant that we say "peace" when we greet one another? (*we wish the other person well; our intentions are peaceful; it's the most important wish we can make*)

- Why is it significant that we say "peace" when we part from one another? (*we offer continued wishes for peace in all activities and relationships*)

Reading Rule Review

Write the following letters and vowels on the chalkboard and ask a student to read them:

מָ טַ לְ בַּ

Reading Rule

When י follows ַ or ָ at the end of a word, the ending has the sound "eye."

Add a *yud* and ask a student to read:

מַי טַי לִי בַּי

Reading Rule

When ו follows יַ or יָ at the end of a word, the ending has the sound "ahv."

Add a *vav* and ask a student to read:

מָיו טָיו לָיו בַּיו

Call on students to read page 58, line 1, third word (בִּמְרוֹמָיו).

PRAYER DICTIONARY

Word Cards

Display Word Cards 44, 46, and 66.

Each of these can be considered "sight words," that is, familiar words that are recognizable on sight. Ask students to read each one in turn and give its English meaning.

Challenge students to explain how each word is used: שָׁלוֹם—when speaking about peace, praying for peace, saying hello or goodbye; יִשְׂרָאֵל—when referring to our patriarch Jacob whose name was changed to Israel, when referring to the Jewish people or to the State of Israel; אָמֵן—at the conclusion of a blessing or prayer.

Reading with Understanding

אָמֵן means "so be it." The word אָמֵן is built on the root אמנ ("faith").

אָמֵן indicates you are affirming what was said in the blessing or prayer.

Display Word Cards 65 and 66 in right-to-left order. Ask students to read the phrase formed by the two Word Cards.

Ask: What is the English meaning of the phrase? (*"and say Amen"*)

Call on a student to read the prayer on page 58 aloud. When the reader says וְאִמְרוּ, the class should respond with אָמֵן.

Ask: What is the significance of saying "Amen"? (*we agree with the prayer for peace*)

Forming Phrases

Display Word Cards 44, 46, and 60–66 in random order.

Call on students to form the following phrases in Hebrew with the Word Cards: "makes peace" (60, 44); "will make peace for us and for all Israel" (61, 44, 62–64, 46); "and say Amen" (65, 66). Students can self-check the phrases on the English side of the Word Cards.

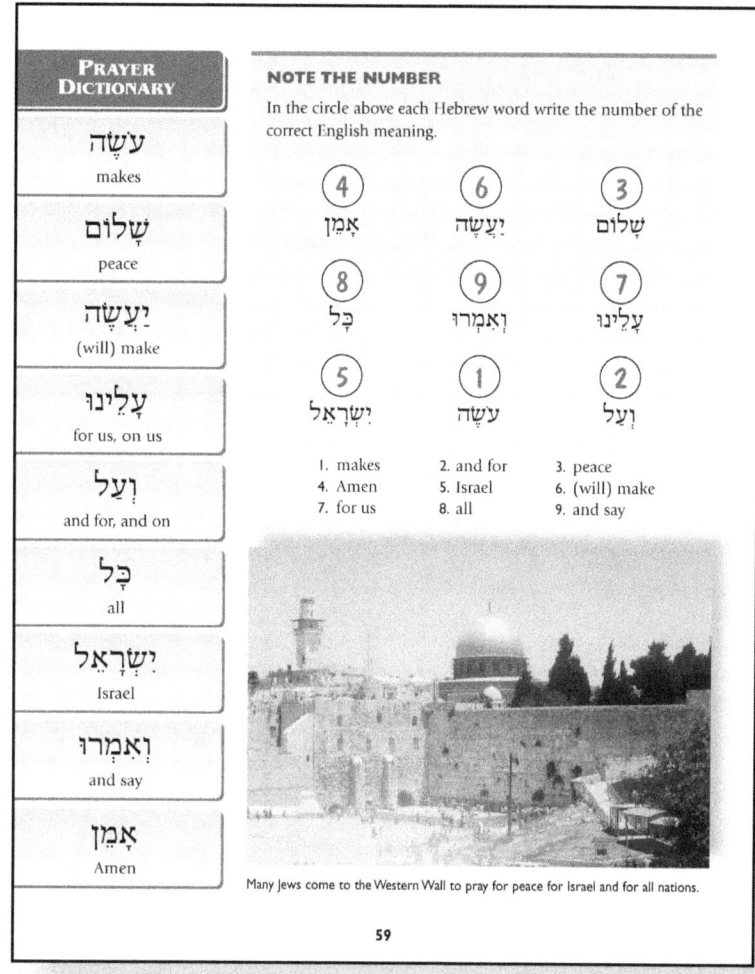

NOTE THE NUMBER

Challenge the students to write the number for as many words in the activity as they can without looking at the Prayer Dictionary. Students should uncover the Prayer Dictionary to check their answers.

Photo Op

Read the caption below the photo to the students.

Explain that visitors to the Western Wall often write prayers on small pieces of paper and then insert the folded papers into the crevices of the wall. The Western Wall is part of the supporting wall of the Temple Mount and is a remnant of the Second Temple, destroyed by the Romans in 70 C.E. Point out, too, the Dome of the Rock, one of the holiest mosques in the Muslim world.

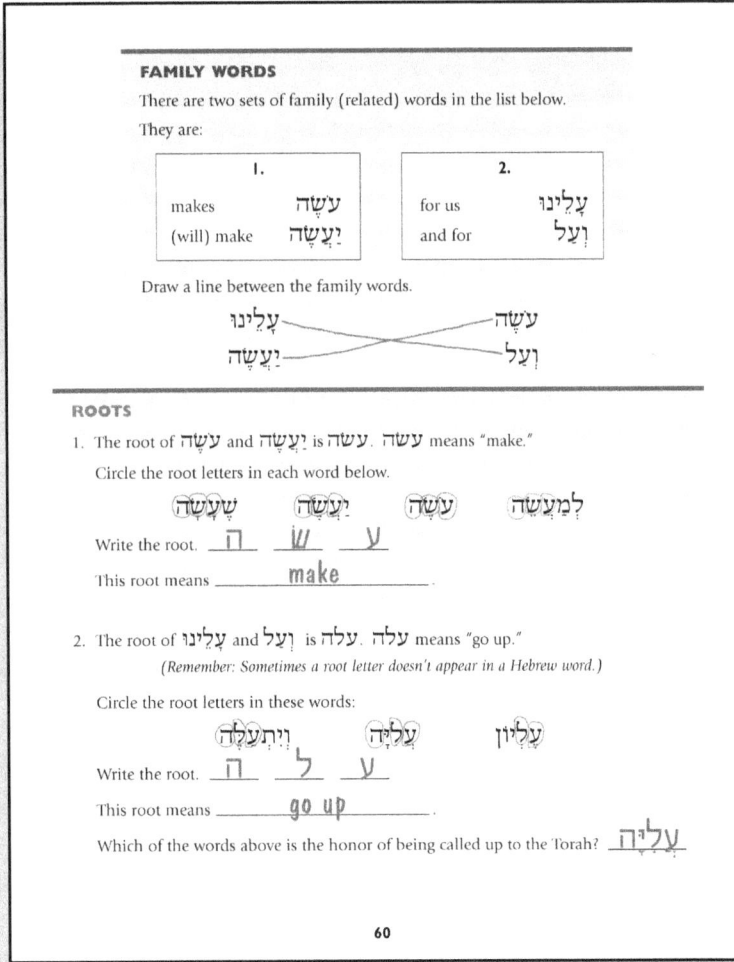

FAMILY WORDS

Complete this section with students.

Direct students to circle these four words in the prayer on page 58.

ROOTS

Read the introduction to exercise 1 with students.

Call on students to read the four words aloud.

Direct students to complete the activity independently.

Read the introduction to exercise 2 with students.

Call on students to read the four words aloud.

Direct students to complete the activity independently.

Word Study

Write the word עֲלִיָּה on the chalkboard. Ask students to read the word aloud.

Explain that this word can mean two things:

1. The honor of being called up to the Torah to recite the Torah blessings and/or to read from the Torah.

2. Going to live in Israel. We call this "making *aliyah*."

Write the root עלה on the chalkboard. Explain that words built on this root are related to "going up."

Ask the Questions

- In what ways does the word "aliyah" ("going up to the Torah") reflect the root? (*the bimah is often raised; we get up from our seats; we go up spiritually to the Torah*)

- In what ways does the word "aliyah" ("going up to Israel") reflect the root? (*we are going up spiritually to Eretz Yisrael, the land promised to us by God*)

Making Aliyah

Ask students: Do you know someone who made *aliyah*? Suggest students write to those people and ask about their experiences as new immigrants in Israel. Tell the class that an immigrant to Israel is known as an עוֹלֶה (masculine) or עוֹלָה (feminine); immigrants are known as עוֹלִים (plural). Write these three words on the chalkboard. Compare them with the word עֲלִיָּה. Ask: What is the root of all three? (עלה)

The Fruit of the Tree

Create two fruit trees. On the roots of one tree, write עשה. On the roots of the other tree, write עלה. Write "make" on the trunk of the first tree and "go up" on the other. Create fruit for the trees with words from the prayer on page 58 and from the exercise on page 60. Add the words עוֹלָה and עוֹלֶה.

THE NEW HEBREW THROUGH PRAYER 2 • הִנֵּנִי   **80**

PLEASED TO MEET YOU

Read this section aloud with students.

If your students know their Hebrew names, they should fill them in to complete the Hebrew sentence: שָׁלוֹם, שְׁמִי _____. If not, they can use their English names. Give each student an opportunity to practice the sentence.

DID YOU KNOW?

Read this section aloud with students.

Ask:

- Has anyone in the class visited יְרוּשָׁלַיִם, the "City of Peace"? Have any of their family members visited יְרוּשָׁלַיִם?

- Does any boy in our class have the Hebrew name דָּוִד or שְׁלֹמֹה? Is there anyone whose brother, father, or grandfather has these names?

Extending the Lesson

- Bring in pictures of Jerusalem. Create a bulletin board display and label it יְרוּשָׁלַיִם—"City of Peace."

- Divide the class into two groups: "David" and "Solomon." Provide the students with historical texts or reference books to research facts about the life of the king for whom their group is named. Each group member should write a fact about his or her king on a white 3" x 5" index card, and a question about the fact on a colored index card. Create teams and play the game "Matching Questions with Answers" described under "Classroom Games" in the front of this guide.

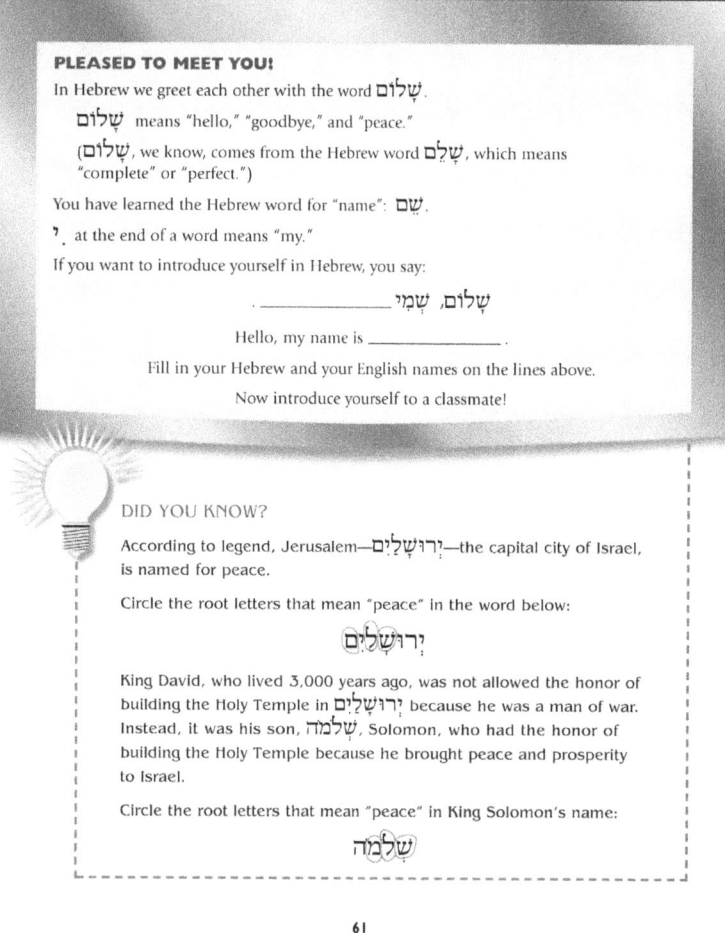

81 LESSON 6

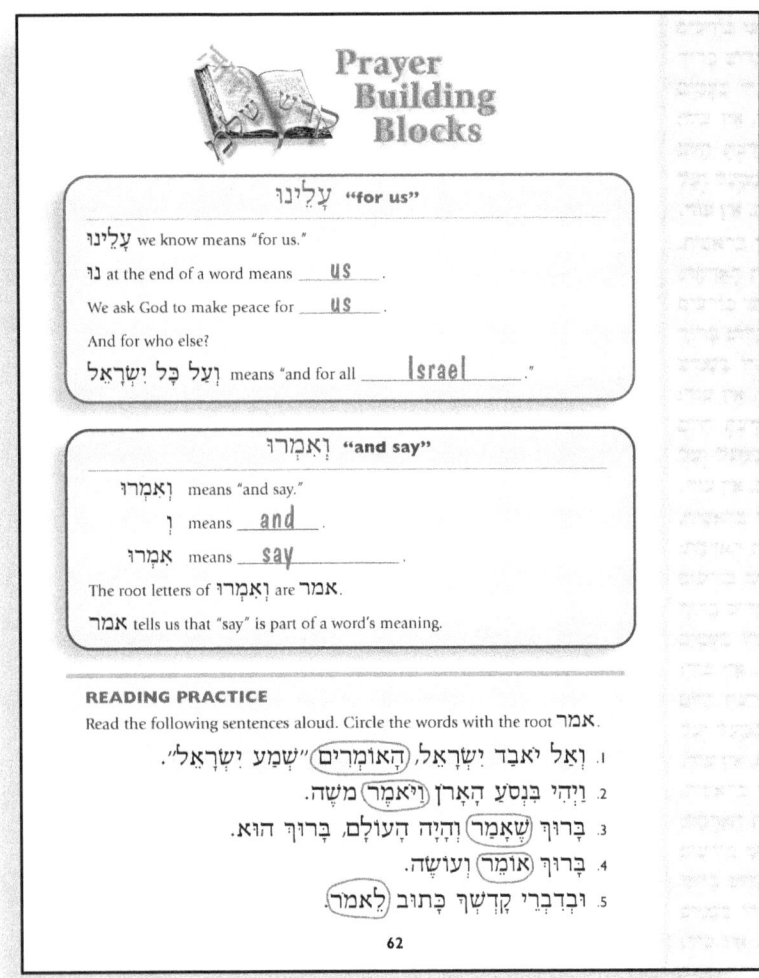

The Fruit of the Tree

Create a fruit tree for the root אמר. Write "say" on the trunk of the tree. Create fruit for the tree, one for each word circled on page 62 built on the root אמר.

Fruit Salad

Remove the fruit from all the fruit trees. Mix up the fruit in a bowl to create a "fruit salad." Have students read the word on each fruit aloud before placing the fruit back on the correct tree.

Extending the Activity

Make a real fruit salad with students and enjoy!

PRAYER BUILDING BLOCKS

עָלֵינוּ "for us"

Write the suffix נוּ on the chalkboard. Review the English meanings: "us" and "our." Ask students for words they already know that conclude with נוּ and for the English meaning of each word. Examples: אֱלֹהֵינוּ ("our God"); אֲבוֹתֵינוּ ("our fathers" or "our ancestors"); אִמּוֹתֵינוּ ("our mothers"); אָבִינוּ ("our father" or "our parent"); קִדְּשָׁנוּ ("who makes us holy"); וְצִוָּנוּ ("and commands us").

Direct students to complete the Building Block and share their answers.

וְאָמְרוּ "and say"

Complete the Building Block with students.

Repeat the activity described previously for Word Cards 65 and 66 on page 59 of the textbook. Call on one student to read the prayer on page 58 aloud. When the reader says וְאָמְרוּ, the class should respond with אָמֵן.

READING PRACTICE

Call on students to read aloud each circled word.

Call on different students to read aloud each complete sentence.

High Five

Each student has a chance to give a "high five" as follows:

- Students make a fist holding one hand upright.
- If they read sentence 1 correctly, they raise their thumbs.

After reading each sentence, students add another finger in turn until they have made a "high five" holding up all five fingers.

FROM THE TANACH

Write the word "Bible" on the chalkboard and "Torah," "Prophets," "Writings" below it. Explain that these are the three sections of the Bible.

Write the Hebrew acronym תַּנַ״ךְ on the chalkboard. Call on students to read the word aloud.

Explain that this is the Hebrew name for the Bible. The three letters of the word represent the Hebrew terms for the three sections of the Bible.

Write the Hebrew terms in the order shown below. Have students circle the first letter in each word to highlight the letters that comprise the word תַּנַ״ךְ. (Remind students that כ changes its form at the end of a word—תַּנַ״ךְ.)

תּוֹרָה (Torah); נְבִיאִים (Prophets); כְּתוּבִים (Writings)

The Prophets

The prophets were people who spoke on behalf of God. They brought hope to our people in times of despair. When our people strayed, they led them back to God and Torah. They lived and taught for a period of 750 years from the time of our exodus from Egypt until our return from exile in Babylonia. Moses was our first and greatest prophet.

Visualizing the Lesson

Write the heading תַּנַ״ךְ on a bulletin board display.

Write the names of the three sections of the Bible in three separate sections of the bulletin board. Use the Hebrew and English term for each one.

- Under the heading תּוֹרָה ("Torah") list the books that make up the Torah: Genesis, Exodus, Leviticus, Numbers, Deuteronomy.

- Under the heading נְבִיאִים ("Prophets") list some of the books in Prophets: Isaiah, Ezekiel, Jeremiah, Amos, Micah.

- Under the heading כְּתוּבִים ("Writings") list some of the books in Writings: Proverbs, Psalms, Job, Megillat Esther.

FROM THE TANACH

The quest for peace—for שָׁלוֹם—has always been important to the Jewish people. Read the following verse from the prophet Isaiah.

And they shall beat their swords into plowshares
And their spears into pruning-hooks;
Nation shall not lift up sword against nation,
Neither shall they learn war any more.

(Isaiah 2:4)

Now read the last two lines of the verse in Hebrew.

לֹא־יִשָּׂא גוֹי אֶל־גוֹי חֶרֶב
וְלֹא־יִלְמְדוּ עוֹד מִלְחָמָה׃

1. Isaiah lived more than 2,500 years ago. Why are his words still important today?
   There is still not peace in the world today; we always strive for peace.

2. List the words in the verse that are the opposite of peace.
   beat, swords, spears, sword, war

3. In one sentence, describe Isaiah's ideal world.

The prophet Micah, who lived at around the same time as Isaiah, spoke almost the exact words in *his* wish for peace. Why do you think it is significant that the two prophets spoke almost the identical words?

63

Into the Text

Read the top portion of page 63 with students.

Call on students to read the Hebrew.

Form groups of 2 or 3 students each. Group members should discuss ideas in response to the three questions on the page and write their responses on the lines. Have groups share their insights with the class.

Discuss the last question together with students.

Create a Bulletin Board Display

Entitle a bulletin board display עֲשֵׂה שָׁלוֹם and add the quotation from Isaiah. Ask students to bring in newspaper articles about people or nations working to make peace, and post them on the bulletin board.

A CLOSER LOOK

Read the introduction together with the students.

Birkat Hamazon: Ask a student to read lines 1–3 up to the words עַד עוֹלָם.

Call on the class to read עֹשֶׂה שָׁלוֹם together.

Kaddish: Ask a student to read lines 1–2.

Call on the class to read עֹשֶׂה שָׁלוֹם together.

A Musical Note

Teach the students to chant עֹשֶׂה שָׁלוֹם with the melody used in your synagogue.

AN ETHICAL ECHO

Read the paragraph together with students.

Write the heading עֲשֵׂה שָׁלוֹם ("Make Peace") on the chalkboard or on poster board.

Create two columns entitled "At Home" and "Outside Our Home."

List the ways to make peace described in the paragraph. (*At Home: talk things over, take "time-outs," apologize, hug each other; Outside Our Home: understand people have different points of view, respect each other, find solutions*)

THINK ABOUT THIS!

Read this section together with students. Discuss individual responses to the questions at the conclusion of the paragraph.

Now direct students' attention back to the "Make Peace" lists.

Ask students to add techniques for making peace that have worked inside their own homes and outside their homes, for example, at school, on the playground, during sports.

An Art Form

Micrography is an art form in which significant words woven into the design of a picture symbolize a concept. Have the students draw a light pencil outline to represent their homes. Then, using a pen or fine-point marker, have them write the phrase שלום בית (without vowels) on the lines forming the outline of their homes. The writing should be small so that the phrase can be repeated many times along the sketch lines. Finally, direct the students to erase the pencil lines of the home. The significant phrase שלום בית now creates the shape of their homes.

Variation

Instead of the phrase שלום בית, repeat two or three words or phrases that create peace in the home, such as "hugs," "smiles," "honor," "respect." Perhaps alternate the selected words with the phrase שלום בית.

Photo Op

Ask students if they think the young girl trusts the woman and why. (*girl is leaning against woman, smiling, holding her arm; older woman is looking down affectionately, touching girl's hand*)

FLUENT READING

Each line below contains the Hebrew word for "peace."

Practice reading the lines. Then circle the Hebrew word for "peace" in each line.

1. הַפּוֹרֵשׂ סֻכַּת (שָׁלוֹם) עָלֵינוּ, וְעַל כָּל עַמּוֹ יִשְׂרָאֵל,
וְעַל יְרוּשָׁלָיִם.

2. (שָׁלוֹם) רָב עַל יִשְׂרָאֵל עַמְּךָ תָּשִׂים לְעוֹלָם.

3. כִּי אַתָּה הוּא מֶלֶךְ אָדוֹן, לְכָל (הַשָּׁלוֹם).

4. בָּרוּךְ אַתָּה יְיָ, הַמְבָרֵךְ אֶת עַמּוֹ יִשְׂרָאֵל (בַּשָּׁלוֹם).

5. וְרַחֲמִים וְחַיִּים (וְשָׁלוֹם) וְכָל־טוֹב, וּמִכָּל־טוֹב לְעוֹלָם אַל־יְחַסְּרֵנוּ.

6. (שָׁלוֹם) עֲלֵיכֶם, מַלְאֲכֵי הַשָּׁרֵת, מַלְאֲכֵי עֶלְיוֹן.

7. שִׂים (שָׁלוֹם) טוֹבָה וּבְרָכָה, חֵן וָחֶסֶד וְרַחֲמִים עָלֵינוּ
וְעַל כָּל יִשְׂרָאֵל עַמֶּךָ.

8. בָּרוּךְ אַתָּה, יְיָ אֱלֹהֵינוּ, מֶלֶךְ הָעוֹלָם, יוֹצֵר אוֹר
וּבוֹרֵא חֹשֶׁךְ עֹשֶׂה (שָׁלוֹם) וּבוֹרֵא אֶת הַכֹּל.

66

WORKSHEET

Duplicate and hand out copies of the worksheet for Lesson 6 to review vocabulary and concepts underlying the prayer.

FAMILY EDUCATION

Duplicate and send home copies of "As a Family: Sh'lom Bayit" (at the back of this guide).

FLUENT READING

- Call on individual students, who will each read a line.

- Place the numbers 1–8 in a box or bag. Have each student select a number at random and read the corresponding line.

- Describe a word on a line. The student must read the correct word and then read the complete line. Examples: Line 1: a term for the Jewish people (עַמּוֹ יִשְׂרָאֵל); the "City of Peace" (יְרוּשָׁלָיִם); line 4: the two words built on the root "bless" or "praise" (הַמְבָרֵךְ, בָּרוּךְ); line 8: the word with a "double-duty dot" (חֹשֶׁךְ).

Expert Reading

Have the class form two groups by counting off 1-2, 1-2, 1-2. All the 1s form a group. All the 2s form another group. The 1s meet and practice the odd-numbered lines: 1, 3, 5, 7. The 2s meet and practice the even-numbered lines: 2, 4, 6, 8. Group members should assist each other with reading skills. Each group member selects one line and becomes the "expert" on reading that line. Group "experts" alternate reading lines 1–8.

Note: Depending upon the size of the group: some lines might have more than one expert; some group members might be experts on more than one line.

FRIDAY NIGHT SERVICE

Write the word עֶרֶב ("evening") on the chalkboard.

Remind students that the Jewish day begins the evening before. Ask for examples. (*Erev Shabbat, Erev Rosh Hashanah, Erev Sukkot, Erev Pesaḥ*)

Write the word שַׁבָּת on the chalkboard to form the phrase עֶרֶב שַׁבָּת.

Pose the Questions

- When does *Erev Shabbat* begin? (*Friday evening at sundown*)

- What do we celebrate on *Erev Shabbat*? (*arrival of Shabbat; creation; the natural world; family; freedom to live a Jewish life*)

- What words describe *Erev Shabbat*? (*peace, family, light, ritual, Shabbat meal, singing, services, community*)

- How do we prepare for *Erev Shabbat*? (*prepare the candles, wine, and ḥallah, and set the table; prepare a special meal; say the blessings*)

Note: The term *Erev Shabbat* may also be used to refer to Friday itself.

Direct students to "Friday Night Service" on page 67 in their texts.

Read the first two paragraphs aloud with the students.

Create a bulletin board and label it "A Palace in Time."

Surround the "palace" with words having to do with Shabbat based on the discussions you have just had. As students study the next three lessons, add terms that reflect the spirit of Shabbat (*the Shabbat bride; a sign of the Covenant; brit; creation; angels of peace; memory of the work of creation; memory of the going out from Egypt*)

Read the last two paragraphs aloud with the students.

FRIDAY NIGHT SERVICE

Are there special occasions you just can't wait for—that you look forward to for weeks in advance? Maybe it's your school's big holiday concert. Or maybe it's summer vacation, when you're off to camp with lots of other kids to swim, play softball, and tell ghost stories.

Shabbat is that kind of occasion for many Jews, who look forward to it all week long. Shabbat is a peaceful end to our week—a day to devote to ourselves, our family, and friends. It's a day when we can put aside the weekly demands of school and work and enjoy an unhurried pace. Rabbi Abraham Joshua Heschel called Shabbat "a palace in time"—a holy place that opens its doors to us once a week, inviting us to enter.

Friday night—the beginning of Shabbat—is an important time to spend with our families. Often the table is set for a special celebration—perhaps with a fancy tablecloth and, of course, candles, wine, and ḥallah. We say the blessings, perhaps sing Shabbat songs, and eat a special meal.

The Friday night Kabbalat Shabbat service marks the beginning of Shabbat in the synagogue. The prayers of the service speak of God the Creator, of the promises God made to the Jews, and of the wondrous gift of Shabbat. We pray as a community with our friends, our neighbors, and our family. And we say "hi" to them as well, catching up with what has happened since last Shabbat, and talking about what to expect in the week to come.

LESSON 6
Worksheet

Name: _____

עֹשֶׂה שָׁלוֹם

1. Write three meanings for the word שָׁלוֹם. _____ _____ _____

   Write two meanings for the word שָׁלֵם. _____ _____

2. Connect the root to the matching English.

peace	עשׂה
go up	אמר
make	עלה
say	שׁלמ

3. Write the correct number of the Hebrew word next to the matching English word.

   _____ Israel   1. יְרוּשָׁלַיִם

   _____ peace   2. כָּל

   _____ Amen   3. שָׁלוֹם

   _____ and say   4. עָלֵינוּ

   _____ for us   5. יִשְׂרָאֵל

   _____ all   6. וְאִמְרוּ

   _____ Jerusalem   7. אָמֵן

4. Write each English phrase below next to the matching Hebrew.

   and for all Israel   May God who makes peace in the heavens

   and say Amen   make peace for us

   _____ עֹשֶׂה שָׁלוֹם בִּמְרוֹמָיו

   _____ וְאִמְרוּ אָמֵן

   _____ הוּא יַעֲשֶׂה שָׁלוֹם עָלֵינוּ

   _____ וְעַל כָּל יִשְׂרָאֵל

5. Write the common root for the words and the phrase below. _____ _____ _____

   Write the English meanings for each word and phrase on the line below it.

   שָׁלֵם   יְרוּשָׁלַיִם   שְׁלֹמֹה   שְׁלוֹם בַּיִת   שָׁלוֹם

   _____ _____ _____ _____ _____

HINENI — THE NEW HEBREW THROUGH PRAYER 2 © Behrman House Publishers

LESSON 7
לְכָה דוֹדִי

LEARNING OBJECTIVES
Prayer Reading Skills

- Recognizing an acrostic
- The terms כַּלָּה ("bride"); חָתָן ("groom")
- The prefix בְּ ("in")
- The phrase *Kabbalat Shabbat* ("Welcoming Shabbat")
- The roots הלכ ("go" or "walk"); קבל ("receive" or "welcome"); שמר ("keep" or "guard"); זכר ("remember"); בוא ("come")

Prayer Concepts

- Lechah Dodi is a hymn that was written about 500 years ago
- Shabbat is compared to a bride or a queen
- Mystics in the sixteenth century went into the fields to welcome Shabbat
- The commandments "Remember Shabbat" and "Keep Shabbat" are highlighted at the beginning of Lechah Dodi
- We light at least two candles on Friday evening to welcome Shabbat. The two candles represent the two commandments

BEYOND THE TEXTBOOK

- The double *sh'va*
- Double letters with *sh'va*
- Family letters

ABOUT THE PRAYER

Lechah Dodi is sung toward the end of the Kabbalat Shabbat service in which we receive, or welcome, Shabbat. In the song, Shabbat is compared to a bride. The idea of Shabbat as a bride developed in Talmudic times, and was further developed by the mystics who lived in Safed during the sixteenth century. Men and boys dressed in white robes would go in procession to the hills chanting psalms and calling upon the "bride," Shabbat, to enter their homes. The words of Lechah Dodi were written by the mystic Shlomo Halevi Alkabetz. He reveals his name, Shlomo Halevi, in the acrostic letter at the beginning of each verse in the song.

INSTRUCTIONAL MATERIALS

Text pages 68–75

Word Cards 67–74

Worksheet 7

Family Education: "As a Family: A Special Day" (at the back of this guide)

SET INDUCTION
Preparing for the Bride

Write the heading "The Traditional Wedding Ceremony" on the chalkboard. Beneath it write three sub-headings: "Dressing the Bride," "Setting the Scene," "The Ceremony." Discuss with students items that might fall under each heading. List their responses on the chalkboard. For example:

- items needed to dress the bride (*white gown, veil, wedding bouquet*)
- items needed to set the scene, i.e., create a wedding atmosphere (*guests, attendants*)
- the wedding ceremony (*procession, wine, blessings, rings, ḥuppah, rabbi, prayer book*)

Add a fourth heading: "Erev Shabbat." Ask students for key words to describe ways we welcome Shabbat in the home and in the synagogue. (*family, nice clothes, delicious dinner, candles, wine, ḥallah, ḥallah cover, flowers, white tablecloth, blessings, prayers, songs, siddur*) Write their responses on the chalkboard.

Compare the lists for a wedding ceremony with the list for Shabbat. Discuss items and rituals that are similar. Discuss feelings that are similar when one anticipates the arrival of a bride and the arrival of Shabbat.

7 לְכָה דוֹדִי

How do you welcome people you love? Maybe you give your grandmother a kiss and your favorite cousin a hug. Or maybe you and your friends exchange "high fives." These greetings are signs that you are happy to see them. On Friday nights, we welcome Shabbat with greetings that express our joy at its arrival—a service called Kabbalat Shabbat ("Welcoming Shabbat" or "Receiving Shabbat") and a hymn called לְכָה דוֹדִי.

In Lechah Dodi, we greet Shabbat as if it were a bride or a queen—radiant and beautiful. We have anticipated the arrival of Shabbat all week, just as we look forward to the arrival of those we love the most.

Practice reading the first verses of לְכָה דוֹדִי and the last verse aloud.

1. לְכָה דוֹדִי לִקְרַאת כַּלָּה, פְּנֵי שַׁבָּת נְקַבְּלָה:
2. שָׁמוֹר וְזָכוֹר בְּדִבּוּר אֶחָד הִשְׁמִיעָנוּ אֵל הַמְיֻחָד
3. יְיָ אֶחָד וּשְׁמוֹ אֶחָד לְשֵׁם וּלְתִפְאֶרֶת וְלִתְהִלָּה:
4. לִקְרַאת שַׁבָּת לְכוּ וְנֵלְכָה כִּי הִיא מְקוֹר הַבְּרָכָה
5. מֵרֹאשׁ מִקֶּדֶם נְסוּכָה סוֹף מַעֲשֶׂה בְּמַחֲשָׁבָה תְּחִלָּה:
6. בּוֹאִי בְשָׁלוֹם עֲטֶרֶת בַּעְלָהּ גַּם בְּשִׂמְחָה וּבְצָהֳלָה,
7. תּוֹךְ אֱמוּנֵי עַם סְגֻלָּה, בּוֹאִי כַלָּה, בּוֹאִי כַלָּה:

Let us go, my beloved, to meet (toward) the Bride, let us greet Shabbat.
"Keep" and "Remember" in one Commandment, the one and the only God made us hear.
Adonai is One and God's name is One, for honor and glory and praise.
To greet (toward) Shabbat come let us go, for it is the source of blessing.
From the beginning of time Shabbat is appointed; though last in creation, it was first in God's thought.
Come in peace, crown of your husband, in joy and in gladness,
In the midst of the faithful of the treasured people. Come, O Bride! Come, O Bride!

INTO THE TEXT

Call on students to read aloud the first paragraph of the introduction.

Ask students how they can welcome Shabbat into their homes.

Have students read aloud the second paragraph of the introduction.

Highlight the following concepts:

- just as a bride is beautiful, so too is Shabbat.
- just as the bride is anticipated and welcomed with joy and ceremony, so too is Shabbat.

Direct students to Lechah Dodi (lines 1–7).

Note: The full version of the hymn appears on page 75.

A First Reading

Ask the class to read line 1 in unison.

Call on individual students to read the first verses of the hymn (lines 2–3, 4–5) and the last verse (lines 6–7).

PRAYER DICTIONARY

Vocabulary Practice

First Round

Display each Word Card and have students practice reading the Hebrew. Then turn each Word Card over so students can read the English translations.

Second Round

Display each Word Card. In this round ask students for the English meaning of each.

Direct students to complete the activities "Word Match" and "What's Missing?" to reinforce vocabulary.

Memory Game

Have students close their textbooks. Call on individual students to read the sentence formed by Word Cards 67–71 including the words that are not there. (לִקְרַאת שַׁבָּת)

Tell students to close their eyes. Remove one Word Card. Have students open their eyes. Call upon a student to read the sentence including the missing words. Repeat the activity until all the Word Cards have disappeared and the last student is "reading" the sentence that is not there.

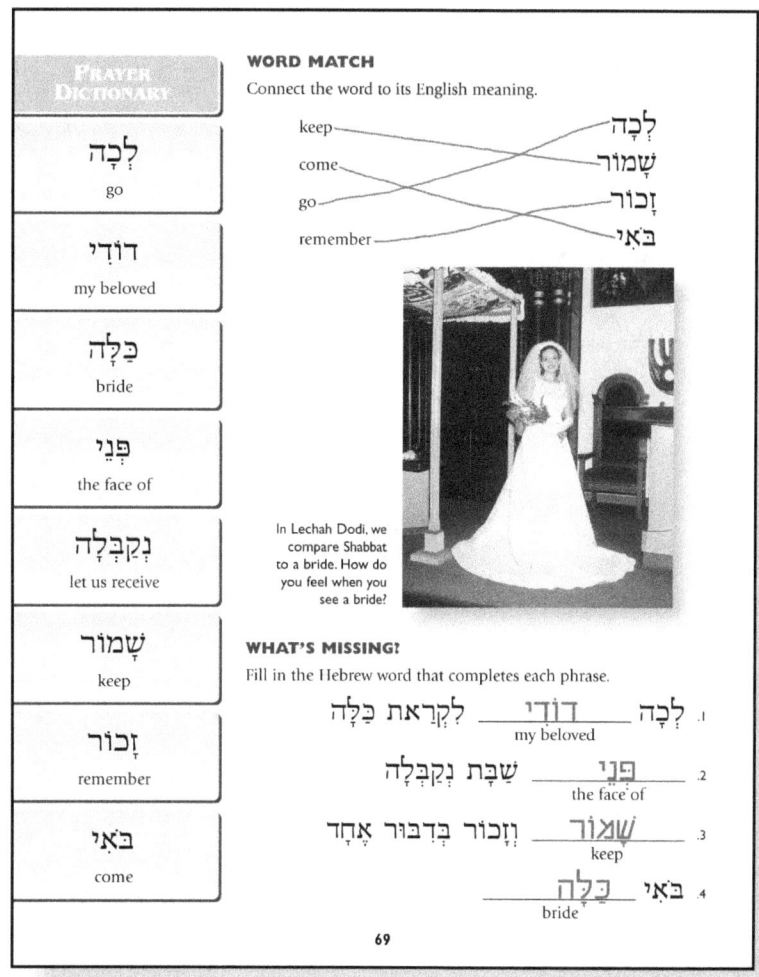

Photo Op

Read the caption with students. Ask if any of them have attended a wedding. What did they observe? How did they feel? What was most meaningful? What did they enjoy most?

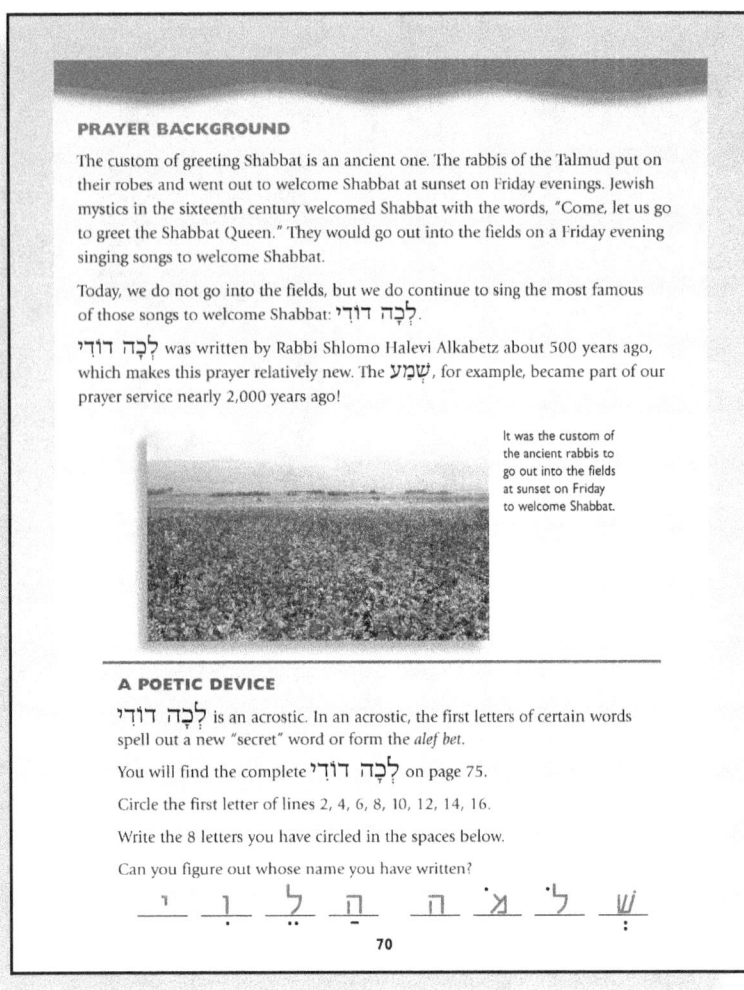

PRAYER BACKGROUND

Read the first paragraph aloud with the students.

Explain that the Talmudic period was approximately 200–500 C.E. Point out to students that we perpetuate, yet change and adapt, our traditions over time, for example, the tradition of welcoming Shabbat.

Photo Op

Read the caption with students.

Ask: What might be the significance of walking out into the fields to welcome Shabbat? (*see the day ending and Shabbat beginning at sunset; "feel" God's presence when in nature; walking back feels like actually escorting Shabbat into the home*)

Read the second paragraph aloud with students.

A Musical Note

Teach students the melody in your synagogue for line 1 of Lechah Dodi.

Read the third paragraph aloud with the students.

A POETIC DEVICE

Read the section aloud with students.

Allow several minutes for students to complete the activity.

Writing an Acrostic

Encourage students to write an acrostic using their own names. Decide on a theme for the acrostic—one theme for the entire class or an individual theme for each student. (*God; Shabbat; prayer; Jewish tradition; Jewish ethics; personal qualities; personal interests*)

Direct students to write the letters of their names down the left side of a piece of paper. Using the first letter on each line, have students write a word, sentence or phrase on each line reflecting the selected theme.

PRAYER BUILDING BLOCKS

לְכָה דוֹדִי "let us go, my beloved"

Read the first three sentences of the Building Block.

Write the root הלכ on the chalkboard.

Write לְכָה below the root. Sometimes a root letter does not appear in a word built on that root. What root letter does not appear in לְכָה? (ה *before the* ל)

A Point of Law

Add the term הֲלָכָה to the words on the chalkboard.

Explain that הֲלָכָה means "Jewish law." It is the way the Jewish people are expected to "go" or to "walk" in their relationship with each other and with God.

Direct students to page 68, line 4. Which two words are built on the root הלכ? (לְכוּ, וְנֵלְכָה). Have students circle the words in their textbooks. Add the words to the list on the chalkboard. Which root letter does not appear in either word? (ה)

Practice reading page 68, lines 4–5 with students both in unison and individually. Teach students the melody for the verse. Sing line 1 and lines 4–5 with the students.

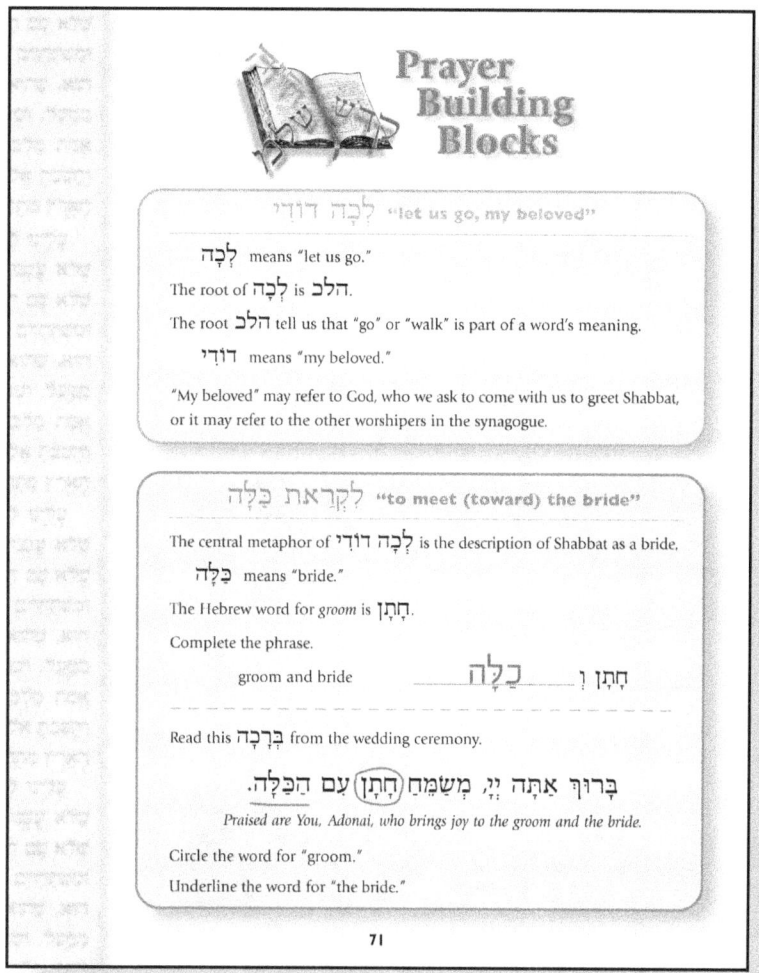

The Fruit of the Tree

Create a fruit tree with the root הלכ. Write "go" and "walk" on the trunk.

Add fruit with the words לְכָה, לְכוּ, וְנֵלְכָה, הֲלָכָה.

Four more roots will be taught in this lesson:

קבל, שמר, זכר, בוא

Create a fruit tree each time a new root is introduced, and make new fruit with the words found in each activity.

לִקְרַאת כַּלָּה "to meet (toward) the bride"

Read and complete the Building Block with students.

The word מְשַׂמֵּחַ means "brings joy."

The word עֹנֶג means "joy." The phrase עֹנֶג שַׁבָּת means "Shabbat joy."

How do we add to the joy of Shabbat? (*families having dinner together; singing together; synagogue services; oneg after services*)

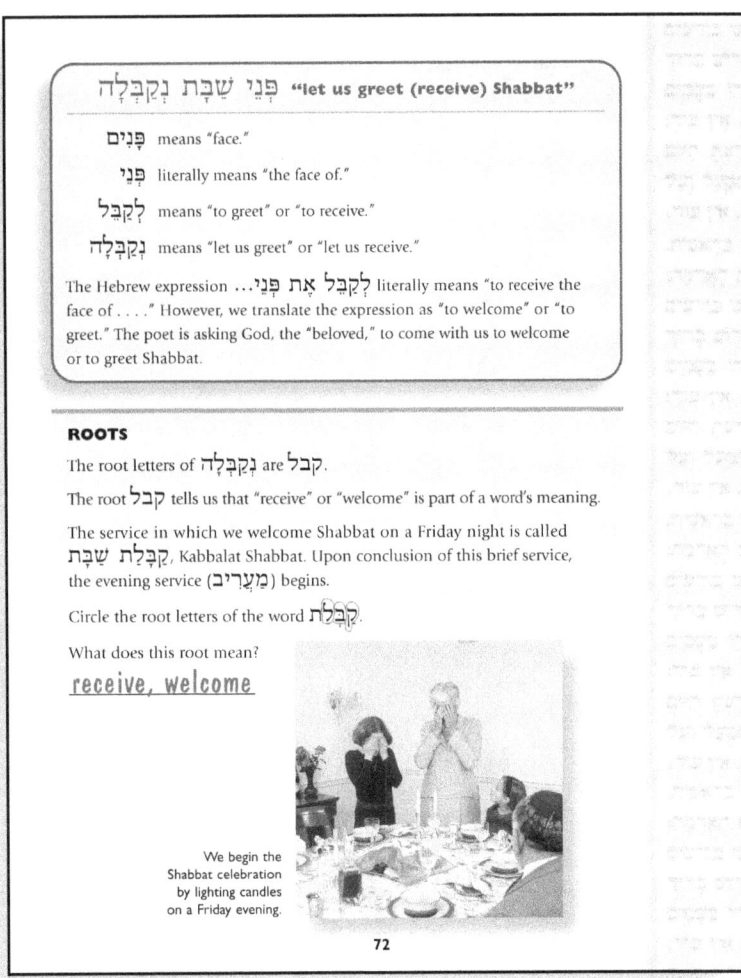

פְּנֵי שַׁבָּת נְקַבְּלָה
"let us greet (receive) Shabbat"

Call on students to read the Building Block phrase aloud.

Read the explanation of the Building Block with students.

Ask: What do you think the "face of Shabbat" looks like? (*smiles; friendships; joy; community; prayer*)

Read and sing line 1 on page 68 together.

ROOTS

Read and complete this section together with students.

Ask students to describe the service to welcome Shabbat in your synagogue.

Photo Op

Direct students to the photo and caption. Ask students if they know why the women are covering their eyes in the photo. Explain: Usually we say a blessing and then do an action; for example, we say the Hamotzi blessing and then take the first bite of bread. However, we light the Shabbat candles first and then recite the blessing. (The reason is that once we say the blessing, Shabbat begins. Since the Torah tells us not to light a match on Shabbat, we light the match—and the candles—first, cover our eyes, and then say the blessing.) When we uncover our eyes, it's as if we are symbolically seeing the light "for the first time."

שָׁמוֹר וְזָכוֹר "keep and remember"

Read the Building Block together with students.

Write the following Hebrew and English phrases on the chalkboard.

זֵכֶר לִיצִיאַת מִצְרָיִם
memory of the going out from Egypt

זִכָּרוֹן לְמַעֲשֵׂה בְרֵאשִׁית
memory of the work of creation

Call on students to read each phrase.

Pose the Questions

- Which Shabbat prayer contains these phrases? (*Kiddush*)

- Which word in each phrase means "memory"? (זִכָּרוֹן, זֵכֶר)

- Why is Shabbat a memory of the work of creation? (*God finished creating the world in six days and rested on the seventh day, Shabbat*)

- Why is Shabbat a memory of the going out from Egypt? (*only a free people can rest, celebrate, and worship together; the Jewish people were "reborn" after their liberation from Egypt*)

Direct students to page 68, lines 2 and 3. Have them circle the words "keep" (שָׁמוֹר) and "and remember" (וְזָכוֹר).

- Read line 2 in unison with students. Call on individual students to read the complete line.

- Read line 3 in unison with students. Call on individual students to read the complete line.

- Read lines 2 and 3 together with students. Teach students the melody. Then sing lines 1–5 together.

READING PRACTICE

Call on students to read each circled word aloud.

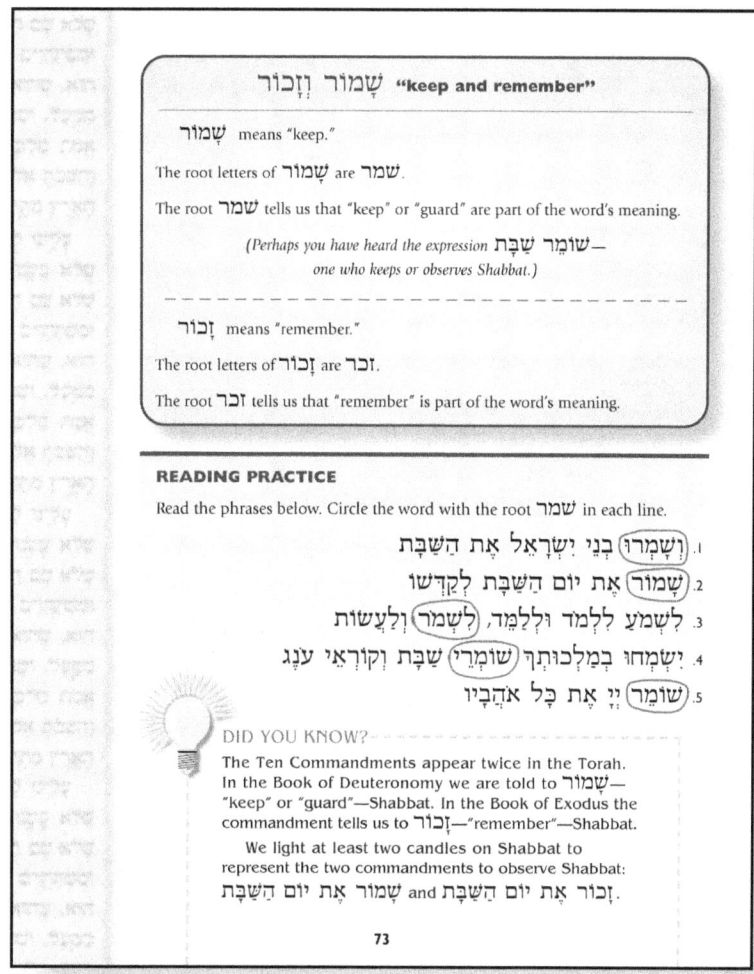

Playing Cards

Randomly distribute playing cards with the 1–5 of hearts to five students and the 1–5 of diamonds to five other students. If necessary, do the same with clubs and spades until all the students have one card. Direct students with hearts to form a group of hearts, with diamonds to form a group of diamonds, and so on with clubs and spades.

Warm-Up: Each member of each group is responsible for one line (1–5). Let group members assist each other in the practice warm-up session.

Play: Group members place their cards face down. If they read their line correctly, they turn the card face up. The goal is to have all five cards face up at the conclusion of the five lines. Repeat with each group.

DID YOU KNOW?

Ask students questions about this section; for example: Which books in the Torah contain the Ten Commandments? Why do we light at least two candles on Shabbat?

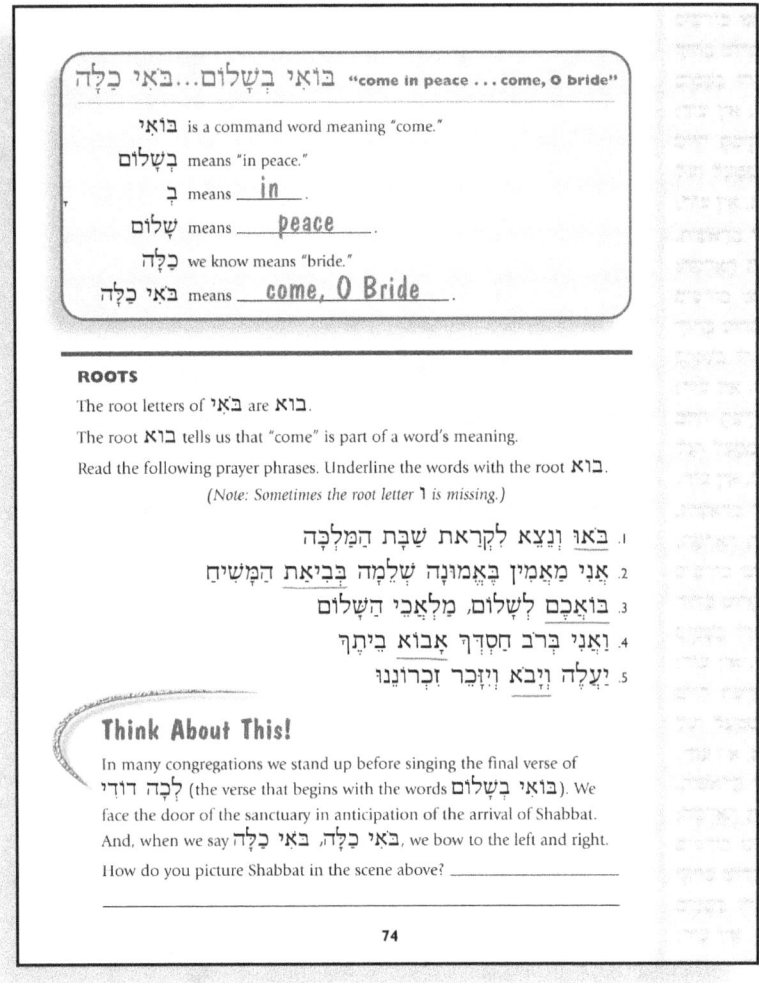

בּוֹאִי בְשָׁלוֹם...בֹּאִי כַלָּה
"come in peace . . . come, O bride"

Have students complete the Building Block individually and share their answers.

Direct students to page 68, lines 6–7. Tell students to find and circle the two Hebrew phrases "come in peace" and "come, O bride!"

Reading Partners

Have students count off A-B, A-B, A-B, and so on to form reading partners. Have partners read lines 6–7 twice, alternating words. For the first reading, A should begin. For the second reading, B should begin.

Each partner should then read the complete verse, lines 6–7.

ROOTS

Call on students to read each underlined word aloud.

Ask students to read words in each line built on other roots they know and to give the English for each root.

line 1: מלכ ("rule"); שבת ("rest")

line 2: אמנ ("faith"); שלמ ("whole," "complete," "peace")

line 3: שלמ ("whole," "complete," "peace")

line 4: חסד ("kindness")

line 5: זכר ("remember"); עלה ("go up")

Call on individual students to read each line.

THINK ABOUT THIS!

Read this section aloud with students. Allow several minutes for students to fill in their responses to the question. Call on students to share their thoughts.

Teach students the melody for the last verse of the song (lines 6–7).

Have students stand and sing this verse. Show them how to bow at the indicated places.

FLUENT READING

Double Sh'va

Write the following words on the chalkboard, broken up as shown:

נַפְ שְׁךָ   חַסְ דְּךָ   וְנִשְׂ מְחָה.

The first *sh'va* in each word is not sounded. The second *sh'va* is sounded ("a" as in "alone").

Ask students to read each word correctly. Then have them find and circle one of these words on line 17 in the prayer. (וְנִשְׂמְחָה) Call on individual students to read lines 16–17.

Double Letter with Sh'va

Write the following words on the chalkboard, broken up as shown:

הִ נְנִי   הַ לְלוּ   יָה   הִתְ עוֹ רְרִי

When a double letter appears in a word, and the first one has a *sh'va*, the *sh'va* is sounded ("a" as in "alone").

Call on three students to circle the double letters in each word and read each complete word. Ask students to find and circle one of these words on line 10 in the prayer. (הִתְעוֹרְרִי) How many times does the word appear? (*twice*) Call on individual students to read lines 10–11.

Vocabulary Know-How

Which word in line 15 means "groom"? (חָתָן) "bride"? (כַּלָּה)

Letter Families

Write the following letter families on the chalkboard: בּב כּכְךָ פּפְף תּת שׁשׂ.

Divide the class into five groups. Assign one set of letter families to each group. Groups should meet and look for words that contain members of their letter family and practice reading the words and the lines. (*Example:* בּב—*line 8:* לִבְשִׁי בִּגְדֵי)

Note:

- Several words reflect more than one letter family. (*Examples:* הַבְּרָכָה, תּוֹךְ)
- Sometimes the same word is found with different members of the letter family. (*Example: line 15*—כַּלָּה; *line 19*—כַלָּה)

Point out to students the acrostic use of the author's name—שלמה הלוי. (*lines 2, 4, 6, 8, 10, 12, 14, 16*)

FLUENT READING

Practice reading the complete לְכָה דוֹדִי.

1. לְכָה דוֹדִי לִקְרַאת כַּלָּה פְּנֵי שַׁבָּת נְקַבְּלָה:
2. שָׁמוֹר וְזָכוֹר בְּדִבּוּר אֶחָד הִשְׁמִיעָנוּ אֵל הַמְיֻחָד.
3. יְיָ אֶחָד וּשְׁמוֹ אֶחָד לְשֵׁם וּלְתִפְאֶרֶת וְלִתְהִלָּה:
4. לִקְרַאת שַׁבָּת לְכוּ וְנֵלְכָה כִּי הִיא מְקוֹר הַבְּרָכָה.
5. מֵרֹאשׁ מִקֶּדֶם נְסוּכָה סוֹף מַעֲשֶׂה בְּמַחֲשָׁבָה תְּחִלָּה:
6. מִקְדַּשׁ מֶלֶךְ עִיר מְלוּכָה קוּמִי צְאִי מִתּוֹךְ הַהֲפֵכָה.
7. רַב לָךְ שֶׁבֶת בְּעֵמֶק הַבָּכָא וְהוּא יַחֲמוֹל עָלַיִךְ חֶמְלָה:
8. הִתְנַעֲרִי מֵעָפָר קוּמִי לִבְשִׁי בִּגְדֵי תִפְאַרְתֵּךְ עַמִּי.
9. עַל-יַד בֶּן-יִשַׁי בֵּית-הַלַּחְמִי קָרְבָה אֶל נַפְשִׁי גְאָלָהּ:
10. הִתְעוֹרְרִי הִתְעוֹרְרִי כִּי בָא אוֹרֵךְ קוּמִי אוֹרִי.
11. עוּרִי עוּרִי שִׁיר דַּבֵּרִי כְּבוֹד יְיָ עָלַיִךְ נִגְלָה:
12. לֹא תֵבוֹשִׁי וְלֹא תִכָּלְמִי מַה-תִּשְׁתּוֹחֲחִי וּמַה-תֶּהֱמִי.
13. בָּךְ יֶחֱסוּ עֲנִיֵּי עַמִּי וְנִבְנְתָה עִיר עַל-תִּלָּהּ:
14. וְהָיוּ לִמְשִׁסָּה שֹׁאסָיִךְ וְרָחֲקוּ כָּל-מְבַלְּעָיִךְ.
15. יָשִׂישׂ עָלַיִךְ אֱלֹהָיִךְ כִּמְשׂוֹשׂ חָתָן עַל-כַּלָּה:
16. יָמִין וּשְׂמֹאל תִּפְרוֹצִי וְאֶת-יְיָ תַּעֲרִיצִי.
17. עַל-יַד אִישׁ בֶּן-פַּרְצִי וְנִשְׂמְחָה וְנָגִילָה:
18. בּוֹאִי בְשָׁלוֹם עֲטֶרֶת בַּעְלָהּ גַּם בְּשִׂמְחָה וּבְצָהֳלָה:
19. תּוֹךְ אֱמוּנֵי עַם סְגֻלָּה בּוֹאִי כַלָּה, בּוֹאִי כַלָּה.

75

WORKSHEET

Duplicate and hand out copies of the worksheet for Lesson 7 to review vocabulary and concepts underlying the prayer.

FAMILY EDUCATION

Duplicate and send home copies of "As a Family: A Special Day" (at the back of this guide).

LESSON 7
Worksheet

Name: _____

לְכָה דוֹדִי

1. Fill in the missing words in the first and last phrases of לְכָה דוֹדִי below. Select the words from the following list:

   שַׁבָּת   דוֹדִי   בֹּאִי   כַּלָּה

   לְכָה _____ לִקְרַאת _____ פְּנֵי _____ נְקַבְּלָה.

   Let us go, <u>my beloved</u>, to meet (toward) the <u>Bride</u>, let us greet <u>Shabbat</u>.

   _____ כַּלָּה, _____ כַּלָּה.

   <u>Come</u>, O Bride! <u>Come</u>, O Bride.

2. Draw a line to connect each root to the matching English in the left column, and to a word built on that root in the right column.

English	Root	Word
keep, guard	הלכ	שָׁמוֹר
welcome, receive	קבל	לְכָה
go, walk	שמר	בֹּאִי
come	זכר	קַבָּלַת
remember	בוא	זָכוֹר

3. Write the English meaning of each commandment below the Hebrew.

   שָׁמוֹר אֶת יוֹם הַשַּׁבָּת   זָכוֹר אֶת יוֹם הַשַּׁבָּת

   _____   _____

4. Below are the names of the five books in the Torah. Circle the two books that contain the Ten Commandments commanding us to observe Shabbat.

   Genesis   Exodus   Leviticus   Numbers   Deuteronomy

5. What is the קַבָּלַת שַׁבָּת service? _____

6. Why is Shabbat compared to a bride?

   _____

LESSON 8
וְשָׁמְרוּ

LEARNING OBJECTIVES
Prayer Reading Skills
- The prefixes בְּ ("on the," "in the"); וְ ("and"); לְ ("for")
- The suffix ם ָ ("their," "them")
- The plural form: ים ‎ ‎ ות
- The roots עשׂה ("make"); שׁבת ("rest"); שׁמר ("keep," "guard")

Prayer Concepts
- Shabbat is a sign of the covenant, *brit*, between God and the children of Israel
- Terms: "covenant," "Israel," "children of Israel"
- V'shamru, recited before the Amidah on Friday night, is part of the Amidah on Shabbat morning
- Ethical Echo: שְׁמִירַת הַלָּשׁוֹן ("guarding your tongue")

ABOUT THE PRAYER

V'shamru comes from the Torah (Exodus 31:14–17). God spoke these words to Moses just before giving him the Ten Commandments. We are to keep, or guard, Shabbat as a sign of the everlasting covenant, *brit*, between God and the Jewish people, the children of Israel. Shabbat is a holy time.

INSTRUCTIONAL MATERIALS

Text pages 76–85

Word Cards 46, 75–84

Worksheet 8

Family Education: "As a Family: A Refreshing Day" (at the back of this guide)

SET INDUCTION
Signs of the Times

Discuss with students signs or symbols that represent the rules of society; for example, a stop sign, one-way traffic sign, no-parking sign, no-smoking sign, no-littering sign.

Discuss the purpose of these signs with the students.

- What agreement does the sign indicate between individuals and groups? (*an expectation that we are responsible for each other and will follow the rules of society*)
- What is the purpose of having a sign to indicate an agreement? (*a graphic reminder of society's expectations and our responsibilities*)

A Sign of the Covenant

Explain that Shabbat is a sign, אוֹת, of the covenant or agreement, בְּרִית, between God and the children of Israel. We honor Shabbat and make it holy. We have symbols and ritual objects to remind us of Shabbat and its meaning.

Ask students to name Shabbat symbols and ritual objects and list them on the chalkboard; for example, candlesticks and candles, wine and Kiddush cup, ḥallah and ḥallah cover, synagogue, family meal, sunset, people in prayer, Torah, and Havdalah ritual items.

Discuss what each symbol and ritual object represents.

וְשָׁמְרוּ 8

Do you have something precious that you protect or guard? Maybe it's a diary where you write down your secret thoughts and wishes, kept hidden under your pillow. Or maybe you have a bike you received as a birthday present, that you keep safe with a lock during school hours.

In a similar way, the Jewish people consider Shabbat to be sacred, and guard it as a gift from God. וְשָׁמְרוּ ("and [you] shall keep" or "and [you] shall guard") comes from the Torah, and reminds us of our promise to God to guard, cherish, and observe Shabbat and keep it holy. V'shamru is said before the Amidah during the Friday night service. In reciting it, we declare that we are guarding Shabbat because it is God's special creation—and we remember that by celebrating Shabbat we are strengthening our ties to God.

Practice reading וְשָׁמְרוּ aloud.

1. וְשָׁמְרוּ בְנֵי-יִשְׂרָאֵל אֶת-הַשַּׁבָּת, לַעֲשׂוֹת אֶת-הַשַּׁבָּת
2. לְדֹרֹתָם בְּרִית עוֹלָם. בֵּינִי וּבֵין בְּנֵי יִשְׂרָאֵל אוֹת הִיא לְעֹלָם,
3. כִּי שֵׁשֶׁת יָמִים עָשָׂה יְיָ אֶת-הַשָּׁמַיִם וְאֶת-הָאָרֶץ,
4. וּבַיּוֹם הַשְּׁבִיעִי שָׁבַת וַיִּנָּפַשׁ.

And the children of Israel shall keep the Shabbat, to make the Shabbat as an eternal covenant for their generations. Between Me and the children of Israel it is a sign forever, that in six days Adonai made the heavens and the earth, and on the seventh day Adonai rested and was refreshed.

76

First Hebrew Sentence: (וְשָׁמְרוּ...עוֹלָם)

Read the sentence aloud with students.

Ask:
- What is the Hebrew word for Israel? (יִשְׂרָאֵל)
- What is the Hebrew word for covenant? (בְּרִית)

Second English Sentence: ("Between Me . . . refreshed")

- Who is "Me?" (*God*)
- What is a "sign forever"? (*Shabbat*)
- What does the sign, Shabbat, represent? (*in six days, Adonai made the heavens and the earth, and on the seventh day Adonai rested and was refreshed*)

Second Hebrew Sentence: (בֵּינִי...וַיִּנָּפַשׁ)

Read the second Hebrew sentence aloud with students.

The word אוֹת means "sign." Have students circle the Hebrew and English words in the prayer.

INTO THE TEXT

Read the first paragraph with students.

Pose the Questions

- What do you have that is precious to you?
- How do you guard it and care for it?
- Does this precious item connect you with anyone else, such as the person who gave it to you or the people you share it with? (*an instrument that we take care of, practice, and play for the enjoyment of others; art supplies that allow us to create pictures for others to enjoy; a computer program that allows us to explore the world of science*)

Read the second paragraph with students.

- Name objects that we know exist but that we cannot touch or see (*God; love; trust; air; a breeze; a sound*)
- How do we know of their existence? (*we can sense them—trust and love; we see manifestations of them—wind and God's creations; we use them to survive—air; we hear them—sound*)
- How do we "keep" and "guard" time for specific activities? (*we put the time aside, e.g., a birthday celebration on one's birthday or the seder during Pesah; we perform rituals, such as lighting candles and reciting blessings over bread and wine on Shabbat*)
- Why do we guard our time for these activities? (*they are precious and meaningful to us*)

A First Reading

Direct students to the prayer:

First English Sentence: ("And the children . . . generations.")

Ask the following:

- What does "eternal covenant" mean? (*an agreement that lasts forever*)
- To what generations does the sentence refer? (*generations of the Jewish people*)

PRAYER DICTIONARY

Word Cards

Write the letters שׁ and שׂ on the chalkboard.

Display Word Cards 46, 75, 77, 81, 83, and 84 in random order on the edge of the chalkboard.

Call on individual students to read the following:

- the four words with שׁ
- the two words with שׂ

Ask students for the meaning of the words they know. Show the translation on the back of the Word Cards.

Hand out Word Cards 46, 75–84 in random order to eleven students, and have them look only at the Hebrew side of their card.

Say an English word or phrase. The student holding the correct Word Card should come forward with the matching Hebrew word or phrase.

SEARCH AND CIRCLE

Have students complete the exercise at the top of page 77 independently. Have them cover the Prayer Dictionary to test themselves and then uncover it to check their answers.

Reading Practice

Review the answers together. Direct the student giving an answer to read all three Hebrew choices aloud. Then the student should say which word is correct. Alternative: Another student should say which word is correct.

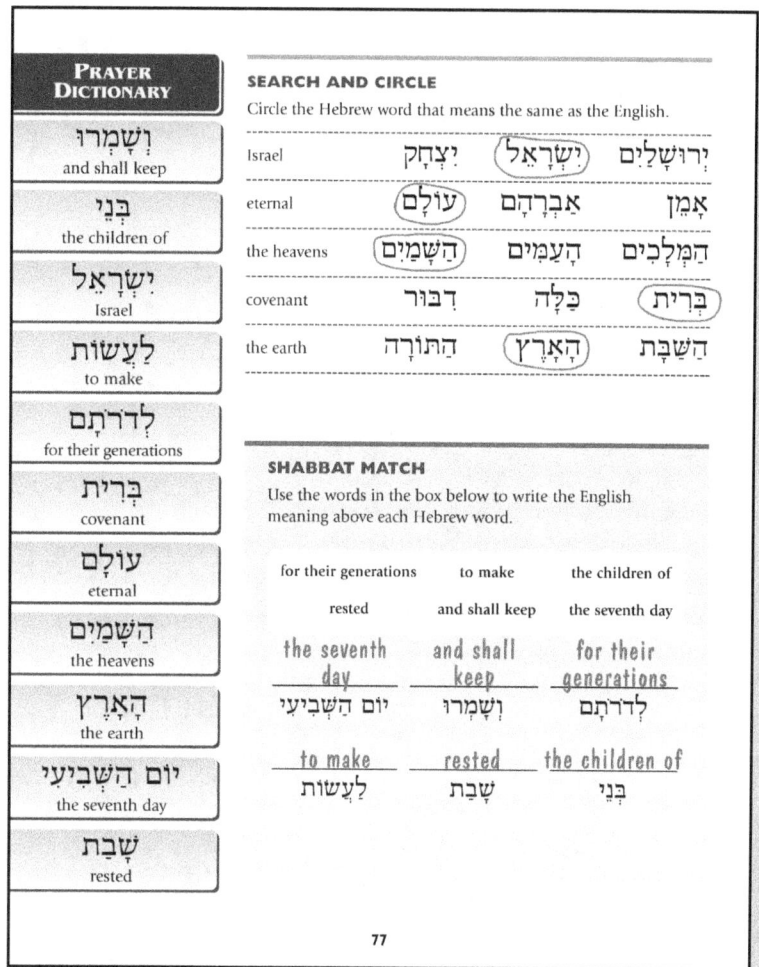

SHABBAT MATCH

Follow the procedure described in the "Search and Circle" activity above.

Prayer Building Blocks

וְשָׁמְרוּ בְנֵי-יִשְׂרָאֵל אֶת-הַשַּׁבָּת
"and the children of Israel shall keep the Shabbat"

Call on students to read the Building Block phrase aloud.

Allow students time to complete the Building Block activity individually.

Call on students to share their answers.

Keeping Shabbat

Based on the students' responses to the last question in the Building Block, make a list with them of the ways we can keep Shabbat. Label the list in Hebrew and in English with the Building Block phrase.

Fruit of the Tree

Add the word וְשָׁמְרוּ to the fruit of the שמר tree.

AN ETHICAL ECHO

Read "An Ethical Echo" aloud with students.

Discuss the concepts. ("guarding the tongue"—keeping the tongue "locked" behind our lips; thinking before we speak; thinking about the harm we can do with our words; "the tongue of evil"—doing harm with our words; hurting others intentionally or unintentionally)

THINK ABOUT THIS!

Ask students the following questions:

- Have you ever been hurt by someone else's words?
- Did you ever hurt another person because you did not "guard your tongue"?
- What are other ways you can hurt someone besides physically? (*making unkind remarks; drawing pictures that could be hurtful; ignoring someone; excluding someone from your group*)

Serious Fun

Draw a picture of a large tongue on the chalkboard or on poster board.

Have the students write ways in which we can hurt others if we do not "guard our tongue." Begin with the three examples in "An Ethical Echo" (gossip, rumors, lies). Students can add other insights. (*ruin reputations, destroy someone's good name; hurt another's feelings; cause feelings of rejection*)

בְּנֵי־יִשְׂרָאֵל "the children of Israel"

Have students complete the Building Block independently.

Review their answers.

Review the family letters בּ and ב. בְּנֵי and בְנֵי are the same words written with different members of the same letter family.

Direct students to page 76, lines 1 and 2.

- Call on a student to read the complete phrase in line 1 containing the Building Block "the children of Israel."
(וְשָׁמְרוּ בְנֵי־יִשְׂרָאֵל אֶת־הַשַּׁבָּת)

- Call on a student to read the complete phrase in line 2 containing this Building Block.
(בֵּינִי וּבֵין בְּנֵי יִשְׂרָאֵל אוֹת הִיא לְעֹלָם)

DID YOU KNOW?

Read the section aloud with students.

Introduce the names of the twelve sons of Jacob, who was also known as Israel (Reuben, Simeon, Levi, Judah, Issachar, Zebulun, Gad, Asher, Dan, Naphtali, Joseph, and Benjamin), and Jacob's daughter, Dinah.

Extending the Lesson

The name Israel means "to struggle with God." Jacob was given that name when he struggled, or wrestled, with an angel of God. Many of us struggle to understand God and what God expects from us.

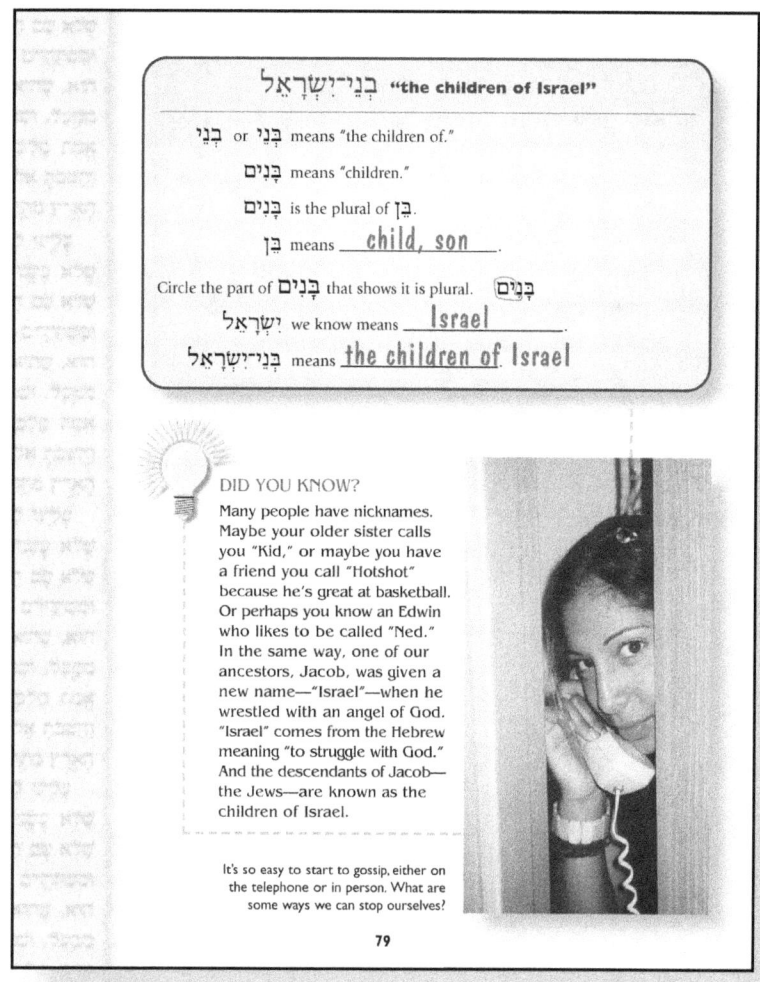

Photo Op

Direct students to the photo and caption.

Discuss ways we can stop ourselves from spreading gossip. (*resolve ahead of time not to do it; say "I don't want to talk about it"*)

Ask: Have any of you been in the position of choosing whether or not to pass on gossip?

Did you give in to the temptation? Did it make you feel important to be "in the know"? Did it make you uncomfortable to pass on gossip? Or did you resist the temptation?

> ## לַעֲשׂוֹת אֶת־הַשַׁבָּת לְדֹרֹתָם בְּרִית עוֹלָם
> **"to make the Shabbat as an eternal covenant for their generations"**
>
> לַעֲשׂוֹת means "to make."
>
> The root of לַעֲשׂוֹת is עשה.
>
> What is the meaning of this root? ____make____
>
> Underline the word with the same root in this line from וְשָׁמְרוּ:
>
> כִּי שֵׁשֶׁת יָמִים עָשָׂה יְיָ אֶת־הַשָׁמַיִם וְאֶת־הָאָרֶץ
>
> Now underline the words with the same root in עֹשֶׂה שָׁלוֹם.
>
> עֹשֶׂה שָׁלוֹם בִּמְרוֹמָיו, הוּא יַעֲשֶׂה שָׁלוֹם עָלֵינוּ וְעַל כָּל־יִשְׂרָאֵל
>
> ---
>
> בְּרִית עוֹלָם means "eternal covenant."
>
> עוֹלָם can mean "eternal (forever)" or "world."

DID YOU KNOW?

As a bond with God, our ancestor Abraham agreed to circumcise his son, Isaac, in return for God's gift of watching over the Jewish people. To this day, Jewish baby boys are circumcised in a בְּרִית מִילָה ceremony (many people call it a *bris*) when they are eight days old. We now celebrate the birth of a baby girl, too, with a ceremony called שִׂמְחַת בַּת ("joyful celebration for a daughter"). A *bris* or *simḥat bat* is the grandest celebration of all—a celebration of the day you were born!

80

לַעֲשׂוֹת אֶת־הַשַׁבָּת לְדֹרֹתָם בְּרִית עוֹלָם

"to make the Shabbat as an eternal covenant for their generations"

Call on students to read the Building Block phrase aloud.

Read and complete the first part of the Building Block with students: לַעֲשׂוֹת.

The Fruit of the Tree

Add the words לַעֲשׂוֹת and עָשָׂה to the fruit of the עשׂה tree.

Read the second part of the Building Block with students: בְּרִית עוֹלָם.

DID YOU KNOW?

Ask students to describe *brit milah* and baby-naming ceremonies they have attended.

Torah Study

Bring in several *ḥumashim* to class and together read about the covenant between God and Abraham. (Genesis 15 and 17)

THE NEW HEBREW THROUGH PRAYER 2 • הִנֵּנִי   104

A SPECIAL AGREEMENT

Read the section aloud with students.

For Discussion

Ahad Ha'am, a leader in the Zionist movement, said, "More than the Jewish people have kept Shabbat, Shabbat has kept the Jewish people." What do you think this means? (*keeping Shabbat has kept the Jewish people connected to God, to Torah, and to one another*)

Read and complete the second part of the Building Block with students: לְדֹרֹתָם.

Display Word Cards 78–80

(לְדֹרֹתָם בְּרִית עוֹלָם).

Call on students to read the phrase and to translate it into English.

Direct students to page 76, first sentence

(וְשָׁמְרוּ...עוֹלָם).

- Call on individual students to read the sentence.
- Read the sentence in unison.
- Teach students to sing the sentence with the melody used in your synagogue.

Have students complete the last part of the building block. Allow them to check each other's work.

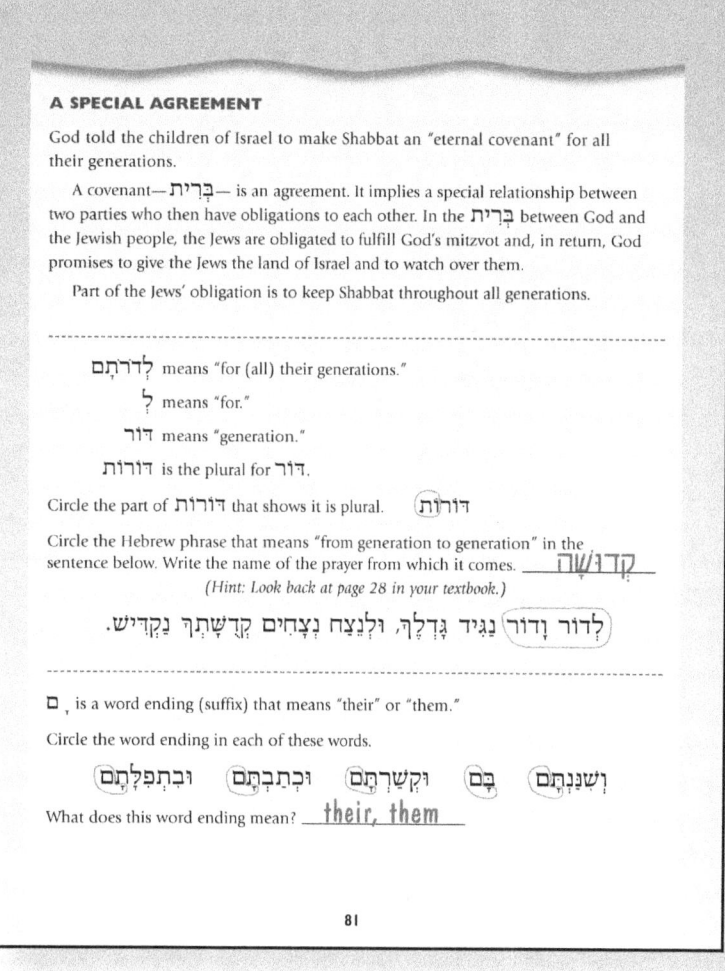

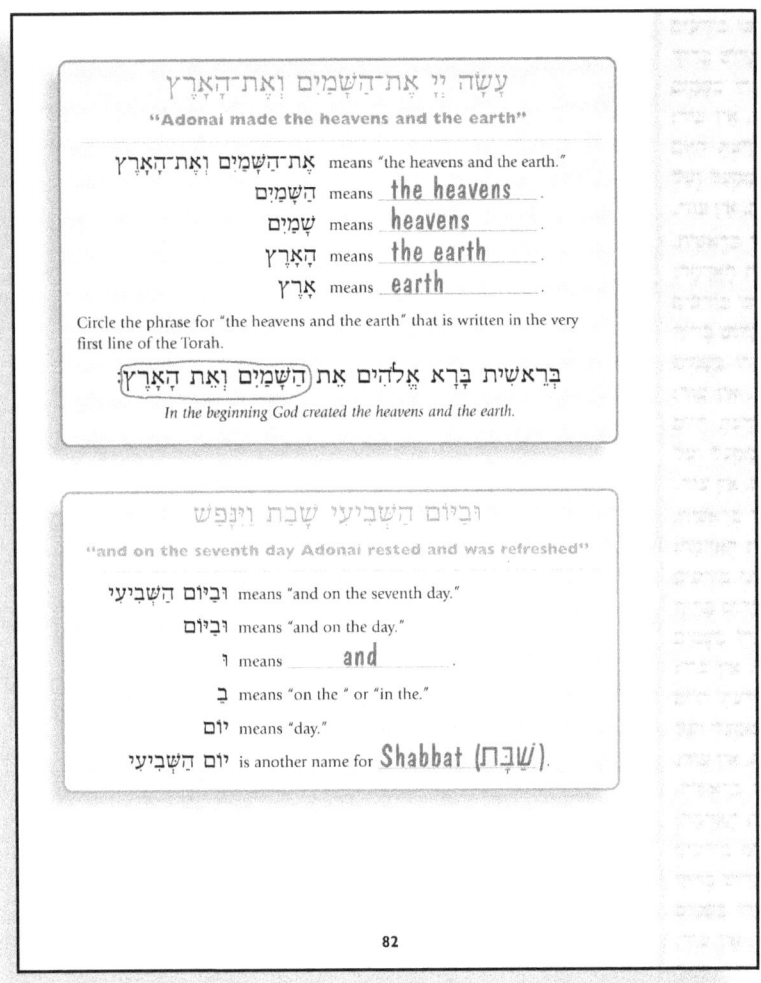

Half and Half

Divide the class in half.

One half should read the first sentence (line 1–line 2, third word).

The other half should read the second sentence (line 2, fourth word–line 4).

Reverse the reading assignments for the two halves of the class.

Read lines 1–4 in unison with students.

Call on individual students to read lines 1–4.

Sing Along

Teach students to sing V'shamru with the melody used in your synagogue.

עָשָׂה יְיָ אֶת־הַשָּׁמַיִם וְאֶת־הָאָרֶץ
"Adonai made the heavens and the earth"

Call on students to read the Building Block phrase aloud.

Have students complete the Building Block independently.

Direct students to page 76, lines 2–3.

- Ask students to find the Building Block phrase there and read it aloud (*line 3*).
- Read line 2, beginning with the fourth word (בֵּינִי), and all of line 3 in unison with students.

Call on individual students to read the same lines.

- Read lines 1–3 in unison with students.

Call on individual students to read lines 1–3.

וּבַיּוֹם הַשְּׁבִיעִי שָׁבַת וַיִּנָּפַשׁ
"and on the seventh day Adonai rested and was refreshed"

Call on students to read the Building Block phrase aloud.

Have students complete the Building Block independently.

Direct students to page 76, lines 3–4.

- Ask students to find the Building Block phrase there and read it aloud. (*line 4*)
- Read lines 3–4 in unison with students.

Call on individual students to read lines 3–4.

REST ON SHABBAT

Read the section aloud with students.

Direct students to page 76, line 4. Ask students to read the Hebrew line and its English meaning.

Ask:

Which phrase means "rested and was refreshed"? (שָׁבַת וַיִּנָּפַשׁ)

What does it mean to be "refreshed"? (*renewed enthusiasm in mind and body; ready to start again; concerns are put aside*)

Does God need to "rest and be refreshed"? (*the phrase is metaphorical, since God isn't human; we use language rooted in human experience to help us understand God*)

The Fruit of the Tree

Create a fruit tree with the root שבת. Write "rest" on the trunk of the tree. Add the words found in this section.

Call on a student to read the English selection from Genesis 2:2–3.

Explain that this is the description of the first Shabbat (Genesis 2:1–3). This passage from the Torah is part of the Shabbat evening service in the siddur.

Prior to reading the Hebrew passage, have students search for words or phrases that are repeated twice:

יוֹם הַשְּׁבִיעִי, מִכָּל-מְלַאכְתּוֹ, אֲשֶׁר, אֱלֹהִים

Have students follow the directions below the passage.

Read the passage aloud in unison with students.

Call on individual students to read the passage.

Note: Students will be introduced to the complete passage at the conclusion of Lesson 9.

IN YOUR OWN WORDS

Allow time for students to write their responses. Call on students to share their insights.

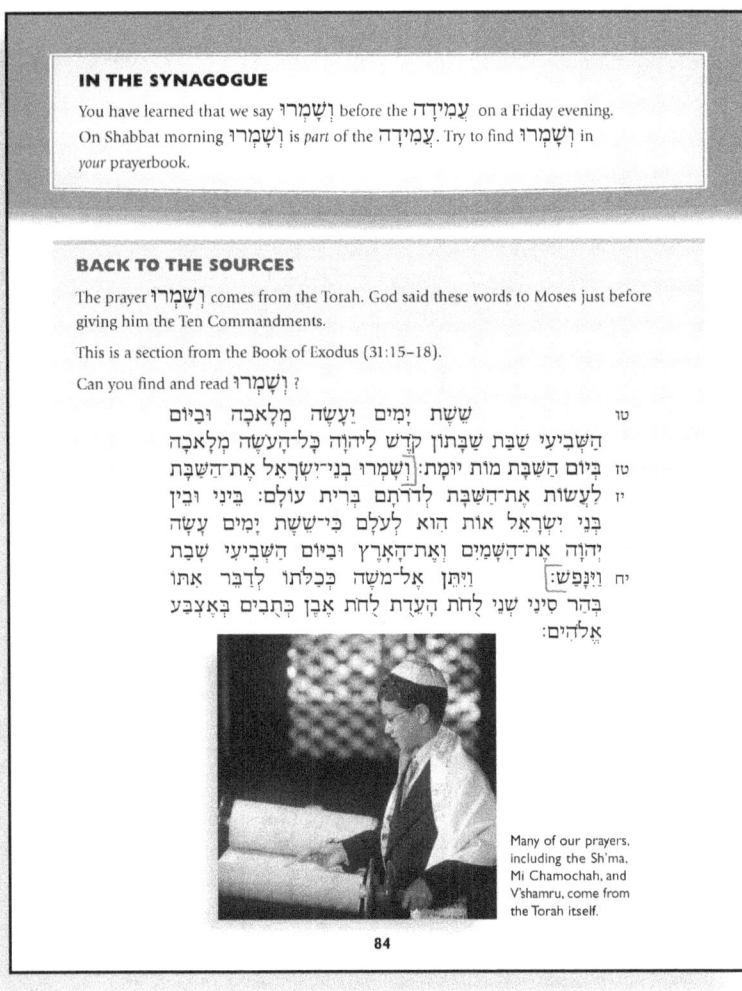

Photo Op

Visit the sanctuary with students. Open one *Sefer Torah* to the Ten Commandments in Exodus and another *Sefer Torah* to the Ten Commandments in Deuteronomy.

Allow individual students the opportunity to read the passages directly from each *sefer Torah*.

Note: The Sh'ma leads directly into the V'ahavta.

BACK TO THE SOURCES

Read the introduction with students.

Have students find and read V'shamru.

Torah Study

Bring several ḥumashim to class.

- Help students locate Exodus 31:15–18.

  Read the commandment directing us to make Shabbat a sign of the covenant forever (31:16–17).

- Help students locate Exodus 20:1–14 (The Ten Commandments).

  Read the commandment telling us to *remember* Shabbat (20:8–11).

- Direct students to locate Deuteronomy 5:6–18 (The Ten Commandments).

  Read the commandment telling us to *observe* Shabbat (5:12–15).

- Explain to students that the Ten Commandments appear twice in the Torah, since the Torah recounts the narrative of the Exodus twice—the first in retelling the actual events and the second in Moses' recollection of the events as he reviews Israelite history at the end of his life. Both versions of the Ten Commandments are considered equally authoritative.

FLUENT READING

Read the introduction with students.

Word Study

Have students find and read:

- the four words in lines 1, 6, and 7 built on the root אהב ("love")
- the phrase in line 4 meaning "forever and ever" (לְעוֹלָם וָעֶד)
- a related word in line 6 (לְעוֹלָמִים)

Reading Rule

Write צוֹ on the chalkboard.

וֹ has the sound "oh" if it follows a letter that has no other vowel.

Write מַצּוֹת on the chalkboard. Call on students to read the word. (*matzot*)

Write צְוֹ on the chalkboard.

וֹ has the sound "vo" if it follows a letter that already has a vowel.

Write מִצְוֹת on the chalkboard. Call on students to read the word. (*mitzvot*)

Call on students to read the last word in line 1 and then to read lines 1–2.

Call on students to read the fourth word in line 4 and then to read the complete line.

Reading Rule

The vowel ַ is read first when ח comes at the end of a word.

Write the following words on the chalkboard:
חַג רוּחַ נָשִׂיחַ בָּחַר מָשִׁיחַ.

Call on students to read each word.

Which word is found on line 3 in the prayer on page 85? (נָשִׂיחַ)

Call on students to read lines 3 and 4. Call on students to read lines 1–4.

Assign five groups of students the five sentences in the prayer (lines 1–2, 3–4, 5, 6, 7).

Allow students time to practice. Call on each group in turn to read their assigned sentence in unison.

Read the complete prayer in unison with the class.

Teach students to sing the prayer with the melody used in your synagogue.

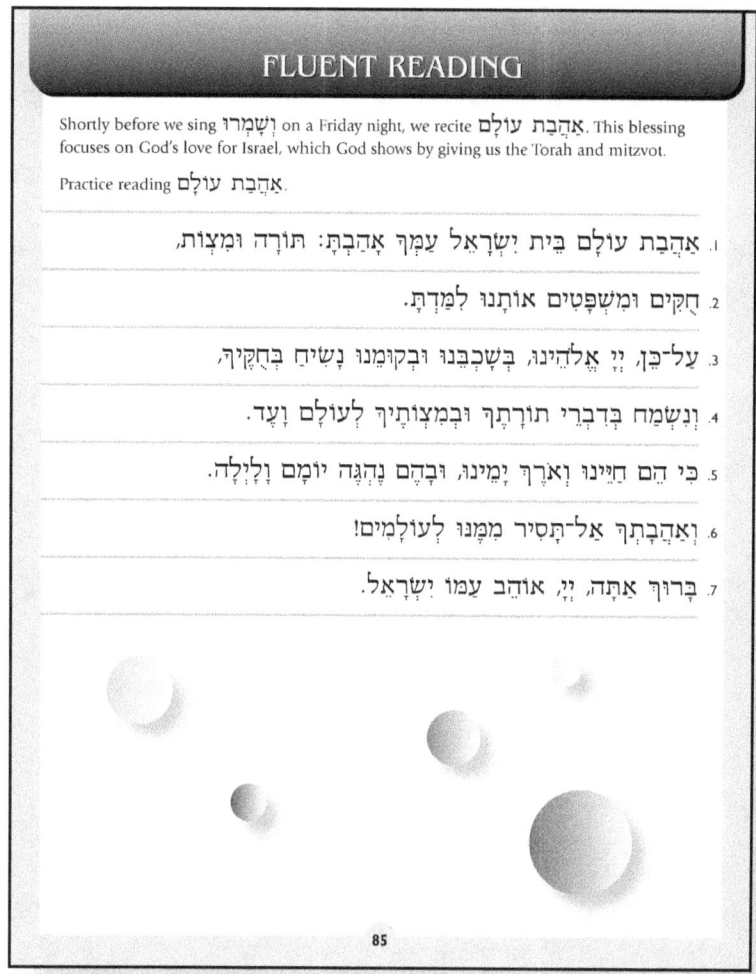

WORKSHEET

Duplicate and hand out copies of the worksheet for Lesson 8 to review skills and concepts.

FAMILY EDUCATION

Duplicate and send home copies of "As a Family: A Refreshing Day" (at the back of this guide).

LESSON 8
Worksheet

Name: _____

וְשָׁמְרוּ

1. Connect the root to the matching English.

English	Hebrew
rest	קדש
bless	שבת
make	זכר
remember	ברכ
keep/guard	שמר
holy	עשה
love	אהב

2. Write the root of each word.

   לַעֲשׂוֹת ___ ___ ___   שָׁבַת ___ ___ ___   וְשָׁמְרוּ ___ ___ ___

   וַיְקַדֵּשׁ ___ ___ ___   וַיְבָרֶךְ ___ ___ ___   אָהַבְתָּ ___ ___ ___

3. Write the English phrase from the list below next to the matching Hebrew phrase.

   rested and was refreshed   keep and remember   guarding the tongue

   children of Israel   eternal covenant   the heavens and the earth

   בְּנֵי יִשְׂרָאֵל _____   בְּרִית עוֹלָם _____

   שָׁמוֹר וְזָכוֹר _____   שְׁמִירַת הַלָּשׁוֹן _____

   אֶת־הַשָּׁמַיִם וְאֶת־הָאָרֶץ _____   שָׁבַת וַיִּנָּפַשׁ _____

4. Whose name was changed to יִשְׂרָאֵל? _____

   Who are the "children of Israel"? _____

5. Give three ways that we "keep" Shabbat.

   _____

   _____

LESSON 9
שָׁלוֹם עֲלֵיכֶם

LEARNING OBJECTIVES
Prayer Reading Skills
- The prefixs מִ ("from"); הַ ("the"); לְ ("for")
- The suffixes כֶם ("your"); ִי ("my")
- The roots מלכ ("rule"); קדש ("holy"); ברכ ("bless"); בוא ("come"); יצא ("depart," "go out")

Prayer Concepts
- Shalom Aleichem is traditionally sung around the Shabbat table after the candles have been lit
- The song expresses our hope for peace
- The hymn is based on a legend in which a "good angel" and an "evil angel" follow us home after Friday evening services
- Ethical Echo: צְדָקָה ("justice")

ABOUT THE PRAYER
Shabbat is a day of peace. The wish for peace is an integral theme in Shabbat songs and prayers. Shalom Aleichem speaks of the angels of peace that are welcomed into each Jewish home on Shabbat.

INSTRUCTIONAL MATERIALS
Text pages 86–95

Word Cards 16, 44, 85–91

Worksheet 9

Family Education: "As a Family: Angels of Peace" (at the back of this guide)

SET INDUCTION
An Angel of Peace
Introduce the following concept: We all have the potential to be angels of peace. Each of us can come into a situation as a messenger of peace, and then depart having made a difference because we were there.

Discuss the term "peace." Students often think of peace as the opposite of war. Broaden the discussion to include other categories such as peace of mind, peace of the heart, peace of the spirit, peace of the soul, and peace of time and place.

Discuss situations in the above categories in which each of us can make a difference by helping to create a sense of peace.

AS A FAMILY
Have students create a class mural with a table set for Shabbat, with glowing candles, wine, a Kiddush cup, two ḥallot, siddurim, flowers, and a white tablecloth. Have students write their last names around the table. Entitle the mural "Shabbat Peace."

Send home "As a Family: Angels of Peace," at the back of this guide. Each family will write words of peace on the page. (*love, family, smiles, gathering, freedom, creation, song, friendships, dove, handshakes*)

Ask each student to bring the family's responses to class. List the words on the chalkboard. Then have students add their words to the mural where their own names are written.

9 שָׁלוֹם עֲלֵיכֶם

Do you and your dad ever turn the radio up full-blast in the car and sing along together? Or maybe you and your friends watch a music video and sing the latest songs as a group. Singing together builds a bond—a feeling of togetherness and community.

We sing the שָׁלוֹם עֲלֵיכֶם hymn at home on Friday night, between lighting the candles and reciting the Kiddush. As we sing it, we strengthen our ties to each other and the good feelings we share.

Shalom Aleichem means "peace be upon you" and is another way we express our hope for peace and well-being.

Practice reading שָׁלוֹם עֲלֵיכֶם aloud.

1. שָׁלוֹם עֲלֵיכֶם, מַלְאֲכֵי הַשָּׁרֵת, מַלְאֲכֵי עֶלְיוֹן,
2. מִמֶּלֶךְ מַלְכֵי הַמְּלָכִים, הַקָּדוֹשׁ בָּרוּךְ הוּא.
3. בּוֹאֲכֶם לְשָׁלוֹם, מַלְאֲכֵי הַשָּׁלוֹם, מַלְאֲכֵי עֶלְיוֹן,
4. מִמֶּלֶךְ מַלְכֵי הַמְּלָכִים, הַקָּדוֹשׁ בָּרוּךְ הוּא.
5. בָּרְכוּנִי לְשָׁלוֹם, מַלְאֲכֵי הַשָּׁלוֹם, מַלְאֲכֵי עֶלְיוֹן,
6. מִמֶּלֶךְ מַלְכֵי הַמְּלָכִים, הַקָּדוֹשׁ בָּרוּךְ הוּא.
7. צֵאתְכֶם לְשָׁלוֹם, מַלְאֲכֵי הַשָּׁלוֹם, מַלְאֲכֵי עֶלְיוֹן,
8. מִמֶּלֶךְ מַלְכֵי הַמְּלָכִים, הַקָּדוֹשׁ בָּרוּךְ הוּא.

Peace upon you, O ministering angels, angels of the Supreme,
From the Ruler of rulers, the Holy Blessed One.
Come in peace, O angels of peace, angels of the Supreme,
From the Ruler of rulers, the Holy Blessed One.
Bless me with peace, O angels of peace, angels of the Supreme,
From the Ruler of rulers, the Holy Blessed One.
Depart in peace, O angels of peace, angels of the Supreme,
From the Ruler of rulers, the Holy Blessed One.

86

- Read aloud the third English phrase in each verse. (*"angels of the Supreme"*)
- Read the third Hebrew phrase next to each circled number.
- Read aloud the second English line of each verse. (*"from the Ruler of rulers, the Holy Blessed One"*)
- Read aloud the second Hebrew line of each verse. (*lines 2, 4, 6, 8*).

Discuss with students what they notice about the pattern in this hymn. (*words and phrases are repeated in regular patterns*)

INTO THE TEXT

Read the first paragraph aloud with students.

Discuss occasions on which they sing together with family or friends. Ask students to describe the feelings generated when they sing with others.

Read the second and third paragraphs with students.

Ask students if they have ever sung Shalom Aleichem on a Friday night.

Write the words "come," "bless," and "depart" on the chalkboard.

Explain that Shalom Aleichem describes angels who come into our homes in peace on Shabbat, bless our homes with peace, and depart in peace.

Note: Shalom Aleichem is a "hymn"—a song of praise or honor to God.

A First Reading

The hymn is divided into four verses of two lines each. Ask students to do the following:

- Circle the line number on which each Hebrew verse begins. (*1, 3, 5, 7*)
- Lightly circle the first English phrase introducing each verse. (*"peace upon you," "come in peace," "bless me with peace," "depart in peace"*)
- Read the first Hebrew phrase in each verse next to the circled number.
- Read aloud the second English phrase in each verse. (*"O ministering angels," "O angels of peace"*)
- State the verse number in which the second phrase is different from that of the others. (*the first verse*)
- Read the second Hebrew phrase next to each circled number.

THE NEW HEBREW THROUGH PRAYER 2 • הִנֵּנִי **112**

PRAYER DICTIONARY

Call on individual students to read aloud each word in the Prayer Dictionary and its English translation.

Capital Letters

Ask: Why are the words "Supreme," "Ruler," and "Holy Blessed One" capitalized? (*all are names for God*)

Word Cards

Display all the Word Cards (16, 44, 85-91) in random order.

Call on students to point out the following Word Cards and to translate them:

- the two Word Cards that make up the name of the hymn (*44 and 85*)
- the four Word Cards that introduce verses 1–4 (*44, 89, 90, 91*)
- the two Word Cards that conclude the first line of each verse (*86 and 16*)
- the two Word Cards that make up the second line of each verse (*87 and 88*)

Nine X Nine

Distribute the nine Word Cards to nine students.

Direct each of the nine students to read a line that contains the word or phrase on the card.

SERIOUS SYNONYMS

Have the students complete the activity individually by referring to the Prayer Dictionary for correct spelling and vocabulary review.

Alternative

Tell students to cover the Prayer Dictionary. Use the Word Cards on display to test vocabulary knowledge. Then, uncover the Prayer Dictionary for students to check their answers.

Ask: What other names do we have for God? (*Adonai, Shaddai, El, Elohim*)

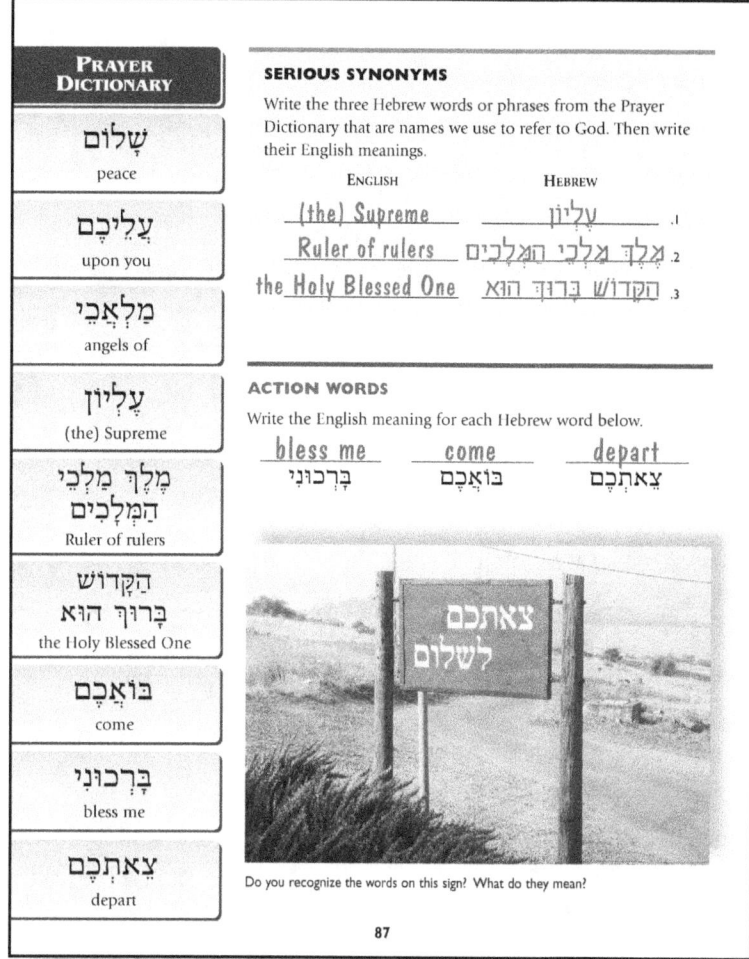

ACTION WORDS

Have students complete the exercise following the same procedure described above for "Serious Synonyms."

Ask students to number the words below the Hebrew in the order in which they appear in the hymn.

(3: צֵאתְכֶם 1: בּוֹאֲכֶם 2: בָּרְכוּנִי)

Photo Op

Display Word Card 91. Have students read the Hebrew and give the English meaning of the word. Ask them to compare the words on the sign to the first phrase on line 7 of the prayer on page 86. (*same phrase*)

What does the sign say? (*depart in peace*)

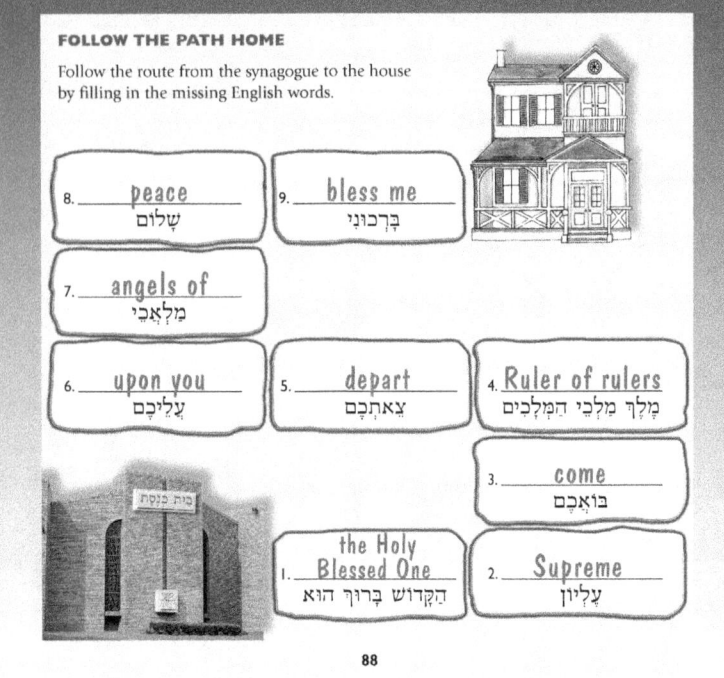

THE LEGEND OF THE HYMN

Bring an English dictionary to class. Have the students look up the meaning of the word "legend." Choose a student to read the paragraph aloud.

Ask what we can do to be sure the good angel prevails. (*prepare our homes to welcome Shabbat*)

FOLLOW THE PATH HOME

Before students set off on the path from the synagogue to the house, direct their attention to the Hebrew words at the top of the synagogue. Choose someone to read the phrase, בֵּית כְּנֶסֶת ("synagogue").

Have the students follow the path "home." Tell them that if they "stumble," they can look in the Prayer Dictionary for help.

Enhancing the Concept

Explain that the term בֵּית כְּנֶסֶת is one of several Hebrew terms for "synagogue." It literally means "House of Assembly or Gathering." Two other terms for "synagogue" are בֵּית מִדְרָשׁ ("House of Study") and בֵּית תְּפִלָּה ("House of Prayer").

- How does each term reflect the ways we use a synagogue? (*House of Assembly: gatherings, celebrations, meetings, Shabbat and holiday dinners; House of Study: religious school classes, adult education classes, Torah study; House of Prayer: weekday, Shabbat, and holiday services*)

- Why is "House of Assembly," בֵּית כְּנֶסֶת, the term most frequently used? (*it reflects all three uses: gathering for special events, for classes, for prayer*)

PRAYER BUILDING BLOCKS

שָׁלוֹם עֲלֵיכֶם "peace upon you"

Read the Building Block with the students.

- Ask: What is the meaning of the words בּוֹאֲכֶם ("come") and צֵאתְכֶם ("depart")?
- Direct students to fill in the names of the three other prayers with the word שָׁלוֹם.

Call on students to read aloud the names of all four prayers.

מַלְאֲכֵי עֶלְיוֹן "angels of the Supreme"

Complete the Building Block with the students.

You may also translate the phrase as "angels of the Supreme God" or "angels of the Supreme One."

Reading Review

Call on students to read aloud lines 1, 3, 5, and 7 on page 86.

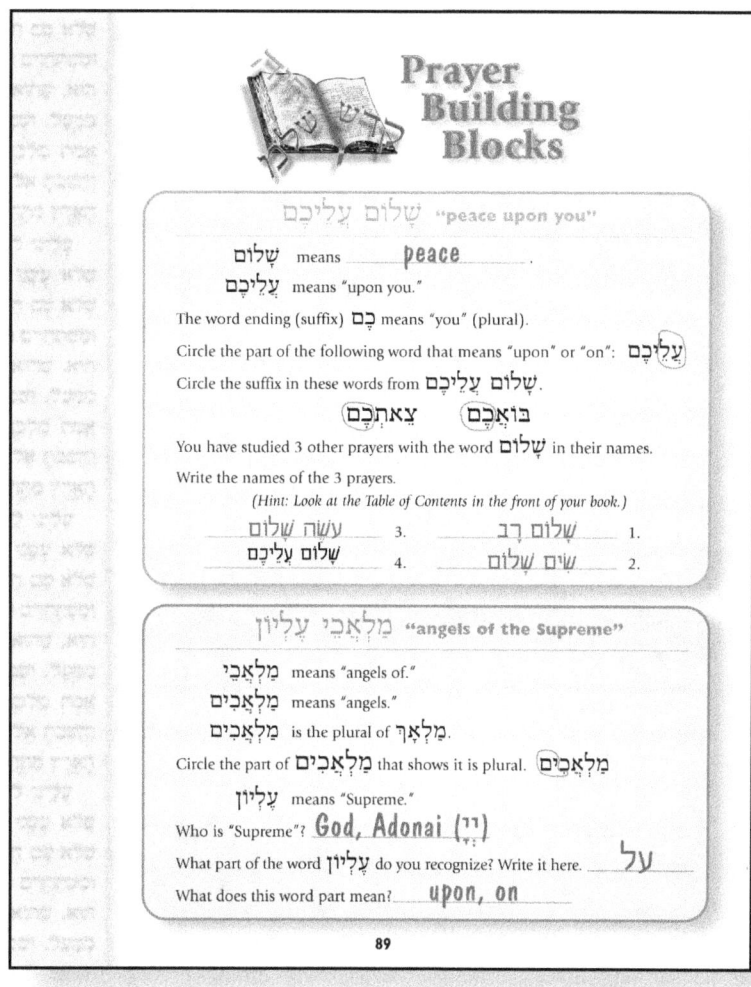

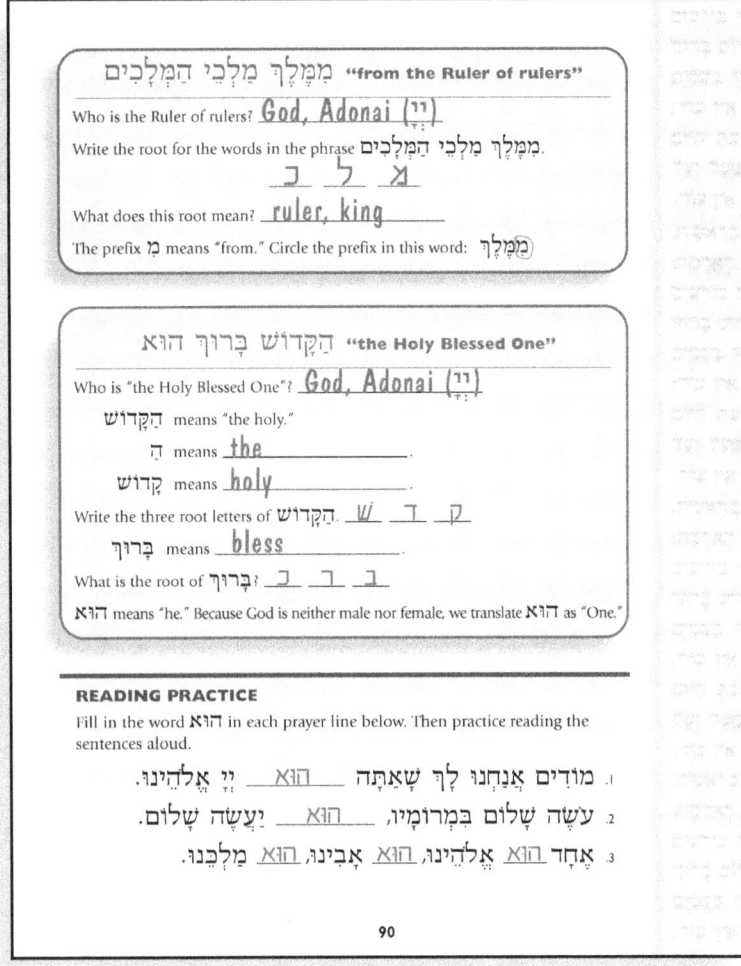

מִמֶּלֶךְ מַלְכֵי הַמְּלָכִים
"from the Ruler of rulers"

Write the words מֶלֶךְ and מַלְאָךְ on the chalkboard. Help students pronounce מַלְאָךְ. (mal-ach)

What is the meaning of each word? ("ruler" and "angel")

Write מַלְכֵי beneath מֶלֶךְ. Write מַלְאֲכֵי beneath מַלְאָךְ and point out the differences between the words. Review the meanings. ("ruler of" and "angels of")

Call on students to read each set of words.

Have students complete the Building Block independently and share their answers.

Tongue Twister: One Phrase

Call on each student in turn to read the phrase מִמֶּלֶךְ מַלְכֵי הַמְּלָכִים.

Repeat several times around the room. Each time challenge the students to read the phrase faster than the last time, trying not to "twist their tongues."

הַקָּדוֹשׁ בָּרוּךְ הוּא
"the Holy Blessed One"

Have students complete the Building Block independently and share their answers.

Tongue Twister: Two Phrases

Direct students to page 86, lines 2, 4, 6, and 8.

Divide the class into two groups, A and B. Challenge the groups to alternate reading the phrases מִמֶּלֶךְ מַלְכֵי הַמְּלָכִים and הַקָּדוֹשׁ בָּרוּךְ הוּא without "twisting their tongues."

Group A should read the first phrase in line 2 and group B should read the second phrase. The groups should alternate reading the phrases in lines 4, 6, and 8. Then have them switch phrases.

READING PRACTICE

Call on individual students to read each line, stopping before the word הוּא.

The class reads הוּא in unison at each stopping point, and then the reader continues the sentence.

Ask: In which blessing do we read sentence 1? (Lesson 4, הוֹדָאָה, the sixth blessing of the עֲמִידָה) Sentence 2? (Lesson 6, עֹשֶׂה שָׁלוֹם)

Note: Sentence 3 is part of the Kedushah in the *Gates of Prayer* siddur.

PRAYER RHYTHMS

Read the page aloud with the students.

Together sing lines 1 and 2 with the melody used in your synagogue.

Allow time for students to describe in their own words the theme of the hymn.

Call on students to share their ideas.

IN YOUR OWN WORDS

Have students fill in their individual responses and then share their insights with the class.

Sing-Along

Sing all four verses of Shalom Aleichem on page 86 with students.

Divide the class into four groups. Call on each group to sing one verse in turn (lines 1–2, 3–4, 5–6, 7–8). Rotate group assignments and sing along once again.

PRAYER RHYTHMS

We have studied the vocabulary of the first verse of שָׁלוֹם עֲלֵיכֶם. Practice reading this verse again.

1. שָׁלוֹם עֲלֵיכֶם, מַלְאֲכֵי הַשָּׁרֵת, מַלְאֲכֵי עֶלְיוֹן,
2. מִמֶּלֶךְ מַלְכֵי הַמְּלָכִים, הַקָּדוֹשׁ בָּרוּךְ הוּא.

The remaining three verses of שָׁלוֹם עֲלֵיכֶם are identical to one another except for the opening phrase, which varies slightly in each one. Read the opening phrases of the three remaining verses.

1. בּוֹאֲכֶם לְשָׁלוֹם   2. בָּרְכוּנִי לְשָׁלוֹם   3. צֵאתְכֶם לְשָׁלוֹם

Write the word that repeats in all three phrases. ___לְשָׁלוֹם___

What does this word mean? **for peace, to peace**

Look back at the English translation of the שָׁלוֹם עֲלֵיכֶם hymn on page 86. Explain in your own words the theme—the main idea—of the song.

_____
_____

IN YOUR OWN WORDS

How can songs like שָׁלוֹם עֲלֵיכֶם and other זְמִירוֹת (Shabbat songs) enhance a Shabbat family celebration?

_____
_____

THREE OPENING PHRASES

בּוֹאֲכֶם "come"

Have students complete the exercise individually. Review answers.

The Fruit of the Tree

Add the word בּוֹאֲכֶם and the phrase בּוֹאֲכֶם לְשָׁלוֹם to the בוא tree.

בָּרְכוּנִי "bless me"

Have the students complete the first part individually.

Complete the second part together. Call on students to read the eight words aloud, emphasizing the final syllable with its suffix.

Fruit of the Tree

Add the word בָּרְכוּנִי and the phrase בָּרְכוּנִי לְשָׁלוֹם to the ברכ tree.

צֵאתְכֶם "depart"

Read this section aloud with students.

Call on students to read each complete verse. (lines 1–2, 3–4, 5–6, 7–8)

Fruit of the Tree

Create a new fruit tree for the root יצא. Write "depart" and "go out" on the trunk of the tree. Remind students that sometimes a root letter does not appear in a word built on that root.

Add the word צֵאתְכֶם and the phrase צֵאתְכֶם לְשָׁלוֹם to fruit for the tree.

THE HOLIDAY CONNECTION

Read the first part together with students. Discuss the question. Have students write their responses on the line provided.

Direct students to circle the words in lines 1–5 built on the root יצא.

Call on individual students to read each circled word aloud.

Vocabulary Note

Write the word מִצְרַיִם ("Egypt") on the chalkboard.

Ask: What is the meaning of the prefix מִ? (*from*)

Hint: See the first Building Block on page 90.

Add the prefix מִ to the word מִצְרַיִם. (מִמִּצְרַיִם)

Ask: What does the word mean when the prefix is added? (*from Egypt*)

Have students lightly underline, or highlight, the word מִמִּצְרַיִם in lines 1, 3, 4, and 5.

Call on students to read the phrases in lines 1, 3, 4, and 5 that mean "depart from Egypt."

(*line 1*: בְּצֵאת יִשְׂרָאֵל מִמִּצְרַיִם; *line 3*: הוֹצִיאָנוּ מִמִּצְרַיִם; *line 4*: יָצָא מִמִּצְרַיִם; *line 5*: בְּצֵאתִי מִמִּצְרַיִם)

Leaving Egypt

Have half the class be the "voice" and read each line.

Have the other half of the class be the "echo" by reading each line back.

Then have the two halves reverse roles and repeat.

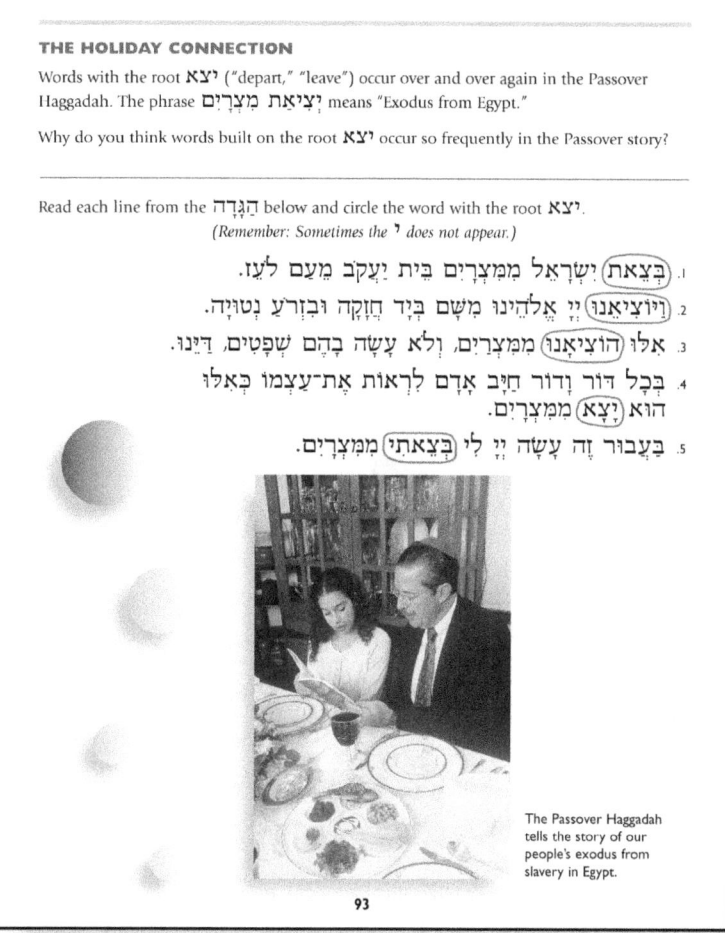

Photo Op

Read the caption aloud.

Explain that the word "haggadah" means "telling."

Direct students' attention to the seder plate in the photo.

Ask them what each item on the seder plate symbolizes. (*Bitter herbs: Jews' bitter lives in Egypt; Ḥaroset: mortar they used when they were slaves; Roasted bone: sacrificial lamb; Greens: springtime, a new beginning; Roasted egg: festival sacrifice, renewal of life*)

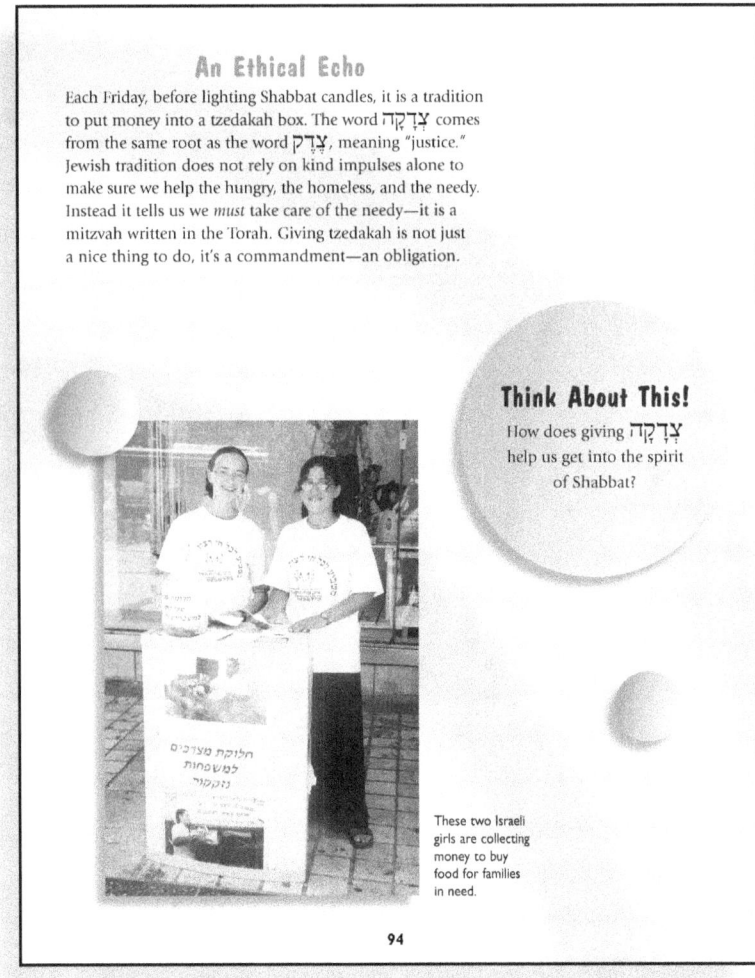

Photo Op

Read the caption aloud.

Encourage students to begin a food drive for needy people in your own community.

AN ETHICAL ECHO

Read the section aloud with students.

A New Tradition

Encourage students to bring in money for tzedakah each week. Discuss with them the role tzedakah plays in helping others physically. (*provide food, clothing, toiletries, toys*) Then ask the following:

- Why do we give tzedakah *before* Shabbat? (*traditionally, we don't handle money on Shabbat; tzedakah helps needy families prepare for Shabbat*)

- How do tzedakah contributions help people who are lonely? (*support services that provide community events such as the Jewish Family Services Passover seder or Ḥannukah party or weekly lunches*)

- How do tzedakah contributions help people avoid embarrassment? (*provide jobs; school supplies; wedding dresses; baseball mitts; winter coats*)

- How do tzedakah contributions help prevent ignorance? (*support schools by providing books and funding teachers in communities and countries that are impoverished*)

THINK ABOUT THIS!

Discuss the question with the students. (*Shabbat is a time of peace and joy; giving tzedakah helps bring peace and joy into the lives of others; Shabbat is a time for families to come together; giving tzedakah helps other families who are in need*)

FLUENT READING

Read the introduction aloud with students.

Note: This passage is also an introduction to the Kiddush.

Direct students to lines 1–2 (Genesis 2:1–2).

Ask students to read the word or phrase that means:

- "God" (אֱלֹהִים)
- "the heavens and the earth" (הַשָּׁמַיִם וְהָאָרֶץ)
- "on the seventh day" (בַּיּוֹם הַשְּׁבִיעִי)
- "had made" (עָשָׂה)

Read lines 1–2 in unison with the students. Then call on individual students to read the lines.

Direct students to lines 3–6. Students have read these lines before in Lesson 8, page 83.

Have students open their textbooks to page 83 and read the English translation of these lines: "And God rested . . . had made."

Divide the class in half. One half should read aloud from the Hebrew selection on page 83; the other half should read page 95, lines 3–6.

Individual students should then read page 95, lines 1–6.

Teach students the melody for this passage.

A Visit to the Sanctuary

Open a *Sefer Torah* to the וַיְכֻלּוּ passage.

Have the class be the "voice," reading a phrase, line, or sentence on 95 in their textbooks.

Have an individual student be the "Torah echo," reading the same phrase, line, or sentence directly from the Torah.

Allow each student the opportunity to be the "Torah echo."

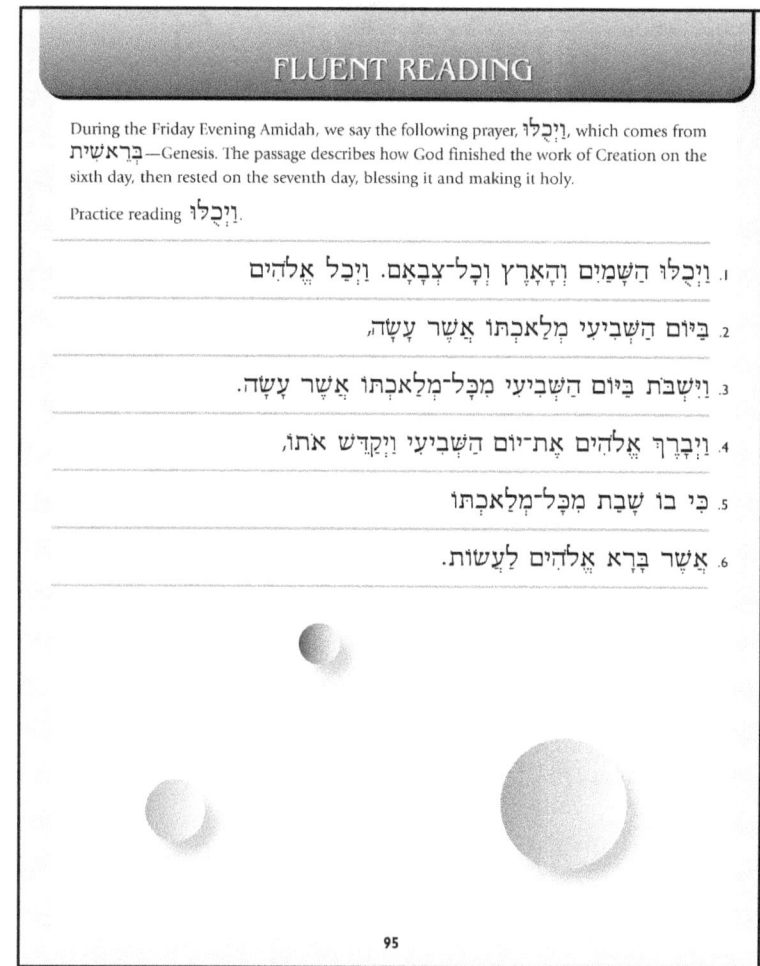

WORKSHEET

Duplicate and hand out copies of the worksheet for Lesson 9 to review skills and concepts.

FAMILY EDUCATION

Duplicate and send home copies of "As a Family: Angels of Peace" (at the back of this guide), if you did not already do so to reinforce the concept of Shabbat Peace at the beginning of this chapter.

LESSON 9
Worksheet

Name: _____

שָׁלוֹם עֲלֵיכֶם

1. Number the first Hebrew phrase in each verse of שָׁלוֹם עֲלֵיכֶם in the order it appears in the hymn.

   Number the matching English in the same order.

   _____ Bless me with peace   צֵאתְכֶם לְשָׁלוֹם _____

   _____ Peace upon you   בּוֹאֲכֶם לְשָׁלוֹם _____

   _____ Depart in peace   שָׁלוֹם עֲלֵיכֶם _____

   _____ Come in peace   בָּרְכוּנִי לְשָׁלוֹם _____

2. Unscramble the Hebrew words in each phrase to match the English translation.

   from the Ruler of rulers   _____ מַלְכֵי הַמְּלָכִים מִמֶּלֶךְ

   the Holy Blessed One   _____ הוּא בָּרוּךְ הַקָּדוֹשׁ

3. Write the English for each word: _____ מַלְאָךְ _____ מֶלֶךְ

   Complete each of the phrases below with one of the following words: מַלְאֲכֵי מַלְכֵי

   _____ עֶלְיוֹן   _____ הַשָּׁלוֹם   _____ הַשָּׁרֵת

   angels of the Supreme   angels of peace   ministering angels

   מִמֶּלֶךְ _____ הַמְּלָכִים

   from the Ruler of rulers

4. Write the English for each root below.

   שׁלמ   מלכ   ברכ   קדשׁ   יצא   בוא

   _____   _____   _____   _____   _____   _____

5. Name one thing you can do to be among מַלְאֲכֵי הַשָּׁלוֹם, "the angels of peace."

   On Shabbat: _____

   At all times: _____

HINENI—THE NEW HEBREW THROUGH PRAYER 2 © Behrman House Publishers

III. ENRICHMENT AND SUPPLEMENTARY MATERIALS

FAMILY EDUCATION

Name: _____

Family Tree

The first blessing in the Shabbat morning Amidah is the Avot. In it we recall our ancestors Abraham and Sarah and all the generations who came after them. Jewish family trees are offshoots of the family tree of this, the first Jewish family!

בָּרוּךְ אַתָּה יְיָ, אֱלֹהֵינוּ וֵאלֹהֵי אֲבוֹתֵינוּ,
אֱלֹהֵי אַבְרָהָם, אֱלֹהֵי יִצְחָק, וֵאלֹהֵי יַעֲקֹב

Baruch Atah Adonai Eloheinu veilohei avoteinu,

Elohei Avraham, Elohei Yitzḥak, Veilohei Ya'akov

Praised are You, Adonai, our God and God of our fathers,

God of Abraham, God of Isaac, and God of Jacob

Some synagogues include the names of the patriarchs (*avoteinu*) *and* the matriarchs (*eemoteinu*):

בָּרוּךְ אַתָּה יְיָ, אֱלֹהֵינוּ וֵאלֹהֵי אֲבוֹתֵינוּ וְאִמּוֹתֵינוּ,
אֱלֹהֵי אַבְרָהָם, אֱלֹהֵי יִצְחָק, וֵאלֹהֵי יַעֲקֹב,
אֱלֹהֵי שָׂרָה, אֱלֹהֵי רִבְקָה, אֱלֹהֵי לֵאָה וְרָחֵל

Baruch Atah Adonai Eloheinu Veilohei avoteinu v'eemoteinu,

Elohei Avraham, Elohei Yitzḥak, Veilohei Ya'akov,

Elohei Sarah, Elohei Rivka, Elohei Leah veRaḥeil

Praised are You, Adonai, our God and God of our fathers and mothers,

God of Abraham, God of Isaac, and God of Jacob,

God of Sarah, God of Rebecca, God of Leah and Rachel

With your child, trace the roots of your family back as many generations as you can. List the names of parents, grandparents, and great-grandparents. Choose one story about a previous generation for your child to share with the class and write it in the space below.

_____

_____

_____

Hineni —The New Hebrew Through Prayer 2 © Behrman House Publishers
www.behrmanhouse.com/family

Name: _____

My Hero

אַתָּה גִּבּוֹר לְעוֹלָם, אֲדֹנָי

Atah gibor l'olam, Adonai

You are mighty, Adonai

The second blessing of the Amidah is גְּבוּרוֹת—G'vurot ("powers"). The Hebrew word גִּבּוֹר (*gibor*) means "mighty" or "powerful." It also means "hero." A hero uses his or her powers to make a difference to family, friends, and community.

Think about the powers we have to change the world for the better. Think about people who are your heroes.

Below list the names or kinds of people you consider to be heroes. Why do they deserve that title? How do or did they use their powers to make a difference in the lives of your family, community, or the world as a whole?

_____

_____

_____

_____

_____

_____

HINENI—THE NEW HEBREW THROUGH PRAYER 2 © Behrman House Publishers
www.behrmanhouse.com/family

Holy Times

קָדוֹשׁ, קָדוֹשׁ, קָדוֹשׁ יְיָ צְבָאוֹת,
מְלֹא כָל הָאָרֶץ כְּבוֹדוֹ.

Kadosh, kadosh, kadosh Adonai tz'va'ot,
m'lo chol ha'aretz k'vodo.

Holy, Holy, Holy is Adonai of the heavenly legions,
the whole earth is full of God's glory. (Isaiah 6:3)

The third blessing of the Amidah is known as the קְדוּשָׁה (*Kedushah*), which means "holiness" or "sanctification." The prophet Isaiah had a vision of God sitting on a divine throne surrounded by angels who called to one another with the words *"kadosh, kadosh, kadosh"* ("holy, holy, holy") as they praised God's earth and God's glory.

Holy moments in our own lives may make us want to echo the words of the angels in Isaiah's vision. Think of the times in your life that were holy. Please share one or two with us in the space below.

_____

_____

_____

_____

_____

HINENI —THE NEW HEBREW THROUGH PRAYER 2 © Behrman House Publishers
www.behrmanhouse.com/family

Name: _____

A Family Thanksgiving

מוֹדִים אֲנַחְנוּ לָךְ...וְעַל נִסֶּיךָ שֶׁבְּכָל יוֹם עִמָּנוּ

Modim anaḥnu lach . . . v'al nisecha sheb'chol yom imanu

We thank You . . . and (for) Your miracles that are with us every day

---

The sixth and next-to-last blessing of the Amidah is the הוֹדָאָה *(Hoda'ah)*, which means "thanksgiving." In the Hoda'ah we thank God for the miracles in the world around us.

Think about the miracles you see and experience every day. On the lines below, write about the miracles that are part of *your* family's world. Thinking about the miracles in our lives reminds us of all the things for which we are thankful.

_____

_____

_____

_____

_____

_____

_____

Name: _____

Words of Peace

שִׂים שָׁלוֹם (בָּעוֹלָם), טוֹבָה וּבְרָכָה,
חֵן וָחֶסֶד וְרַחֲמִים עָלֵינוּ וְעַל כָּל יִשְׂרָאֵל עַמֶּךָ.

Sim shalom (ba'olam), tovah u'vrachah,
ḥein va'ḥesed v'raḥamim aleinu v'al kol Yisrael amecha

Grant peace (in the world), goodness and blessing,
graciousness and kindness and mercy upon us and upon all Israel Your people.

This blessing, שִׂים שָׁלוֹם (*Sim Shalom*), which means "Grant peace," is the final blessing of the Shabbat Morning Amidah. When the Jewish people make a wish as a community, it is a wish for peace. In Sim Shalom we ask God to inspire us to make peace and to act kindly toward others. Some congregations add the phrase "in the world" to the prayer to indicate that our wish is for peace for *everyone*.

The root of the Hebrew word שָׁלוֹם (*shalom*) has the general meaning of "completion" or "wholeness." This suggests that, for Jews, the desire to live in peace is integrally related to our desire to live lives of integrity and wholeness.

A first step toward living in peace is to try to create peace within our homes. We can begin by carefully choosing the words we use with our family members. Our words can express kindness, support, love, and respect toward one another. Draw up a mini-dictionary entitled "Words of Peace." What words would you include? List them below.

Words of Peace

_____
_____
_____
_____
_____
_____

Sh'lom Bayit

עֹשֶׂה שָׁלוֹם בִּמְרוֹמָיו, הוּא יַעֲשֶׂה שָׁלוֹם עָלֵינוּ
וְעַל כָּל יִשְׂרָאֵל. וְאִמְרוּ, אָמֵן.

Oseh shalom, bim'romav, hu ya'aseh shalom aleinu
v'al kol Yisrael. V'im'ru Amen.

May God who makes peace in the heavens, make peace for us
and for all Israel. And say Amen.

Shalom, שָׁלוֹם, means "peace," but שָׁלוֹם means much more than that. שָׁלוֹם is built on the Hebrew root for "complete" or "perfect." When we create peace we are complete and are helping to perfect our world.

It is often easiest to begin the pursuit of peace within our own families. We call this mitzvah שְׁלוֹם בַּיִת, *Sh'lom Bayit* ("peace in the home"). The fifth of the Ten Commandments tells us, "Honor your father and your mother" (Exodus 20:12; Deuteronomy 5:16). A relationship built on respect between children and parents helps to foster *Sh'lom Bayit*.

Create your own "Ten Commandments" for *Sh'lom Bayit*, peace in your home. Discuss your ideas as a family and write them down on your own family tablets below. Make the Fifth Commandment—"Honor your father and your mother"—the fifth commandment on *your* tablets. Post your "Ten Commandments" in a visible place in your home.

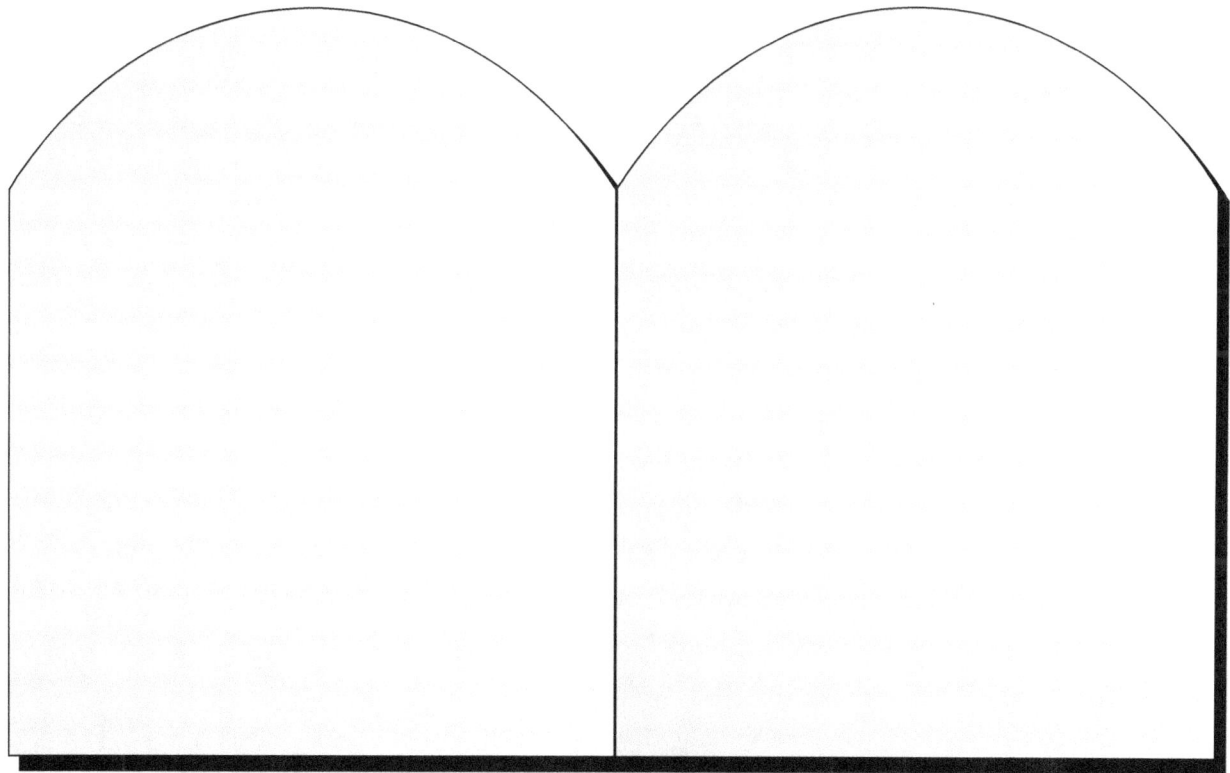

Name: _____

A Special Day

לְכָה דוֹדִי לִקְרַאת כַּלָּה, פְּנֵי שַׁבָּת נְקַבְּלָה.

Lechah dodi likrat kallah, p'nei Shabbat n'kab'lah.

Let us go, my beloved, to meet (toward) the Bride, let us greet Shabbat.

Lechah Dodi is the final song in the Kabbalat Shabbat service, the service in which we welcome Shabbat on Friday night. In Lechah Dodi we greet Shabbat as if it were a bride, and we anticipate its arrival and prepare to greet it as we would prepare to greet a bride.

Think about the special events in your own lives and the ways you prepared for them; for example, a wedding, the birth of a baby, a move to a new house, a bar or bat mitzvah, or a family reunion. Reflect on the details of your preparation as well as your joy and anticipation when the day arrived. List your steps in preparing for the day and describe your feelings when it finally came.

_____

_____

_____

_____

_____

_____

_____

HINENI—THE NEW HEBREW THROUGH PRAYER 2 © Behrman House Publishers
www.behrmanhouse.com/family

A Refreshing Day

וּבַיּוֹם הַשְּׁבִיעִי שָׁבַת וַיִּנָּפַשׁ

U'vayom ha'sh'vee'ee shavat vayeenafash

. . . and on the seventh day Adonai rested and was refreshed.

(Exodus 31:17)

V'shamru (וְשָׁמְרוּ) is taken from the Torah. It teaches us that Shabbat is a sign of the covenant between God and the Jewish people and it reminds us of our promise to God to guard, cherish, and observe Shabbat and keep it holy. The passage ends with the words "in six days Adonai made the heavens and the earth, and on the seventh day Adonai rested and was refreshed." The seventh day is, of course, Shabbat.

We too can stop to rest and refresh ourselves on Shabbat. Discuss and list ways in which your family members can do just that. How has your family acknowledged and observed Shabbat?

_____

_____

_____

_____

_____

_____

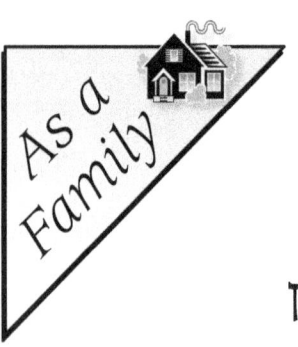

Name: _____

Angels of Peace

בָּרְכוּנִי לְשָׁלוֹם, מַלְאֲכֵי הַשָּׁלוֹם, מַלְאֲכֵי עֶלְיוֹן
מִמֶּלֶךְ מַלְכֵי הַמְּלָכִים, הַקָּדוֹשׁ בָּרוּךְ הוּא.

Barchuni l'shalom, mal'achei hashalom, mal'achei elyon

Mimelech mal'chei ham'lachim, hakadosh baruch hu

Bless me with peace, O angels of peace, angels of the Supreme,

From the Ruler of rulers, the Holy Blessed One.

_____

In the Shabbat song Shalom Aleichem ("peace upon you"), we sing of the angels of peace, who come in peace, bless us with peace, and depart in peace.

Each one of us can be an "angel of peace"—a blessing to those whose lives we touch. As a family, write words or images below that are related to peace (for example, "friendship," "generosity," "kindness," "protest").

Your child will share your word list in class as the students discuss how we become angels of peace on Shabbat and at all times.

_____

_____

_____

_____

_____

HINENI —THE NEW HEBREW THROUGH PRAYER 2 © Behrman House Publishers
www.behrmanhouse.com/family

TECHNIQUES FOR USE WITH SPECIAL NEEDS STUDENTS

Like most classes, yours probably includes a diverse group of students with different learning styles and needs, who achieve mastery at different rates. The variety of activities in *Hineni* offers your students a broad selection of learning opportunities that can be easily modified for students with special learning needs.

Without practice, students frequently lose some of their Hebrew decoding skills over the summer. This is particularly true of students with special learning needs. It is helpful to assess such students' decoding skill levels individually at the very beginning of the new school year and review the letters and vowels with them.

It is important to use a diagnostic-prescriptive approach. By noting students' decoding errors, you can identify their needs, reteach problematic letters and vowels, and provide the necessary practice to bring the students back up to speed. Use your school's primer to reteach basic reading skills. Retest the students to be certain that they have mastered the troublesome items.

Here are some teaching tips that can help you work more effectively with special needs students.

- Be ready to assist the students in decoding new words and phrases. Model the correct pronunciation and phrasing before they read any segment of the book. Do not let them struggle. Reinforce word attack skills by breaking words into syllables. Repeat words and phrases several times, and do not assume that all your students will be able to read them fluently and accurately when they see the same words and phrases again later.

- Students with significant learning difficulties may have trouble keeping up with the class. Prioritize your goals for them. Identify the core elements of the text that you want them to master; this will help them keep up with the rest of the class. Allow extra time for them to finish an assignment, or reduce the number of items they are expected to complete. Offer them other modes of responding, e.g., orally instead of in writing, underlining or circling instead of copying, or working together with an aide or a buddy.

- Although the Hebrew text in *Hineni* has separated and numbered lines, some students may benefit from using an index card or pencil to help track across the line. In some instances, masking the rest of the page to reduce distractions can enable them to read more easily.

- Some students, especially those who are shy, lack confidence, or have learning differences, are reluctant to read aloud in class. You can provide an alternative method of monitoring their reading progress by listening to small groups while the rest of the class is working on the other sections of the lesson. This is also a more efficient use of class time.

- For students who require additional support in order to achieve mastery, enlist parents as partners in the educational process. Short periods of daily practice with an audiotape at home will help the students retain what they have learned in class and build toward fluency and accuracy. Parents can "sign off" on the practice schedule even if they themselves do not feel that they are competent Hebrew readers.

By adapting your teaching techniques to meet the individual learning styles and special needs of your students, you can help every member of your class master the skills in this book.

ANSWERS TO WORKSHEETS

LESSON 1 Worksheet

Name: _____

אָבוֹת וְאִמָהוֹת

1. Write the English translation for each term below.

   עֲבָדָיו _____ שְׁמוֹנֶה עֶשְׂרֵה הַתְּפִלָּה
   standing   eighteen   (the) prayer

2. Circle the suffix in each word below.

   אֲבוֹתֵֽי(נוּ)   ‎ us   our

   What does this suffix mean? __us__ __our__

3. Write the English name below each Hebrew name.

   רָחֵל   יִצְחָק   לֵאָה   שָׂרָה   יַעֲקֹב   רִבְקָה   אַבְרָהָם
   Rachel Isaac   Leah   Sarah   Jacob   Rebecca Abraham

   Write the Hebrew names of the patriarchs in the order in which they appear in אָבוֹת.

   __אַבְרָהָם__ __יִצְחָק__ __יַעֲקֹב__

   Write the Hebrew names of the matriarchs in the order in which they appear in אָבוֹת וְאִמָהוֹת.

   __שָׂרָה__ __רִבְקָה__ __רָחֵל__ __לֵאָה__

   What is the English meaning of אֱלֹהֵי? __God of__

4. Connect each Hebrew word to its English meaning.

   helper   מֶֽלֶךְ
   ruler   עוֹזֵר
   shield   מָגֵן
   rescuer   מוֹשִׁיעַ

   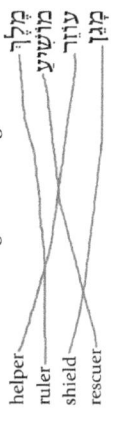

5. In many synagogues we follow several steps when we say the עֲמִידָה. Write three of the steps here. __stand; face toward Jerusalem; take 3 small steps forward at beginning of עֲמִידָה; take 3 small steps backward at end of עֲמִידָה; how at beginning and end of אָבוֹת; bow several times during עֲמִידָה; do not talk__

6. Give one example of what your generation can do to ensure that Judaism continues in the next generation. __continue ritual observance, e.g., observe Shabbat, light Hanukkiyah, celebrate Passover seder; celebrate Jewish life-cycle events; study Torah; learn about our customs; support Israel__

HINENI—THE NEW HEBREW THROUGH PRAYER 2 © Behrman House Publishers

---

LESSON 2 Worksheet

Name: _____

בְּרָכוֹת

1. How many blessings are there in the Shabbat morning עֲמִידָה? __seven__

   Unscramble the letters to spell the name of the first blessing: תוֹבָא __אָבוֹת__
   What is the English meaning of the name? __fathers, ancestors__

   Unscramble the letters to spell the name of the second blessing: תוֹרוּבְגּ __גְבוּרוֹת__
   What is the English meaning of the name? __powers__

2. Write the English meaning next to each Hebrew word or phrase below.

   בִּקוּר חוֹלִים __visiting the sick__   רוֹפֵא חוֹלִים __heals the sick__   גִבּוֹר __mighty, powerful, hero__
   עֲמִידָה __standing (prayer)__   בִּרְכַּת כֹּהֲנִים __Priestly Blessing__   כֹּהֲנִים __priests__

3. Connect the Hebrew root to the matching English.

   bless, praise   ברך
   kindness   חיה
   compassion, mercy   חסד
   life   רחם

4. Using your knowledge of roots, connect each Hebrew word or phrase below to its English meaning.

   the Merciful One   בִרְכַּת הַמָּזוֹן
   Blessing after Meals   גְמִילוּת חֲסָדִים
   acts of loving-kindness הָרַחֲמָן
   Torah of life   תוֹרַת חַיִּים

HINENI—THE NEW HEBREW THROUGH PRAYER 2 © Behrman House Publishers

LESSON 3 Worksheet

Name: _____

קְדֻשָּׁה

1. Write the root of each Hebrew word on the first line below the word.
   Write the English for the root on the second line below the word.

קְדֻשָּׁה	בְּרָכָה	קָדוֹשׁ	יִמְלֹךְ
קדש	ברך	קדש	מלך
holy	bless/praise	holy	rule

2. Complete each word by adding the root letters for "holy."

   1. קָדֻשׁ הַ
   2. קִדַּשׁ יִם
   3. קָדוֹשׁ
   4. קְדֻשַּׁת
   5. קִדַּשְׁתִּי
   6. קְדוֹשִׁי

3. Why do you think the קְדֻשָּׁה contains so many words with the root קדש?
   to focus on God's holiness; we express our awe at God's holiness

4. Word Match!
   Write the number of the Hebrew word or phrase next to the matching English.

   _4_ we will tell (or relate)   הָאָרֶץ .1
   _1_ the earth   נְגִיד .2
   _5_ God's glory   כְבוֹד יהוה .3
   _2_ the Bible   תַּנַ"ךְ .4
   _6_ your greatness   גְּדֻלָּה .5
   _3_ from generation to generation   לְדֹר וָדֹר .6

5. Why do we rise up on our toes when we recite the words קָדוֹשׁ, קָדוֹשׁ, קָדוֹשׁ?
   to symbolize the fluttering wings of the angels in Isaiah's vision;
   to represent the uplifting of the spirit

HINENI—THE NEW HEBREW THROUGH PRAYER 2 © Behrman House Publishers

---

LESSON 4 Worksheet

Name: _____

הוֹדָאָה

1. What is the common meaning for the words below? __thanks__

   הוֹדָאָה   הוֹדוּ   לְהוֹדוֹת   מוֹדִים   מוֹדֶה

   Select and write the correct word from the list above to complete the introductory phrase in the הוֹדָאָה blessing.

   __מוֹדִים__ אֲנַחְנוּ לָךְ

   Select and write the correct word from the list above to complete the final sentence in the הוֹדָאָה blessing.

   לְהוֹדוֹת טוֹב שִׁמְךָ וּלְךָ נָאֶה __לְהוֹדוֹת__.

2. What is the common meaning for the words below? __praise__

   הַלְלוּיָהּ   הַלֵּל   תְּהִלָּה

   What root do these words share? __ה ל ל__

3. What is the English meaning of the suffix ךָ? __you, your__

   Add the suffix ךָ to complete each of the following words from the הוֹדָאָה blessing.

   לְךָ   דָּ   עִמָּ   שִׁמְ   נֶהְלָ   לָ

4. What is the English meaning of the word אֲנַחְנוּ? __we__
   What is the English meaning of the suffix נוּ? __us, our__

   Add the suffix נוּ to complete each of these words from the הוֹדָאָה blessing.

   שַׁע   דֹּר   חַיֵּי   וֵאלֹהֵי   אֱלֹהֵי
   נֵס   נִשְׁמוֹת   יִשְׁעֵ   בְּכָל

5. Complete the English phrase with your own words of appreciation:
   I give thanks to You, God, for _____

HINENI—THE NEW HEBREW THROUGH PRAYER 2 © Behrman House Publishers

LESSON 5 Worksheet

Name: _____

בְּרָכָה שָׁלוֹם:
שָׁלוֹם רָב/שִׁים שָׁלוֹם

1. Which version of בְּרָכָה שָׁלוֹם do we say in the evening service and which do we say in the morning service? Write your answers below.

   Evening שִׁים שָׁלוֹם   Morning שָׁלוֹם רָב

2. Draw lines to connect the Hebrew words to their roots.

   Set 1

   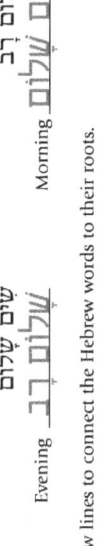

   Set 2

3. The English phrases below are in the order in which we recite them in שִׁים שָׁלוֹם. Number the Hebrew phrases in the correct order to match the English.

   1. grant peace — עָלֵינוּ וְעַל כָּל יִשְׂרָאֵל עַמֶּךָ **4**
   2. goodness and blessing — שִׂים שָׁלוֹם טוֹבָה וּבְרָכָה חֵן וָחֶסֶד וְרַחֲמִים **1**
   3. graciousness and kindness and mercy (compassion) — טוֹבָה וּבְרָכָה **2**
   4. upon us and upon all Israel Your people **3**

4. Write the following English words and phrases under the matching Hebrew words and phrases from שִׁים שָׁלוֹם:

   and a love of kindness   and life   Torah of life   and blessing
   and righteousness   and mercy/compassion   and peace

צְדָקָה	חַיִּים	חֶסֶד וְאַהֲבַת	חַיִּים תּוֹרַת	וּבְרָכָה
and righteousness	and life	and a love of kindness	Torah of life	and blessing

שָׁלוֹם		וְרַחֲמִים		
and peace		and mercy/compassion		

HINENI — THE NEW HEBREW THROUGH PRAYER 2 © Behrman House Publishers

---

LESSON 6 Worksheet

Name: _____

שָׁלוֹם עֲשֵׂה

1. Write three meanings for the word שָׁלוֹם. **peace   hello   goodbye**
   Write two meanings for the word שָׁלֵם. **complete   perfect**

2. Connect the root to the matching English.

   peace — עשׂה
   go up — אמר
   make — עלה
   say — שׁלם

3. Write the correct number of the Hebrew word next to the matching English word.

   5 Israel   1. וִירוּשָׁלַיִם
   3 peace   2. כָּל
   7 Amen   3. שָׁלוֹם
   6 and say   4. עֲלֵינוּ
   4 for us   5. יִשְׂרָאֵל
   2 all   6. וְאִמְרוּ
   1 Jerusalem   7. אָמֵן

4. Write each English phrase below next to the matching Hebrew.

   and for all Israel   May God who makes peace in the heavens
   and say Amen   make peace for us

   הוּא יַעֲשֶׂה שָׁלוֹם בִּמְרוֹמָיו **May God who makes peace in the heavens**
   יַעֲשֶׂה שָׁלוֹם עָלֵינוּ **make peace for us**
   וְעַל כָּל יִשְׂרָאֵל **and for all Israel**
   וְאִמְרוּ אָמֵן **and say Amen**

5. Write the common root for the words and the phrase below. **שׁ ל ם**
   Write the English meanings for each word and phrase on the line below it.

שָׁלוֹם	יְרוּשָׁלַיִם	שְׁלֹמֹה	שָׁלֵם	שָׁלוֹם בַּיִת
whole, complete	Jerusalem	Solomon	peace	peace in the home

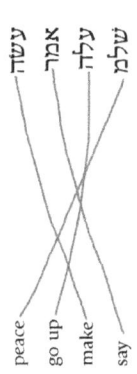

HINENI — THE NEW HEBREW THROUGH PRAYER 2 © Behrman House Publishers

LESSON 7 Worksheet

Name: _____

לְכָה דוֹדִי

1. Fill in the missing words in the first and last phrases of לְכָה דוֹדִי below. Select the words from the following list:

   לִקְרַאת, בֹּא, דוֹדִי, שַׁבָּת, לְכָה

   לְכָה __דוֹדִי__ לִקְרַאת __כַּלָּה__ פְּנֵי __שַׁבָּת__ נְקַבְּלָה.
   Let us go, <u>my beloved</u>, to meet (toward) the <u>Bride</u>, let us greet Shabbat.

   בֹּאִי __כַלָּה__, בֹּאִי __כַלָּה__.
   <u>Come</u>, O Bride! <u>Come</u>, O Bride.

2. Draw a line to connect each root to the matching English in the left column, and to a word built on that root in the right column.

English	Root	Word
keep, guard	הלך	שַׁמֹּר
welcome, receive	קבל	לְכָה
go, walk	שמר	נְקַבְּלָה
come	בא	דוֹדִי
remember	זכר	זָכוֹר

3. Write the English meaning of each commandment below the Hebrew.

   זָכוֹר אֶת יוֹם הַשַׁבָּת   שָׁמוֹר אֶת יוֹם הַשַׁבָּת
   __Remember Shabbat__   __Keep/Guard Shabbat__

4. Below are the names of the five books in the Torah. Circle the two books that contain the Ten Commandments commanding us to observe Shabbat.

   Genesis   (Exodus)   Leviticus   Numbers   (Deuteronomy)

5. What is the לְכָה דוֹדִי service? __the service to welcome Shabbat__

6. Why is Shabbat compared to a bride?
   __We look forward to the arrival of Shabbat just as we look forward to__
   __the arrival of a bride. A bride is beautiful and Shabbat is beautiful.__

LESSON 8 Worksheet

Name: _____

וַיְכֻלּוּ

1. Connect the root to the matching English.

rest	קדשׁ
bless	שׁבת
make	זכר
remember	ברך
keep/guard	עשׂה
holy	שׁמר
love	אהב

2. Write the root of each word.

   וַיְכֻלּוּ __כלה__   שׁוֹמֵר __שׁמר__   וְהָאָרֶץ __ארץ__
   זָכוֹר __זכר__   בְּרָכָה __ברך__   וַיִשְׁבֹּת __שׁבת__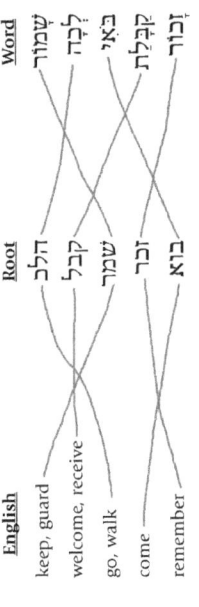

3. Write the English phrase from the list below next to the matching Hebrew phrase.

   keep and remember   guarding the tongue   the heavens and the earth
   rested and was refreshed   eternal covenant   children of Israel

   בְּרִית עוֹלָם __eternal covenant__   בְּנֵי יִשְׂרָאֵל __children of Israel__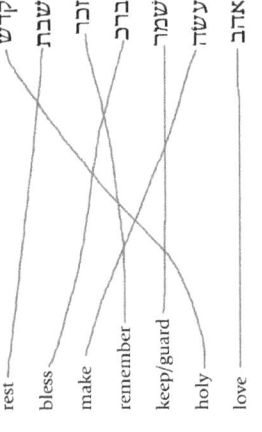
   נְצֹר לְשׁוֹנְךָ __guarding the tongue__   שָׁמוֹר וְזָכוֹר __keep and remember__
   שָׁבַת וַיִנָּפַשׁ __rested and was refreshed__   אֶת־הַשָׁמַיִם וְאֶת־הָאָרֶץ __the heavens and the earth__

4. Whose name was changed to יִשְׂרָאֵל? __Jacob__
   Who are the "children of Israel"? __the Jewish People__

5. Give three ways that we "keep" Shabbat.
   __welcome Shabbat with candles, wine, hallah; say blessings;__
   __attend synagogue services; rest and refresh ourselves__

LESSON 9
Worksheet

Name: _____

שָׁלוֹם עֲלֵיכֶם

1. Number the first Hebrew phrase in each verse of שָׁלוֹם עֲלֵיכֶם in the order it appears in the hymn.

   Number the matching English in the same order.

   3 Bless me with peace   **4** צֵאתְכֶם לְשָׁלוֹם

   1 Peace upon you   **2** בּוֹאֲכֶם לְשָׁלוֹם

   4 Depart in peace   **1** שָׁלוֹם עֲלֵיכֶם

   2 Come in peace   **3** בָּרְכוּנִי לְשָׁלוֹם

2. Unscramble the Hebrew words in each phrase to match the English translation.

   from the Ruler of rulers מַלְכֵי הַמְּלָכִים מִמֶּלֶךְ מַלְכֵי   הַמְּלָכִים מִמֶּלֶךְ מַלְכֵי

   the Holy Blessed One הוּא בָּרוּךְ הַקָּדוֹשׁ חוּא   הַקָּדוֹשׁ בָּרוּךְ הוּא

3. Write the English for each word: מַלְאָךְ <u>angel</u>   מֶלֶךְ <u>ruler</u>

   Complete each of the phrases below with one of the following words: מַלְכֵי מַלְכֵי

   מַלְאֲכֵי הַשָּׁרֵת   מַלְאֲכֵי הַשָּׁלוֹם   מַלְכֵי

   <u>angels of the Supreme</u>   <u>angels of peace</u>   <u>ministering angels</u>

   מִמֶּלֶךְ מַלְכֵי

   <u>from the Ruler of rulers</u>

4. Write the English for each root below.

   שלם   מלך   ברך   קדש   יצא   בוא

   <u>peace</u>   <u>rule</u>   <u>bless</u>   <u>holy</u>   <u>depart</u>   <u>come</u>

5. Name one thing you can do to be among מַלְאֲכֵי הַשָּׁלוֹם, "the angels of peace."

   On Shabbat: <u>invite people for Shabbat dinner in your home; give tzedakah</u>

   At all times: <u>reach out to help others; extend friendship; talk through disagreements</u>

HINENI—THE NEW HEBREW THROUGH PRAYER 2 © Behrman House Publishers

PRAYER DICTIONARY

א	אָבוֹת	fathers	**י**	יִשְׂרָאֵל	Israel
	אֲבוֹתֵינוּ	our fathers	**כ**	כִּבְבוֹדוֹ	God's glory
	אָבִינוּ	our parent		כָּל	all
	אַבְרָהָם	Abraham		כַּלָּה	bride
	אֱלֹהֵי	God of		כֻּלָּנוּ כְּאֶחָד	all of us as one
	אִמָּהוֹת	mothers	**ל**	לֵאָה	Leah
	אִמּוֹתֵינוּ	our mothers		לְבָרֵךְ	to bless
	אָמֵן	Amen		לְדוֹר וָדוֹר	from generation to generation
	אֲנַחְנוּ	we		לְדֹרֹתָם	for their generations
	אַתָּה	you (are)		לְהוֹדוֹת	to thank
ב	בָּאִי	come		לְהוֹשִׁיעַ	to save
	בֶּאֱמֶת	in truth		לְכָה	go
	בּוֹאֲכֶם	come		לְעוֹלָם	eternally
	בְּנֵי	the children of		לַעֲשׂוֹת	to make
	בְּעֵינֶיךָ	in your eyes	**מ**	מוֹדִים	thank, give thanks
	בְּרַחֲמִים	with compassion, mercy		מְחַיֶּה	give life
	בְּרִית	covenant		מִי כָמוֹךָ	who is like you?
	בָּרְכוּנִי	bless me		מַלְאֲכֵי	angels of
	בִּשְׁלוֹמֶךָ	with your peace		מֶלֶךְ	ruler
ג	גִּבּוֹר	might, powerful		מֶלֶךְ מַלְכֵי הַמְּלָכִים	Ruler of rulers
	גָּדְלְךָ	your greatness	**נ**	נַגִּיד	we will tell
ד	דּוֹדִי	my beloved		נוֹדֶה	we will thank, give thanks
ה	הָאָרֶץ	the earth		נְקַבְּלָה	let us receive
	הַגִּבּוֹר	the mighty		נְקַדֵּשׁ	let us sanctify
	הַגָּדוֹל	the great		נָתַתָּ	you gave
	הַקָּדוֹשׁ בָּרוּךְ הוּא	the Holy Blessed One	**ע**	עוֹזֵר	helper
	הַשָּׁמַיִם	the heavens		עוֹלָם	eternal
ו	וְאַהֲבַת חֶסֶד	and a love of kindness		עֶלְיוֹן	supreme
	וְאָמְרוּ	and say		עֲלֵיכֶם	upon you
	וְהַנּוֹרָא	and the awesome		עָלֵינוּ	for us, on us
	וְטוֹב	and may it be good		עַמְּךָ	your people
	וִיהַלְלוּ	(they) will praise		עֹשֶׂה	makes
	וּמָגֵן	and shield	**פ**	פְּנֵי	the face of
	וּמוֹשִׁיעַ	and rescuer	**צ**	צֵאתְכֶם	depart
	וְעַל	and for, and on	**ר**	רַב	great
	וְשָׁמְרוּ	and shall keep		רִבְקָה	Rebecca
ז	זָכוֹר	remember		רָחֵל	Rachel
ח	חַיִּים	life, the living	**ש**	שָׁבַת	rested
	חֵן	graciousness		שִׂים	grant, put
	חֲסָדִים טוֹבִים	acts of loving-kindness		שָׁלוֹם	peace
ט	טוֹבָה	goodness		שָׁמוֹר	keep
י	יוֹם הַשְּׁבִיעִי	the seventh day		שִׁמְךָ	your name
	יִמְלֹךְ	will rule		שָׂרָה	Sarah
	יַעֲקֹב	Jacob	**ת**	תְּהִלָּתְךָ	your praises
	יַעֲשֶׂה	(will) make		תּוֹרַת חַיִּים	Torah of life
	יִצְחָק	Isaac			

WRITING CHART

Script	Print	Name	Letter
		Alef	א
		Bet	בּ
		Vet	ב
		Gimmel	ג
		Dalet	ד
		Hay	ה
		Vav	ו
		Zayin	ז
		Het	ח
		Tet	ט
		Yud	י
		Kaf	כּ
		Chaf	כ
		Final Chaf	ך
		Lamed	ל
		Mem	מ

Script	Print	Name	Letter
		Final Mem	ם
		Nun	נ
		Final Nun	ן
		Samech	ס
		Ayin	ע
		Pay	פּ
		Fay	פ
		Final Fay	ף
		Tsadee	צ
		Final Tsadee	ץ
		Koof	ק
		Resh	ר
		Shin	שׁ
		Sin	שׂ
		Tav	תּ
		Tav	ת

NOTES